Liberty Under Attack

LIBERTY Under ATTACK

Reclaiming Our Freedoms in an Age of Terror

EDITED BY

RICHARD C. LEONE AND
GREG ANRIG, JR.

A Century Foundation Book

PUBLICAFFAIRS
New York

CONTENTS

CONTENTS

Liberty Under Attack

Reclaiming Liberty

RICHARD C. LEONE
AND GREG ANRIG, JR.

For Americans, 9/11 will be remembered forever as the dawn of their understanding of the terrible threat posed by terrorists. Nearly three thousand people died that day in the worst attack so far within the United States. And, since that time, a larger number of Americans have been killed in conflicts in Afghanistan and Iraq—invasions and subsequent occupations justified as a necessary part of the "War on Terror." Whatever the relative merits of these incursions, the continuing attacks on American occupying forces have kept alive the notion that we are "at war," even in the absence of more acts of terrorism at home. The death and destruction in those two countries includes considerably more complex causes than a simplistic notion of a global war on Islamic extremists. But these conflicts clearly have a pervasive and continuing effect on our perceptions, policies, and politics—an impact greater even than reports about real or possible threats of actual terrorist acts in the United States. Together with the attacks in Spain, Britain, Indonesia, and the Middle East, the violence associated with our occupations is a constant reminder that there are suicidal and homicidal individuals, whatever their reasons, eager to kill Americans and their allies.

Although experts had warned for years, even for decades, about the likelihood of terrorist attacks occurring within the United States, most Americans, including those in government and politics, were caught off guard by the 9/11 attacks. Under those circumstances, it was inevitable that not all of their choices regarding security or their other policy responses would be wise. The 9/11 Commission, accounts from former officials like Richard Clarke, and journalistic investigations have documented confusion and missteps within the federal government in the hours, days, and weeks following the attacks on the World Trade Center and the Pentagon. The sudden alteration of the national consciousness completely transformed the government's priorities. Hundreds of billions of dollars would be spent on new activities, wars would be initiated, civil liberties would be abridged, and judicial precedents would be set aside.

This volume seeks to document and analyze those swift and far-reaching changes. In many cases, its authors offer judgments about how effective those measures have been and their implications for the liberties we cherish in the United States. The essays are not simply about the pros and cons of American liberties and the genuine versus imagined tensions between security and freedom; they are a detailed report on the changes wrought in those liberties as a consequence of continuing violence abroad as well as continuing fear of terrorism at home.

In 2003, we published a volume of essays by some of these same authors titled *The War on Our Freedoms: Civil Liberties in an Age of Terrorism*. In the four years since that publication, Americans have learned that some of the concerns that our original book raised have indeed become realities, with significant costs. The war in Iraq has resulted in more American lives lost than the number killed on 9/11, as well as economic costs estimated at over $1 trillion. Top-level decisions to carve out exceptions to the Geneva Conventions led to widespread abuse of prisoners in Iraq, Afghanistan, and Guantánamo, greatly aiding the recruitment efforts of terrorist organizations. The reorganization creating the Department of Homeland Security, according to government reports, contributed to the Federal Emergency Management Agency's (FEMA's) ineffective response to Hurricane Katrina. Eavesdropping programs have been launched to monitor communications of Americans without a warrant, impinging on personal privacy in ways that largely remain secret.

Public reaction to those outcomes has been mostly negative. Nonetheless, the governmental response continues to err heavily on the side of endorsing actions that have produced undemonstrated security benefits, even when they have come with tangible costs, including lost liberties. In September of 2006, for example, Congress approved legislation that would allow the denial of habeas corpus to detainees and would grant executive branch latitude to conduct "coercive interrogations," with support in the Senate from twelve Democrats and all but one Republican. A minimally modified Patriot Act was renewed with even less congressional dissent, despite negligible public evidence that major portions of the law had proven to be effective in fighting terrorism.

The factors contributing to the government's continuing aggressiveness, despite the public's concerns, are complex. They include, however, the persistence of one-party rule, including strong Republican representation in the federal judiciary, until the November 2006 elections switched control of Congress to the Democrats; a deep desire on the part of both political parties to be united in the face of truly threatening and homicidal enemies; the normal inclination to "support" a presidency when large numbers of troops are in harm's way; and the at least partially successful intimidation of possible opponents on matters related to security. Nonetheless, American history teaches one lesson that has continued to hold true throughout the four years since the publication of *The War on Our Freedoms*: greater public awareness of the facts increases the likelihood of wise governmental decision making. Sometimes progress is slow, but our democracy works best when the public is informed. The goal of this volume is to continue that educational process.

The New Normal

It is utterly beyond the realm of possibility that, after 9/11, there would not have been dramatic increases in airline security and that such measures would not have affected people's lives. Further increases in surveillance, such as wiretapping and e-mail screening without court approval, are more problematic. For months there was negligible opposition to the creation of the Orwellian-sounding "Total Information Awareness" agency in the Department of Defense (DoD), headed by John Poindexter—the same John Poindexter who played a central role in Iran-Contra. Later the administration changed the name, altered the leadership, and modified the mission of the office, but the DoD remains involved in domestic "oversight" to an extent that is unclear to the public. The scale of surveillance by the National Security Agency is even broader and has been the subject of important investigative journalism and congressional inquiry. Essays in this volume by John D. Podesta, Stephen J. Schulhofer, and Patrick Radden Keefe address various aspects

4

of the expansion of federal surveillance in conjunction with greater government secrecy.

In the nature of the case, much of what has been done is invisible. The official explanation is always that secrecy is required for reasons related to security—our enemies mustn't know how the government is trying to stop them. It just so happens that secrecy also can be politically convenient, keeping hidden from voters actions that they could find objectionable. But the argument that open debate is a luxury we can't afford, that it would cause dangerous delay and modifications in the administration's plans, denigrates a proven strength of our democracy. Many of the nation's most egregious historical failures were outgrowths of excessive secrecy and manipulated public information—including the Vietnam War, domestic spying during the 1960s and 1970s, Watergate, the Iran-Contra scandal, and, it seems, the Iraq invasion. On the other hand, some of America's greatest achievements emerged largely as a result of often painful public examination. Those accomplishments include the civil rights movement, the eventual defeat of McCarthyism, and post-Watergate political and intelligence reforms.

Given how divided Americans are on questions related to domestic surveillance, much greater public scrutiny, informed by facts about what the government is already doing, would surely be far more beneficial to the country than to the terrorists. Even absent that information, one poll found that 50 percent of respondents thought that "the Bush Administration was . . . wrong in wiretapping [telephone conversations between U.S. citizens living in the United States and suspected terrorists living in other countries] without obtaining a court order," 44 percent thought it was "right," and 7 percent were "unsure" (CNN Poll, May 16–17, 2006). A CBS News poll found that

51 percent of respondents approved "of the government collecting the phone call records of people in the U.S. in order to reduce the threat of terrorism," 44 percent disapproved, and 5 percent were unsure (CBS News Poll, May 16–17, 2006).

The American public remains divided, largely along party lines, on the effectiveness, legality, and morality of the Bush administration's tactics, but a slight majority disapproves. Bush's plummeting overall approval rating has been well documented, but when asked about isolated issues, the public appears less decisive. For example, though Bush's approval rating has been hovering in the low thirties, before the 2006 election 47 percent approved of his handling of the U.S. campaign against terrorism. The low profile assumed by political figures who were troubled by the administration's actions is probably related to the relatively strong public support for those measures—even those that increase surveillance or curtail liberties.

There are a few widely held explanations for this discrepancy. First, enough is going wrong internationally and domestically for the vast majority of voters to have bad feelings toward the president, yet there has not been another terrorist attack on the United States since 9/11 so, therefore, "he must be doing something right." Also, enough fear of a terrorist attack in the United States remains that many Americans are still willing to grant the government significant leeway in its antiterrorist operations.

After five years, clearly the alterations that have been made in the area of civil liberties amount to a rewriting of what were previously accepted as fundamental values for our free society. All these changes, of course, have been justified by a single reason: they will keep us safer from terrorists. Two basic questions need to be asked about each of these "safety measures": Just how important are the "liberties" set aside in the name of the War on

Terror? And, exactly to what extent do these actions actually make us safer?

Blowback

The term blowback, according to the author Chalmers Johnson, was first used by the CIA in a 1954 report about the agency's secret involvement the previous year in replacing Mohammed Mossadegh with Reza Shah Pahlavi as leader of Iran. The word refers to the unintended consequences of a covert action that ultimately undercut the effort's intent—an eventuality that came to pass in Iran when hostility toward the Shah's tyrannical regime led to Ayatollah Khomeini's revolution. To this day, the United States is paying a steep price for its role in trying to manipulate Iran's affairs more than five decades ago.

In the War on Terror, the danger of blowback has been ever present. Some U.S. actions, particularly the invasion of Iraq and the abuse of prisoners at Abu Ghraib, have clearly produced some blowback in the form of larger numbers of radicalized Muslims around the world who have become committed to the jihadist cause. The declassified key judgments in the government's National Intelligence Estimate on "Trends in Global Terrorism," dated April 2006 and released in September, stated that "the global jihadist movement—which includes al-Qa'ida, affiliated and independent terrorist groups, and emerging networks and cells—is spreading and adapting to counterterrorism efforts." That report, which synthesizes intelligence provided by all relevant agencies, went on to conclude that two underlying factors "fueling the spread of the jihadist movement" were "fear of Western domination, leading to anger, humiliation, and a sense of powerlessness," and the "Iraq jihad."

Because the Iraq War and occupation, which has led to the deaths of tens of thousands of Iraqis, and the Abu Ghraib photographs have exacerbated "humiliation and a sense of powerlessness," most expert observers weighing their costs and benefits have concluded that both have done more harm than good in preventing future terrorism against Americans. As for the myriad other policies pursued since 9/11, verdicts are more difficult to reach because a great deal of information about their impact remains publicly unavailable and relatively little time has passed since their implementation. But in the four years since we published *The War on Our Freedoms: Civil Liberties in an Age of Terrorism,* what were then identified as causes for concern have today become, in many cases, causes for alarm.

The Use of Torture and Coercive Interrogation Techniques

The Supreme Court ruled in June 2006, in the *Hamdan* case, that the Bush administration's approach to military commissions was contrary to federal law. Many present and former military lawyers, including Eugene Fidell in this volume, have argued against many of the procedural changes sponsored by the administration. Instead of the ad hoc rules adopted since 9/11, they advocate reliance upon the basic rights provided under the uniform code of military justice.

The Geneva Conventions of 1949 arguably have been the single most important and effective source of progress on international human rights in the past century. More than 190 countries have adhered to their prohibitions against subjecting prisoners of war to "outrages upon personal dignity; in particular, humiliating and degrading treatment" as well as acts of "violence . . . cruel treatment and torture." The highest-ranking U.S. military commanders have long been among the most ardent and consistent enthusiasts of the Geneva Conventions, in recognition of the protections they provide to our soldiers in captivity as well as the clarity they give to U.S. personnel responsible for guarding POWs.

In February 2002, President Bush issued a directive saying that "the United States armed forces shall continue to treat detainees humanely and, to the extent appropriate and consistent with military necessity, in a manner consistent with the principles of Geneva." The president did not elaborate on what he meant by "appropriate and consistent with military necessity," but the directive obviously communicated a qualification to "the principles of Geneva." There was no opportunity for public debate in advance of that decision. Congress convened no hearings. The military never had a chance to explain to the country at large what the risks would be of even suggesting that exceptions might possibly be made to the Geneva Conventions.

The nation didn't learn until three years later that, in private, Secretary of State Colin Powell had objected to qualifying America's commitment to the conventions in any way, emphasizing that a sweeping pronouncement that they don't apply to Taliban or al Qaeda prisoners would pose a multitude of "cons" with the only "pro" being the provision of "maximum flexibility." The cons Powell listed included undermining the protections of the law of war for our troops, both in this specific conflict and in general; a high cost in terms of negative international reaction, with immediate adverse consequences for our conduct of foreign policy; undermining public support for the

United States in allied countries, making military cooperation more difficult to sustain; legal problems raised in European and other countries with extradition or other forms of cooperation in bringing terrorists to justice; and making the government more vulnerable to domestic and international legal challenges and undermining an important legal basis for trying the detainees before military commissions.

As Stacy Sullivan's essay demonstrates, Powell's analysis proved to be prescient. Notwithstanding largely unsubstantiated claims that torture has been effective in producing useful information, the pervasive abuse of prisoners has tarnished America's hard-earned reputation as a beacon for human rights.

Guantánamo Bay

Just three days after the 9/11 attacks, Vice President Dick Cheney spelled out what essentially became the administration's policy with respect to detaining and trying individuals suspected of having ties to al Qaeda or the Taliban. He said,

> The basic proposition here is that somebody who comes into the United States of America illegally, who conducts a terrorist operation killing thousands of innocent Americans . . . is not a lawful combatant. They don't deserve to be treated as a prisoner of war. They don't deserve the same guarantees and safeguards that would be used for an American citizen going through the normal judicial process. . . . They will have a fair trial, but it'll be under the procedures of a military tribunal. . . . We think that guarantees that we'll have the kind of treatment of these individuals that we believe they deserve.

Not long thereafter, the United States began using a detention facility at Guantánamo Bay, Cuba, to hold individuals accused of being enemy combatants. As many as seven hundred citizens of more than forty countries were held there at one point, about half of whom were eventually returned to their native country after a determination that they weren't so very dangerous after all. The others have remained there, without any prospect of facing a trial. Most have been subjected, without charge, to questioning involving some degree of coercion. Hunger strikes, suicides, and other unrest have plagued the facility.

Here, too, the American public is deeply divided. In a recent ABC News/*Washington Post* poll (June 22–25, 2006), 62 percent of respondents "think holding prisoners at the Guantánamo Bay military prison has . . . damaged the United States' image in the rest of the world," but 57 percent support "the federal government holding suspected terrorists without trial at the U.S. military prison in Guantánamo Bay, Cuba," with 37 percent opposing the detentions and 5 percent unsure.

Along with Abu Ghraib, photographs of Guantánamo detainees shackled and prostrate before American guards contributed to the steep decline in favorable international opinion toward the United States. International opinion was also affected by the military commissions the administration eventually designed to try some of the enemy combatants at Guantánamo. Although those commissions were struck down by the Supreme Court in the *Hamdan* case, discussed by Ann Beeson in Chapter 11, Congress subsequently passed legislation allowing for similar commissions with mildly altered rules. Australian Army Colonel Gerald Fogarty, writing in the journal of the U.S. Army War College before the *Hamdan* decision, argued that the U.S. government's reliance on military commissions to try enemy combatants has undermined U.S. influence and effectiveness: "The military commissions empowered under President Bush's military order are the exact types of trials that the United States openly condemns in the international community. . . . The effect of this apparent double standard is to deny the United States the moral high ground it needs to censure other nations in future human rights abuses."

General John Gordon, a retired air force general and former CIA officer who served as both the senior counterterrorism official and homeland security officer on President Bush's National Security Council, concurred: "There was great concern that we were setting up a process that was contrary to our own ideals."

Deportation and Scrutiny of U.S. Muslims

The July 7, 2005, attacks in London by four suicide bombers who were born and raised in the United Kingdom set off extended soul searching in England about the underlying causes behind home-grown Muslim terrorism. They also prompted Prime Minister Tony Blair to propose a sweeping increase in police powers, including the right to detain suspects for as long as ninety days without charge. Blair's plan was greatly watered down in Parliament, in part because of concerns that England's checkered history with regard to civil liberties generally and its isolation in particular of native Muslims may have contributed to the climate that produced the suicide bombers from Leeds.

The consensus seems to be that Muslims in the United States, most of whom are not from the Middle East, are generally better assimilated into mainstream society than they are in Europe. Still, it remains impossible to know the extent to which sympathizers of Islamic jihadists, even in small numbers, may be contemplating plots of their own inside U.S. borders. Aziz Huq's essay takes stock of government actions to date that, at the very least, run the risk of alienating Muslim communities while deterring potentially cooperative individuals from coming forward with information that would be useful for law enforcement. Early on, thousands of Muslims were detained and deported, a "voluntary" special registration was implemented, and mosques were spied on. Well-publicized investigations and accusations of purported sleeper cells produced evidence that seemed far from conclusive about whether the individuals involved were genuinely terrorist threats.

More recently, the FBI has attempted to strengthen relations with Muslim communities in the United States. Whether that commonsense approach will prove to be effective remains unknown, as does whether or not any blowback will arise from the much more aggressive tactics that were initially pursued—and, to some extent, still are.

Although the detainee treatment legislation that Congress passed in September 2006 imposed some modest constraints on interrogation techniques and military tribunal procedures, as Joseph Lelyveld argues in Chapter 10, it left the president with considerable latitude in deciding how to handle enemy combatants. The legislation also allows for the indefinite detainment without trial of enemy combatants. The Supreme Court is likely to review the law, but Congress, including twelve Democratic senators, has once again deferred to a president who in many ways has abandoned policies and principles that have served the country well throughout its history. General John Shalikashvili, a former chairman of the Joint Chiefs of Staff, put it well: "The U.S. has repeatedly faced foes in its past that, at the time they emerged, posed threats of a nature unlike any that it had previously faced. But the U.S. has been far more steadfast in the past in keeping faith with its national commitment to the rule of law."

Invocation of "Unitary Executive" Authority

Many of the Bush administration's directives and statements issued when the president signs laws have included language referring to the "unitary executive branch." The boilerplate typically reads that the executive branch "shall construe" an act or part of an act "in a manner consistent with the constitutional authority of the President to supervise the unitary executive branch and as Commander in Chief and consistent with the constitutional limits of judicial power." According to research by Christopher Kelley of Miami University, Bush's predecessors rarely used the term "unitary executive" in signing statements or executive orders—Clinton never did, George H. W. Bush used it six times, and Reagan used it just once. More than one hundred of Bush's signing statements have used the phrase, however.

What does the "unitary executive" concept mean? John Yoo, the Justice Department lawyer whose work was instrumental in supporting the administration's decision to make exceptions to the Geneva Conventions, is its most forceful advocate. After leaving the government in 2003, Yoo wrote a book, called *The Powers of War and Peace: The Constitution and Foreign Affairs after 9/11*, that attempts to explain and defend the idea. In Yoo's view, the Constitution demonstrates that the founders intended for the president to have unilateral authority to (1) initiate wars without congressional approval; (2) violate or terminate treaties at will; and (3) exercise unilateral authority unchecked by law in all matters related to foreign affairs in times of war. In other words, during wartime a president can operate outside the bounds of established law.

In Chapter 2, David Cole demonstrates how deeply disconnected the "unitary executive" idea is from American history. Lawyers advocating the concept, mainly members of the conservative Federalist Society, say that it is inspired by Alexander Hamilton's writings in the *Federalist Papers*. It is unarguably true that Hamilton was a forceful defender of the need for a vigorous presidency with a degree of independence from the other branches of government. On the other hand, Hamilton also emphasized the importance of congressional checks on presidential power such as Senate confirmation of ambassadors and Supreme Court judges, and ratification of treaties by two-thirds of the Senate. Hamilton biographer Ron Chernow wrote, "In the Federalist Papers, Hamilton was as quick to applaud checks on powers as those powers themselves, as he continued his lifelong effort to balance freedom and order."

Yoo's arguments about the commander-in-chief's constitutional right to ignore laws and unilaterally abrogate treaties dismiss a multitude of legal precedents with the offhanded claim that "everything is different since the 9/11 attacks on U.S. soil by non-state enemies." But that rationale is a flimsy one for such a radical position, which discards accumulated precedents that have served the country well. Again and again through the decades, the Supreme Court has consistently ruled that, in time of war, the president must obtain explicit authorization from Congress for actions that threaten to abridge individual liberties. Indeed, in the Supreme Court's 5–3 ruling in the *Hamdan* case, which struck down the military tribunals the administration uni-laterally designed to try a prisoner seized in Afghanistan, Justice Anthony Kennedy's concurring opinion took direct aim at Yoo's theories precisely because of their dismissal of historic precedents. Unfortunately, that decision came after much damage was already done.

The Suspension of Politics

Alan Brinkley reminds us that this sort of thing has happened before, indeed, that many of the liberties we take for granted were a long time coming. Still, there were aspects of the political acquiescence after 9/11 that were without close precedent. The events came at a time when the administration's natural opposition, the Democratic Party, was deeply riven by differences about the causes of the presidential loss in 2000. That relatively commonplace internal squabble was compounded by lingering uncertainty about the causes of and cures for the loss of both houses of Congress in 1994. Although the Democrats were a long way from consensus, there was one area in which considerable agreement existed: the party needed to shed its image as being weak on national security matters. In this context, the unexpected overnight emergence of domestic terrorism as a threat had particular power. Democrats rushed to line up behind hard-line measures.

An added incentive for doing so was the belief, based on bitter experience, that the so-called "conservative echo chamber," consisting of the administration, its allies in the media, and the large network of right-wing organizations, would be overwhelmingly critical of anyone who appeared out of step with the president's insistence on strong and unprecedented measures to respond to an unparalleled attack. The political fear of being out of the mainstream is normal. In this case, it specifically involved the specter of opening oneself up to later blame for a terrorist attack or simply the opprobrium attached to any sign of weakness on issues related to terrorism. And President Bush's relatively strong ratings on security linger even as the popularity of the specific choices he has made wane.

The political situation itself is not without precedent. American politics has endured several periods when questioning the course of an administration was treated, by some, as tantamount to treason. The Alien and Sedition Acts date from the early years of the republic. "Waving the Bloody Shirt" was the name given to the post–Civil War ploy of questioning the patriotism of any who deviated from the Radical Republican agenda of that period. During the Cold War, there were recurrent outbreaks of what we now loosely term "McCarthyism," tarring opponents as "soft on Communism" or "un-American." For five years, the Republican majorities in all three branches of government have made opposition much more difficult or, at least, less effective. And the president's position has been reinforced by the decades of increasing ideological uniformity within the Republican Party.

The consequences for congressional oversight and debate have been especially noteworthy. In retrospect, for the past five years, what seems to have been most lacking in both the Congress and the press was a willingness to insist on the rules of public give and take that we all claim to cherish. The swift enactment of the Patriot Act was the first clear sign that all principles of legislative oversight and deliberation were up for grabs.

It established a pattern that has recurred in issue after issue. There is continued resistance to Congress fulfilling its historic role and enacting laws that define crimes, process, and punishments. Instead, that authority has been ceded to the administration. Gary Hart's essay explores the role Congress has played (and not played) as the new rules of the game have been invented and implemented by the administration.

Until recently, much of the press joined with this conformity. The issues that normally command the headlines are the threats, thwarted threats, the actual attacks, and the everyday violence related to the occupations in Iraq and Afghanistan. Matters like the rules for trials of detainees and their related court decisions receive much less coverage, particularly on television where most people get their news. Peter Osnos explores many of these questions in depth in his essay.

Given the mainstream news coverage, it is hardly surprising that the continuing violence, threats of violence, and response to violence play the dominant role in shaping public reactions and opinions. In the area of liberties and values, discussion of what has happened, what it means, and whether we need to change course takes place only among a limited part of the citizenry.

America's Strength

Whatever the causes, after 9/11 zeal replaced pragmatism in foreign policy. Politics skewed toward uniformity instead of pluralism. Policy has been formulated and pursued based on fundamentalist certainty rather than on the traditional Anglo-Saxon approach—the latter a process that embraces the virtues of incrementalism, adaptation, and muddling through.

Whatever the merits of individual measures, programs, or even wars, taken together they surely represent a sea change in liberty and policy. The changes in civil liberties clearly rise to a level that invites the question: Has it really become necessary to destroy or suspend some of our freedoms in order to save them? We needn't wait for some future version of the *Pentagon Papers* for answers. We should take stock now. We should assess the impact of being an occupying power in a hostile environment— the effect on the military, on our notions of justice, the truth, and our national character, on the way the world sees us, and on the people whose country we are occupying.

Over the past five years, the number of questions has increased, the concerns have deepened, the missteps have multiplied; but we have just begun the sort of healthy debate that is the best corrective to a mistaken and regrettable policy. For most of us, day to day, things go on quite normally. We read of the legal innovations, Guantánamo prisoners, or secret surveillance, but they do not seem to impinge on our lives. We may note that, since 9/11, in a sense, the normal give and take of politics has been first suspended and then altered because of multiple uncertainties and the natural desire to be unified in the face of undoubted danger. So far, only a minority has asked the most basic questions about what has happened to our government: Have American liberties and the human rights of foreigners been abused by those in power? Are we in fact on the way to becoming a different sort of society because of the threats and actions of terrorists? These are profound questions, and the essays in this volume make a small start at trying to answer them. But they are the right questions; they do not overstate what is at stake.

The results of the 2006 midterm elections may well reflect a heightened understanding of the stakes—and a deep unease about many of the decisions taken in the name of liberty. What happened, in fact, may be very important; it may mark the resumption of normal politics. For five years since the horrible events of 9/11, many of the routine characteristics of American partisan politics have been set aside. The results have not been good. In addition to blundering into an unnecessary war in Iraq, there has been, generally, negligible congressional oversight in many areas. As a result, the public has found it difficult to learn details about how the government was carrying on its business—from enforcement of environmental and health regulations to implementation of the Patriot Act. All of that has been instantly changed by the new lineup in Congress. Decisions will now be held up to the light and argued in a quite different way. Politics may resume its normal bumpy, but somehow-in-the-end-it-all-works-out-right America.

One certainty about human institutions is that they function better when subjected to scrutiny, when they provide transparency that makes that scrutiny informed, and when they are forced by the pressures of outside examination to reconsider their own premises. With the country bogged down in a violent occupation in Iraq and Afghanistan and with a mounting sense that domestic problems are being allowed to drift or being abandoned, the public is uneasy and quite naturally insistent on having their uneasiness addressed directly. Accustomed to the success of slogans and clever spin heavily supported by a large infrastructure of media and quasi-political organizations, the administration and its supporters in Congress may have become complacent about their ability to manage any degree of public unease.

The success of democracy in the United States has been built on open and informed debate, a respect for legal precedents and the rule of law, a belief in the overarching value of human freedom, and, perhaps most of all, a deep understanding of the lessons taught by our history. Nothing about 9/11 changed that. What we have learned more than anything else since 9/11 is that ignoring those sources of our strength poses a greater danger to us than anything terrorists can do.

The essays that follow have a common theme: they pose, in effect, the questions we should have been debating for the past five years. Are the new security measures necessary and effective to offset the additional danger to which we are exposed both because of the intentions of terrorists and as a consequence of the reactions provoked by our policies abroad? Do the measures and the overall strategy of which they are a part merely create the appearance of substantial security, or are they working well? And, does the curtailment of civil liberties, of the rule of law, and of political debate represent a significant and ultimately self-defeating weakening of our liberties at home, a challenge to our values, and a diminution of our standing in the world? Overall, the question that confronts us was perhaps best stated 150 years ago by Abraham Lincoln: "Must a government, of necessity, be too strong for the liberties of its own people, or too weak to maintain its own existence?"

PART I
Discarding Democracy

CHAPTER 1

Past as Prologue?

ALAN BRINKLEY

The history of civil liberties in America, like the history of civil rights, is a story of struggle. Even in peacetime, Americans have engaged in an ever-changing negotiation between the demands of liberty and the demands of order and security. But in times of national emergency, the conflict between these two demands becomes particularly intense—and the relative claims of order and security naturally become stronger. We are now well into what is apparently an open-ended crisis, and it has already become clear that the highly robust view of civil liberties we have embraced in recent decades has not survived unaltered. This adjustment is consistent with every major crisis in our history, all of which have led to abridgments of personal liberty, some of them inevitable and justifiable. In most such crises, and certainly in this one, administrations have used the seriousness of their mission to seize powers far in excess of what the emergency required. At such moments in the past, it was particularly important that vigilant citizens made the case that the defense of our liberties is not an indulgence but an essential part of our democratic life. In our current circumstances, where the "crisis" has no clear beginning or end and could in theory last long beyond our own lifetimes, such vigilance is especially important.

The robust protection of civil liberties we have known in the last several decades is a relatively recent phenomenon, the result of decades, indeed, centuries of effort and struggle against powerful obstacles. The idea—often expressed in the first months after 9/11—that civil liberties always "snap back" after suppression during emergencies has no basis in our history. There is no "norm" to which society naturally returns. The climate for civil liberties is only what we make of it. The question facing Americans today is not whether civil liberties are being abridged. Clearly they are. It is whether these abridgments will be a temporary setback for civil liberties, as in earlier crises, or whether we will enter a new period in our history in which the role of civil liberties in national life will become permanently diminished. Americans have asked these questions before, and the way they have answered them has determined how civil liberties have survived and grown. Understanding how earlier generations have responded to crises similar to our own may help us comprehend both the gravity of our current situation and the steps necessary to improve it.

IT IS A PART OF OUR NATIONAL mythology that the framers of the Constitution guaranteed civil liberties to all Americans through the Bill of Rights and that we are simply the beneficiaries of their wisdom. But not even the framers were confident that the Bill of Rights provided sufficient protection of liberties. Madison opposed the Bill of Rights altogether, arguing that any effort to enumerate rights would serve to limit them—one reason for the largely forgotten (until recently) Tenth Amendment, which states that "powers not delegated to the United States by the Constitution" are "reserved to the States . . . or the people." Proponents of the Bill of Rights feared that the amendments alone would not be sufficient to protect individual liberties—and they were well justified in those fears.

During the first century of the history of the United States, the Bill of Rights had relatively little impact on the lives of most American citizens. There were widespread violations of civil liberties that by modern standards would seem exceptionally oppressive, inspiring one scholar, remarking on the early history of the Bill of Rights, to describe it as "140 Years of Silence." Even ignoring the egregious violations of rights and liberties inflicted on both enslaved and free African Americans, Native Americans, Mexicans, Chinese, and many other groups of immigrants, and the routine limitations on the rights of women, the abridgments of civil liberties were severe and routine. Local governments—which shared the view of the courts that the Bill of Rights applied only to the federal government—routinely banned books, censored newspapers, and otherwise policed "heretical" or "blasphemous" speech. Standards of public decorum and behavior were rigidly enforced, and unconventional conduct was often criminalized. The legal rights of the accused in criminal trials had few effective protections, and obedience to the Fourth, Fifth, and Sixth Amendments was often token or nonexistent. Freedom of religion did not always extend to Catholics, Jews, free thinkers, agnostics, or atheists, and such people had no protection against discrimination in education, jobs, and even place of residence. Perhaps more important, popular support for an expansive view of civil liberties was thin and in some places nonexistent. As a result, there was little pressure on any level of government to work vigorously to defend them. The only exception was the vigorous use of the Bill of Rights to defend property rights.

The Alien and Sedition Acts enacted by Congress in 1798—prompted by the "quasi-war" with France and designed to strengthen the government's authority to deal arbitrarily with aliens and dissenters—produced widespread popular hostility and led to the defeat of President John Adams in 1800. But this powerful reaction should not obscure the degree to which similar abuses of constitutionally protected freedoms by nonfederal governments occurred routinely, even in more normal times. Abraham Lincoln's controversial suspension of the writ of habeas corpus during the Civil War only increased the already excessive vulnerability of the citizenry to arbitrary arrest and imprisonment.

It would be too much to say that the Bill of Rights was an empty shell during the nineteenth century; things would surely have been worse without it. But to a significant degree it remained without content in the absence of popular, legislative, and judicial support—all of which were intermittent and often grudgingly given for over a hundred years.

OUR MODERN NOTION of civil liberties was, in fact, not born with the creation of the Bill of Rights or even with the passage of the Fourteenth Amendment, which bound the states to the protections of the Constitution and federal law. The most important event in defining our modern conception of civil liberties was, rather, the American involvement in World War I, which created some of the most egregious violations of civil liberties in our history—and, as a result, some of the first vigorous defenses of them.

When the United States entered the war in April 1917, the Wilson administration was acutely aware of how much of the public remained hostile to the nation's intervention. It responded much as the Adams and Lincoln administrations had in earlier conflicts—with an aggressive campaign of intimidation and coercion designed to silence critics and root out opposition. At the center of this effort were two pieces of wartime legislation: the Espionage Act of 1917 and the Sedition Act of 1918, which empowered the government to suppress and punish "disloyalty and subversion." The Espionage Act, among other things, permitted the postmaster general, Albert Sidney Burleson, to ban all "seditious" materials from the mails, a task that Burleson approached with great relish by announcing that "seditious" materials included anything that might "impugn the motives of the government and thus encourage insubordination," anything that suggested "that the government is controlled by Wall Street or munitions manufacturers, or any other special interests," anything, in other words, that Burleson considered somehow radical. All publications of the Socialist Party were banned by definition.

The Sedition Act, passed the next year to strengthen the provisions of the Espionage Act, made it a criminal offense to use "any disloyal, profane, scurrilous, or abusive language about the form of government of the United States or the Constitution of the United States, or the flag of the United States, or the uniform of the Army or Navy," or to use any language that might bring those institutions "into contempt, scorn, . . . or disrepute." This second law was particularly useful to the government as an instrument for suppressing radicals and labor unionists. The greatest number of prosecutions under the law was directed against members of the Socialist Party and its radical offshoot, the Industrial Workers of the World (IWW). Eugene Debs, the Socialists' leader, was convicted and imprisoned for questioning American involvement in the war. Bill Haywood, head of the IWW, fled to the Soviet Union to avoid imprisonment. Others were imprisoned for casual remarks about the president or the conduct of the war effort. Hiram Johnson, progressive senator from California, caustically described the provisions of the law: "You shall not criticize anything or anybody in the Government any longer or you shall go to jail."

This state-sponsored repression did not occur in a vacuum. It both encouraged and reflected a widespread popular intolerance of dissent that very quickly became coercive. In 1917, private volunteers formed the American Protective League (APL) to assist the government in the task of maintaining loyalty. The APL received the open endorsement of the attorney general, who called it a "patriotic organization . . . assisting the heavily overworked federal authorities in keeping an eye on disloyal individuals and making reports on disloyal utterances." It received $275,000 in government funds to finance its activities. Its members wore silver badges, as if they were official law-enforcement authorities (although there was no screening process for membership); ordinary citizens were generally unaware of the distinction between them and legitimate authorities. By the end of the war, the organization had 250,000 members—men and women who defined their mission as spying on their neighbors, eavesdropping on suspicious conversations in bars and restaurants, intercepting and opening the mail and telegrams of people suspected of disloyalty, and reporting to the authorities any evidence of disenchantment with the war effort. They made extralegal arrests; they organized "slacker raids" against perceived draft resisters. And they constituted only the largest of a number of such organizations. There were also the National Security League, the American Defense Society, and even a group modeled on the Boy Scouts—the Boy Spies of America.

Much of this repression was directed at labor leaders, radicals, and other dissidents. But its greatest impact fell on immigrants. Both Woodrow Wilson and Theodore Roosevelt denounced "hyphenated Americans" in 1916, and neither discouraged assaults on them. Popular passions against dissidents and immigrants soon ran amok. The primary target, although not the only one, was German Americans. The California Board of Education, for example, banned the teaching of German in the public schools, calling it "a language that disseminates the ideals of autocracy, brutality, and hatred." Libraries removed German books from their shelves. Merchants and others dropped German words from the language ("sauerkraut" became "liberty cabbage," "hamburger" became "liberty sausage"). German faculty members were fired from universities. German musicians were fired from orchestras. There were widespread rumors of plots by German Americans to put ground glass in bandages sent to the front; thus people with German names were barred from the Red Cross. In Minnesota, a minister was tarred and feathered because he was overheard praying with a dying woman in German. In southern Illinois, a man was lynched in 1918 for no apparent reason except that he happened to be of German descent; the organizers of the lynch mob were acquitted by a jury, which insisted that their conduct constituted a patriotic act.

This overwrought nativism—generated, even if partly inadvertently, by government policy and rhetoric—extended to other ethnic groups as well: to the Irish (because of their hostility to the English), to the Jews (because many were hostile to an American alliance with the anti-Semitic Russian government), and to others simply because their ethnic distinctiveness seemed a threat to the idea of "One-Hundred Percent Americanism," a phrase widely used at the time to describe national unity. Immigrant ghettoes in major cities were strictly policed and became frequent targets of vigilante groups. Even many settlement house workers began to feel it their duty to impose a new and more coercive conformity on the immigrants they served. A settlement worker in Chicago said in 1918 that the war had made her realize that "we were a nation only in a very imperfect sense. We were stirred to a new sense of responsibility for a more coherent loyalty, a vital Americanism."

Woodrow Wilson reputedly predicted in early 1917, "Once lead this people into war, and they'll forget there ever was such a thing as tolerance. To fight, you must be brutal and ruthless, and the spirit of ruthless brutality will enter into the very fibre of our national life, infecting Congress, the courts, the policeman on the beat, the man on the street." It proved in large measure to be a self-fulfilling prophecy—and not just for the war. The behavior Wilson predicted, and helped create, continued well after the armistice. In some ways, it intensified, most notably during what has become known as the great Red Scare.

The Red Scare was in part a response to the Bolshevik Revolution in Russia and the tremendous fear it created throughout the capitalist world. It was also a product of the great instability of postwar America, which many middle-class people believed to be orchestrated by revolutionaries. There was widespread labor unrest, racial conflicts in cities, economic turbulence, and a small but frightening wave of terrorist acts by radicals. But the Red Scare was above all a result of the deliberate strategies of ambitious politicians, who saw a campaign against "Bolshe-vism" in America as a useful spur to their careers—and as a way to consolidate the new powers they had gained during the war to override constitutional protections in the name of order.

The Justice Department, under Attorney General A. Mitchell Palmer (who had presidential hopes for 1920), was the leading actor in inflaming the Red Scare. An attempted bomb-ing of Palmer's house helped legitimize the major campaign against radicals that he was already planning and that he launched in 1920. On New Year's Day, he ordered simultaneous federal raids (orchestrated by the young J. Edgar Hoover) on suspected radical centers all over the country. There were 6,000 arrests, amid enormous publicity. They have become known as the Palmer Raids.

The Palmer Raids were supposed to reveal and destroy what Palmer claimed was a national, revolutionary conspiracy. In fact, the raids netted three pistols, no explosives, and only a small smattering of radical literature. Most of the people ar-rested were not radicals at all, and even the relatively few gen-uine radicals rounded up could not be shown to have violated any laws. Most were eventually released, although many re-mained in custody for weeks and even months without facing formal charges, without access to attorneys or even to their own families. Several hundred foreign radicals and presumed radi-cals were deported to Russia, where they arrived—many of them speaking no Russian and knowing nothing of the coun-try—in the middle of a civil war. Palmer himself looked back on this sorry episode a year later without repentance. "Like a prairie fire," he said, "the blaze of revolution was sweeping over every American institution of law and order a year ago. It was eating its way into the homes of the American workman, its sharp tongues of revolutionary heat were licking the altars of the churches, leaping into the belfry of the school bell, crawling into the sacred corners of American homes, seeking to replace marriage vows with libertine laws, burning up the foundations of society."

As during the war, popular vigilante groups took their cue from the government and leaped into the battle. In Washington state, a mob dragged a member of the IWW from jail, where he had been placed after arrest on vague charges of "subversion," castrated him, and hung him. In New York, soldiers and sailors (eager to strike back at people who had opposed the war effort) invaded the offices of a socialist newspaper, smashed the presses, and beat up the staff. And just as German books had been burned, German teachers had been terminated, and German ideas had been suppressed during the war, now books, teachers, and ideas presumed to be radical were burned, terminated, and suppressed.

THE FEDERAL GOVERNMENT'S assault on civil liberties during and after World War I may have been the most egregious in American history. It stifled dissenters who gave no evidence of being a danger to the nation. It permitted the persecution of German Americans who posed no threat to security. It produced a wide-ranging legal assault on men and women based on nothing but their presumed beliefs. And it routinely suspended such ordinary rights as freedom of speech, freedom of association, and freedom from arbitrary arrest.

But in acting so aggressively to abridge civil liberties, the government in these years unintentionally gave birth to a powerful new movement to protect them. Indeed, it is not too much to say that World War I was the birthplace of our modern notion of civil liberties; in its aftermath, the Bill of Rights began to have an expansive meaning in American life for the first time. The backlash against wartime excesses helped create three new forces committed to defending civil liberties in the future: popular support, formidable institutions, and the first serious evidence of judicial backing.

Popular support for civil liberties prior to World War I had been almost entirely theoretical. Most Americans, if asked, would have claimed to support the Bill of Rights. But except for a few dissenters and free thinkers, most took little notice of, and expressed little alarm about, the many ways in which its provisions were made almost meaningless by the operation of state and local governments. People of wealth and standing assumed, generally correctly, that they faced little danger of repression, censorship, and arbitrary arrest. People without property had no realistic expectation that the civil liberties promised by the Constitution meant much to them. As Zechariah Chafee, the great champion of free speech in the 1920s and 1930s, later wrote of this period: "The First Amendment had no hold on people's minds, because no live facts or concrete images were then attached to it. Consequently, like an empty box with beautiful words on it, the Amendment collapsed under the impact of Prussian battalions, and terror of Bolshevik mobs."

The heavy-handed actions of the federal government, however, created popular alarm, where local abuses had not, largely because of the greater suspicion with which Americans viewed broad federal power. The Palmer Raids in particular produced widespread denunciations in the press, destroyed A. Mitchell Palmer's political career, nearly crushed in the bud J. Edgar

Hoover's prospects for bureaucratic advancement, and badly damaged the Wilson administration and the Democratic Party. Republicans, sensing a political opportunity, took up the cause of civil liberties as a way of attacking the Democrats and helped give the issue popular credibility. In the absence of public opinion polls, it is impossible to measure the extent of this shift in public opinion, but it is nevertheless clear that not since the Alien and Sedition Acts of 1798 had violations of civil liberties aroused so much popular and political condemnation.

The war and its aftermath energized the small and once largely powerless community of civil liberties activists, who suddenly saw an opportunity to establish their cause in the public mind. Among them was Roger Baldwin, a settlement house worker in St. Louis who, inspired by a speech by Emma Goldman, became deeply committed early in the century to resisting state efforts to limit individual freedoms. He became a civil liberties activist during World War I, and he spent the rest of his long and active life building institutional support for protections of this relatively new concept. (He believed, with some justification, that he was responsible for introducing the term "civil liberties" into American public discourse.)

In 1917, Baldwin and a few other critics of government policies created the National Civil Liberties Bureau, whose original purpose was to criticize state repression and build support for protecting personal freedoms. Baldwin's approach to this task was deliberately controversial. He rejected the suggestions of some of his allies that he target only the most indefensible violations (such as the government's brutal treatment of conscientious objectors). He insisted, rather, that the best way to establish the principle of robust civil liberties would be to defend the most unpopular people and causes. He was especially outspoken on behalf of the radical anarchists of the Industrial Workers of the World, arguing that by standing up for the Wobblies he was casting light not just on the role of government but also on the role of industrial capital in repressing the rights of individuals.

The National Civil Liberties Bureau attracted relatively little attention during the war itself. But the reaction to the 1919 Palmer Raids suddenly thrust it into prominence. In January 1920, it was reorganized and renamed the American Civil Liberties Union (ACLU). Baldwin suddenly found himself with a host of prominent supporters, among them Clarence Darrow, Jane Addams, Felix Frankfurter, Helen Keller, Norman Thomas, and John Dewey, and he began to envision a larger role for his organization. It would no longer simply denounce assaults on liberty; it would use its influence to attack them through the legal system.

The third great contribution to the creation of the modern regime of civil liberties was the slow but growing support for the idea within the judiciary. Protecting civil liberties did not become a major part of the Supreme Court's agenda until the Warren Court decisions of the 1950s and 1960s, and even then the courts at lower levels were slow to embrace the cause. But the gradual shift in judicial thinking on the issue began to be visible within months after the end of World War I, less in the actual decisions of the courts than in several notable dissents that created the intellectual foundation for an expanded legal notion of free speech.

The most important figure in this process was Oliver Wendell Holmes. During and immediately after the war, Holmes showed no more inclination than any other members of the Supreme Court to challenge the government's aggressive use of the Espionage and Sedition acts to silence opposition. Early in 1919, the Court accepted an appeal on behalf of Charles Schenk, a socialist who had been convicted of violating the Espionage Act by passing out leaflets denouncing the war and encouraging young men to resist the draft. Holmes wrote the majority opinion, which affirmed both Schenk's conviction and the constitutionality of the law. "The question in every case," he wrote in a controversial decision, "is whether the words used are used in such circumstances and are of such a nature as to create a clear and present danger that they will bring about the substantive evils that Congress has a right to prevent." Schenk's "words," he insisted, were designed to undermine the draft and were therefore unprotected speech. "When a nation is at war," he added, "many things that might be said in time of peace are such a hindrance to its effort that their utterance will not be endured so long as men fight, and that no Court could regard them as protected by any constitutional right."

Holmes's decision evoked a storm of protest from eminent legal scholars whose opinion the justice evidently respected, and by November 1919, he had clearly revised his views about protected speech. In *Abrams v. U.S.*, the court reviewed the conviction of Jacob Abrams, a Russian immigrant who had been convicted under the Sedition Act for distributing leaflets criticizing President Wilson's decision to dispatch American troops to Russia in 1918, during the civil war that followed the Bolshevik Revolution. As in the Schenk case, there was no evidence that Abrams's actions had in any way impeded the course of the war. But a lower court had claimed that it was enough to justify a conviction that his actions *might* have jeopardized American policy. The Supreme Court agreed, upholding both the conviction and the law. But this time, Holmes (joined by

Justice Louis Brandeis) vigorously and famously dissented in language that many consider the classic initial argument for a robust view of the First Amendment. Defenders of the Sedition Act, Holmes said, had rested their case on the overwhelming importance of sustaining support for the war and the dangers dissenters posed to that effort. But no one should be so confident that the passions of the moment are irrefutable, Holmes suggested, for

> when men have realized that time has upset many fighting faiths, they may come to believe even more than they believe the very foundations of their own conduct that the ultimate good desired is better reached by free trade in ideas—that the best test of truth is the power of the thought to get itself accepted in the competition of the market, and that truth is the only ground upon which their wishes safely can be carried out. That, at any rate, is the theory of our Constitution. It is an experiment, as all life is an experiment. Every year, if not every day, we have to wager our salvation upon some prophecy based upon imperfect knowledge. While that experiment is part of our system, I think that we should be eternally vigilant against attempts to check the expression of opinions that we loathe and believe to be fraught with death. . . . I had conceived that the United States, through many years, had shown its repentance for the Sedition Act of 1798.

A year later, Louis Brandeis made another significant contribution to the case for expanding the definition of free speech. In a dissent against the court's ruling in *Gilbert v. Minnesota*, in which the Court upheld a Minnesota law under which Joseph Gilbert had been convicted of speaking against the draft,

Brandeis wrote: "I have difficulty in believing that the liberty guaranteed by the Constitution . . . does not include liberty to teach, either in the privacy of the home or publicly, the doctrine of pacifism. . . . I cannot believe that the liberty guaranteed by the Fourteenth Amendment [that is, the Fourteenth Amendment's guarantee of First Amendment and other protections to all citizens] includes only liberty to acquire and to enjoy property." And in 1927, still dealing with the fallout from wartime repression, Brandeis wrote yet another influential opinion in *Whitney v. California*. He concurred on technical grounds with the 1919 conviction of Anita Whitney for joining a communist party in California and advocating the overthrow of the U.S. government, but he dissented sharply from the Court's expansive view of the state's power to suppress "dangerous" speech:

> Those who won our independence by revolution were not cowards. They did not fear political change. They did not exalt order at the cost of liberty. To courageous, self-reliant men, with confidence in the power of free and fearless reasoning applied through the processes of popular government, no danger flowing from speech can be deemed clear and present [a not very subtle slap at Holmes's Schenk decision], unless the incidence of the evil apprehended is so imminent that it may befall before there is opportunity for full discussion. If there be time to expose through discussion the falsehood and fallacies, to avert the evil by the processes of education, the remedy to be applied is more speech, not enforced silence. . . . It is therefore always open to Americans to challenge a law abridging free speech and assembly by showing that there was no emergency justifying it. . . . The fact that speech is likely to result in some violence or in destruction of property is not enough to

justify its suppression. There must be the probability of serious injury to the State. Among free men, the deterrents ordinarily to be applied to prevent crime are education and punishment for violations of the law, not abridgment of the rights of free speech and assembly.

In these and other dissents, Holmes, Brandeis, and a slowly expanding group of other judges and justices began laying out much of what became the legal and moral basis for our modern conception of civil liberties.

As the United States prepared to enter World War II, no one in authority was unaware of the enormous price the nation (and the Democratic Party) had paid for the legal and popular repression of 1917 through 1920. Nor were officials unaware of the new bulwarks defending civil liberties—the ACLU and other, related organizations and the still frail but nevertheless visible body of precedent in the courts. As a result, there was no equivalent to the Alien and Sedition Acts in World War II, no government encouragement of vigilante action against dissenters (who were, in any case, many fewer than in the previous war), no demonization of German Americans or Italian Americans. Although the government censored press reports from the front, there was no effort to interfere with what newspapers printed at home. Loud and often vicious attacks on the president and the Congress went unpunished and largely ignored.

But the new regime of civil liberties was not yet strong enough to protect racial minorities against the repressive passions the war helped unleash. African Americans, Mexicans, and others continued to confront the longstanding barriers to liberty that had been part of American racial practices for centuries. Even those who joined the military were required to serve in segregated units and were often denied the most elementary rights of protest and self-protection. A catastrophic explosion at Port Chicago in Los Angeles in 1944 left 320 navy workers, two-thirds of them African Americans, dead. When black workers refused to return to work at Port Chicago several weeks later, claiming correctly that little had been done to increase safety at the site, they were court-martialed, given fifteen-year prison terms, and dishonorably discharged.

Most vulnerable of all were the small communities of Japanese Americans on the Pacific Coast. In the aftermath of Pearl Harbor, many Californians, not implausibly, feared enemy attacks on the Pacific Coast. Less plausibly, they feared that the slightly more than 100,000 Japanese Americans in California (two-thirds of them American citizens) might be conspiring with the Japanese government to facilitate such attacks.

As in World War I, far from attempting to dampen these fears, public officials inflamed and legitimized them. Earl Warren, the California attorney general, stated publicly: "To assume that the enemy has not planned fifth column activities for us in a wave of sabotage is simply to live in a fool's paradise." John L. DeWitt, commander of army forces on the West Coast, proposed the relocation of "enemy aliens" to a site far from the coast and rejected all suggestions that distinctions be made between aliens and citizens or between the loyal and disloyal. "The Japanese race is an enemy race," he insisted. "Racial affinities are not severed by migration." Even second- and third-generation Japanese Americans could not be trusted because, he said, "the racial strains are undiluted."

DeWitt won the support of Secretary of War Henry Stimson, who then persuaded President Roosevelt (despite the strenuous objections of Attorney General Francis Biddle) to sign an executive order authorizing the removal of all people of Japanese ancestry from the Pacific Coast. This act—not the most far-reaching but surely one of the most extreme and shameful violations of civil liberties in American history—was not an inevitable result of popular sentiment, which could have been mollified by appropriate assurances from people in authority and which, in any case, subsided relatively quickly after Pearl Harbor. It was a result of deliberate decisions by men in the War Department whose single-minded commitment to the pursuit of victory in the war left little room for consideration of such abstract notions as civil liberties and civil rights. It did not much matter to them whether or not the Japanese were truly disloyal. If they were in error, they believed, it was better to err on the side of security. Relocation was a way of avoiding the difficult task of determining individual loyalty and also a way of assuaging (rather than trying to change) public opinion. That the victims of this action were Japanese, a people whom both the federal government and the popular culture were energetically demonizing through an extraordinarily racist propaganda campaign, made the decision still easier.

The question of the constitutional validity of the internment orders reached the Supreme Court in May 1943. Only a week before the case arrived, the justices had overturned a state court ruling (and one of the Court's own decisions of three years before) upholding the expulsion of Jehovah's Witnesses from public schools because they refused to salute the flag on religious grounds. But consistent with its historic reluctance to challenge wartime governments on constitutional issues, it showed no such sensitivity to civil liberties in deciding the case of Fred Korematsu, a San Francisco welder who had resisted relocation two years earlier. In a 6–3 decision announced in 1944, the Court ruled, in effect, that the internment policy was constitutional simply because the military claimed it was necessary. Justice Hugo Black, justly remembered as a great civil libertarian through most of his career, brusquely dismissed Korematsu's claim as without merit, even though he conceded there was no evidence of the plaintiff's disloyalty. Justice Frank Murphy, dissenting, stated bluntly: "This exclusion of 'all persons of Japanese ancestry, both alien and non-alien,' from the Pacific Coast area on a plea of military necessity in the absence of martial law ought not to be approved. Such exclusion goes over 'the very brink of constitutional power,' and falls into the ugly abyss of racism." The American Civil Liberties Union and, indeed, almost the entire civil liberties community remained virtually silent throughout.

Just as the Espionage Act, the Sedition Act, and the Palmer Raids created a series of efforts to avoid the mistakes of the past, the Japanese American internment became a case study of security measures run amok for several decades after World War II. Even at the height of Cold War hysteria, when civil liberties violations were widespread, there was never a serious effort to intern communists and subversives (although the 1950 McCarran Act made provisions—never implemented—for such internment camps). But a civil liberties regime constantly fighting the last war is not always well prepared for the next one. In the 1950s, the defenses for civil liberties painstakingly built up in the four decades since the Palmer Raids proved a frail protection for the left when confronted with the second great Red Scare. Accustomed to protecting citizens from prosecution for exercising free speech, defenders of civil liberties seemed unable to frame an effective response to newer violations: people being dismissed from jobs, being blacklisted in their professions, being libeled by public officials on the basis of their presumed beliefs and past associations, or in some cases being jailed because of their reluctance to testify against others.

A familiar pattern emerged after the demise of McCarthy: a widespread, retroactive repudiation of the "guilt-by-association" tactics of the communist hunters and a heightened sensitivity about protecting academic freedom and challenging arbitrary prosecutions and job dismissals on political grounds. This aggressive effort to create bulwarks against a repetition of the harrowing events of the early 1950s also contributed to the dramatic growth in the protection of political, cultural, and religious dissent in the 1960s and to the expansion of legal protections available to those accused of crimes. Interest in civil liberties was so intense in the 1960s that during the Vietnam War, with some notable exceptions, the usual wartime infringements of civil liberties were surprisingly rare. Reporters in Vietnam were permitted to cover the war with little censorship or control by the military. Opponents of the draft openly denounced the system without significant legal jeopardy. A powerful antiwar movement emerged with only minor, and largely incompetent, assaults from the government it was challenging—with the notable exception of the violence and deaths at Kent State University and Jackson State University in 1970.

By the end of the Vietnam War, it seemed to many Americans that civil liberties were now firmly established and well defended, that despite the continued need for vigilance, the largest battles had been won. And in the glow of that apparent victory, it became tempting to think of the growth of civil liberties protections in the twentieth century as part of a consistent, linear, progressive story that could be expected to continue indefinitely into the future. But the real lesson of the growth of civil liberties in the twentieth century is not that progress is inevitable but that society's definition of civil liberties is fluid and constantly changing, that new situations create new threats for which prior experiences are often poor preparation, and that public support for protecting basic freedoms is highly contingent and can evaporate freely.

Well before September 11, 2001, a large segment of right-wing opinion had become firmly committed to the idea that "the sixties" had produced an irresponsible and excessive regime of civil liberties. According to this view, radicals, dissenters, and foreigners do not deserve the protections they have received, the press has become a dangerous and even subversive force that must somehow be curbed, and it should be the task of conservative politics to roll back these rights and increase the ability of the state to protect itself from its challengers.

One powerful orthodoxy of conservative (and military) opinion—despite an almost complete absence of evidence to support it—was that an unrestrained and critical press had undermined the ability of Americans to fight effectively in Vietnam. As a result, beginning in the early 1980s when the press was entirely excluded from the American invasion of Grenada, reporters faced significant new barriers to covering wars. In World War II, photographers and reporters were among the first Americans on the beaches of Normandy. The great war photographer Robert Capa was, in fact, ahead of the troops, taking dramatic pictures of thousands of young men landing and, in many cases, dying in the waves behind him. In Grenada, Panama, Kuwait, and Kosovo, the American government—claiming to be concerned about the "safety" of reporters despite the insistence of the press that they themselves were not deterred by possible danger—almost never let the media anywhere near the fighting. The token freedom granted to reporters in post-invasion Iraq has been largely mooted by levels of security that severely hamper the mobility of journalists. The public has had to rely on official military accounts of what has happened, many of which later turn out to be incomplete or false.

At the same time, aggressive efforts to fight crime produced a series of attacks on the legal protections of accused criminals, protections the Warren Court had painstakingly constructed. Police and prosecutors pushed hard and sometimes successfully to expand their ability to conduct random searches. Despite many protests, law enforcement relied heavily on racial profiling. The erosion of legal services gradually made a mockery in some places of the right of the accused (and most alarmingly of those facing the death penalty) to be represented effectively by counsel. By the end of the twentieth century, in other words, civil liberties—while far better protected than they had been a half century and more before—were already under assault from forces who believed they had expanded too far and too fast and thus had become a threat to social order. The attacks of 9/11 became, among other things, a vehicle for advancing an assault on civil liberties that was already under way for other reasons.

The aggressive efforts by the government to seize new powers and to curb traditional liberties in the early twenty-first century cannot be wholly dismissed as cynical or gratuitous. Some alteration in our understanding of rights is appropriate and necessary in dangerous times, as even the most ardent civil libertarians generally admit. But the history of civil liberties in times of emergency suggests that governments seldom react to crises carefully or judiciously. They acquiesce to the most alarmist proponents of repression. They pursue pre-existing agendas in the name of national security. They target unpopular or vulnerable groups in the population not because there is clear evidence of danger but because they can do so at little political cost. During World War I, the victims of government repression were labor leaders, anarchists, socialists, and German Americans, none of whom posed any danger to the war effort but all of whom were widely disliked. In World War II, the victims were Japanese Americans, who were stripped of all the rights of citizenship not because there was any evidence that they were disloyal but because they were feared on largely racial grounds. In the present emergency, the victims are mostly Arab Americans and foreign nationals, who have been subject to mass arrests and considerable harassment on the basis of virtually no evidence of danger or disloyalty.

Citizens naturally react to great crises viscerally and often vent their fears in the form of demands for unconscionable actions. It should be government's duty to see beyond the understandably passionate feelings of the public and to frame a reasoned response to the dangers we face—not to defend all civil liberties reflexively, certainly, but to give them considerable weight in choosing how to balance the competing demands of freedom and order. Our government has conspicuously failed to uphold that balance since 2001 and, indeed, has worked hard to institutionalize the abridgments of civil liberties that they have imposed on many groups of citizens in recent years. Popular opposition to these changes—from the press, from politicians, and even at times from the civil liberties community itself—has been strikingly frail in relation to the tremendous strength of the forces of repression. But if there is any reason for optimism in these dark times, it lies in the American history of constantly changing understandings of civil liberties and the frequent popular backlashes against limiting them. As in the past, the hope of halting, or reversing, the current trend toward a regime of much more limited freedom rests, in the end, with the public—with those organizations and individuals who care about civil liberties and with those who believe that the more than two century-long struggle to legitimize and strengthen their place in American life is one that must continue.

CHAPTER 2

What Bush Wants to Hear

DAVID COLE

F ew lawyers have had more influence on President Bush's legal policies in the War on Terror than John Yoo. This is a remarkable feat, because Yoo was not a cabinet official, not a White House lawyer, and not even a senior officer within the Justice Department. He was merely a mid-level attorney in the Justice Department's Office of Legal Counsel with little supervisory authority and no power to enforce laws. Yet by all accounts, Yoo had a hand in virtually every major legal decision involving the U.S. response to the attacks of September 11, and at every point, as far as we know, his advice was virtually always the same—the president can do whatever the president wants.

Yoo's most famous piece of advice was in an August 2002 memorandum stating that the president cannot constitutionally be barred from ordering torture in wartime—even though the United States has signed and ratified a treaty absolutely forbidding torture under all circumstances, and even though Congress has passed a law pursuant to that treaty, which without

This article appears in the November 17, 2005, issue of the *New York Review of Books*. Reprinted with permission from the *New York Review of Books*, © 2005 NYREV, Inc.

any exceptions prohibits torture. Yoo reasoned that, because the Constitution makes the president the commander-in-chief, no law can restrict the actions he may take in pursuit of war. By this reasoning, the president would be entitled by the Constitution to resort to genocide if he wished.

Yoo is now back in private life, having returned to the law faculty at the University of California at Berkeley. Unlike some other former members of the administration, he seems to have few if any second thoughts about what he did and has continued to aggressively defend his views. His book, *The Powers of War and Peace: The Constitution and Foreign Affairs after 9/11*, shows why Yoo was so influential in the Bush administration. It presents exactly the arguments that the president would have wanted to hear. Yoo contends that the president has unilateral authority to initiate wars without congressional approval and to interpret, terminate, and violate international treaties at will. Indeed, ratified treaties, Yoo believes, cannot be enforced by courts unless Congress enacts additional legislation to implement them. According to this view, Congress's foreign affairs authority is largely limited to enacting domestic legislation and appropriating money. In other words, when it comes to foreign affairs, the president exercises unilateral authority largely unchecked by law—constitutional or international.

Yoo is by no means the first to advance such positions. Many conservatives favor a strong executive, especially when it comes to foreign affairs, and they are generally skeptical about international law. What Yoo offers that is new is an attempt to reconcile these modern-day conservative preferences with an influential conservative theory of constitutional interpretation: the "originalist" approach, which claims that the Constitution must be interpreted according to the specific understandings held by the framers, the ratifiers, and the public when the Constitution and its amendments were drafted.

The problem for originalists who believe in a strong executive and are cynical about international law is that the framers held precisely the opposite views—they were intensely wary of executive power, and as leaders of a new and vulnerable nation, they were eager to ensure that the mutual obligations they had negotiated with other countries would be honored and enforced. During the last two centuries, of course, executive power has greatly expanded in practice, and the attitude of many U.S. leaders toward international law has grown increasingly disrespectful as the relative strength of the United States compared to other nations has increased. But these developments are difficult to square with the doctrine of "original intent," which, at least as expressed by Justice Antonin Scalia and other extreme conservatives, largely disregards the development of the law for the past two centuries. Yoo's task is to reconcile the contemporary uses of American power with his belief in original intent. His views prevailed under the Bush administration and therefore should be examined not only for their cogency and historical accuracy but for their consequences for U.S. policy in the War on Terror.

War

On its face, the Constitution divides power over foreign affairs. It gives Congress substantial responsibility, especially with respect to war. Congress has the power to raise and regulate the military; to declare war and issue "Letters of Marque and Reprisal," which authorize lesser forms of conflict; to define offenses against the law of nations; and to regulate international commerce. The Senate must confirm all treaties and all appointments of ambassadors. The president is named as the "commander-in-chief" and appoints ambassadors and makes treaties subject to the Senate's consent. In addition, the words "executive power" have, since the beginning of the republic, been regarded as giving the president an implicit authority to represent the nation in foreign affairs.

These divisions of responsibility were conceived for widely recognized historical and philosophical reasons. The Constitution was drafted following the Revolutionary War, in which the colonies rebelled against the abuses of the British monarchy, the prototypical example of an unaccountable executive. The new nation so distrusted executive power that the first attempt to form a federal government, the Articles of Confederation, created only a multi-member Continental Congress, which was in turn dependent on the states for virtually all significant functions, including imposing taxes, regulating citizens' behavior, raising an army, and going to war. That experiment failed, so the Constitution's drafters gave Congress more power and revived the concept of a branch of government headed by a single executive. But they insisted on substantial limits on the power of the new executive branch and, accordingly, assigned to Congress strong powers that had traditionally been viewed as belonging to the executive—including the power to declare war.

Many of the framers passionately defended the decision to deny the president the power to involve the nation in war. When Pierce Butler, a member of the Constitutional Convention, proposed giving the president the power to make war, his proposal was roundly rejected. George Mason said that the president was "not to be trusted" with the power of war and that it should be left with Congress as a way of "clogging rather than facilitating war." James Wilson, another member, argued that giving Congress the authority to declare war "will not hurry us into war; it is calculated to guard against it. It will not be in the power of a single man, or a single body of men, to involve us in such distress; for the important power of declaring war is vested in the legislature at large." Even Alexander Hamilton, one of the founders most in favor of strong executive power, said that "the Legislature alone can interrupt [the blessings of peace] by placing the nation in a state of war." As John Hart Ely, former dean of Stanford Law School, has commented, although the original intention of the founders on many matters is often "obscure to the point of inscrutability," when it comes to war powers, "it isn't."

In the face of this evidence, Yoo boldly asserts that a deeper historical inquiry reveals a very different original intention—namely, to endow the president with power over foreign affairs virtually identical to that held by the king of England, including the power to initiate wars without congressional authorization. He argues that the power to "declare War" given to Congress was not meant to include the power to begin or authorize a war but simply the power to state officially that a war was on—a statement that would be "a courtesy to the enemy" and would authorize the executive to exercise various domestic wartime powers. At most, Yoo contends, the clause giving Congress power to "declare War" was meant to require congressional approval for "total war," a term Yoo never defines, but it left to the president the unilateral decision to engage in all lesser hostilities. He quotes dictionaries from the founding period that defined "declare" as "to pronounce" or "to proclaim," not "to commence." He points out that the Constitution did not give Congress the power to "engage in" or to "levy" war, terms used in other constitutional provisions referring to war. And he notes that, unlike some state constitutions of the time, the federal Constitution did not require the president to consult Congress before going to war.

All the evidence Yoo cites, however, can be read more convincingly to corroborate the view he seeks to challenge—namely, that the Constitution gave the president only the power, as commander-in-chief, to carry out defensive wars when the country came under attack and to direct operations in wars that Congress authorized. British precedent is of limited utility here, since the framers consciously departed from so much of it. Dictionary definitions of "declare" also offer little guidance, since Yoo ignores that there is a world of difference between someone's "declaring" his or her love for wine or Mozart and a sovereign's declaring war. "Declare War" was, in fact, a legal term of art, and there is evidence that it was used at the time to mean both the commencement of hostilities and a statement officially recognizing that war was ongoing. The use of the word "declare" rather than "levy" or "engage in" simply reflects the division of authority under which the president actually levies—or carries on—the war once it is begun. Indeed, the framers famously substituted "declare" for "make" in enumerating Congress's war powers for just this reason. And the framers had no reason to require the president to consult with Congress before going to war since it was Congress's decision, not the president's.

Most troubling for Yoo's thesis, his account renders the power to "declare War" a meaningless formality. At the time of the Constitution's drafting, a formal "declaration of war" was not necessary for the exercise of war powers under either domestic or international law, so Yoo's hypothesis that the declaration served that purpose fails. Yoo's further suggestion that the clause recognizes a distinction between "total wars," which must be declared, and lesser wars, which need not be, has no historical basis. Despite his ostensible commitment to originalism, Yoo cites no evidence whatsoever to suggest that any such distinction existed for the founding generation. Nor does he ever explain what the distinction might mean today. And the fact that the text grants Congress both the power to "declare War" and to issue "Letters of Marque and Reprisal" strongly suggests an intent that Congress decide on all forms of military conflict other than repelling attacks. Once these explanations evaporate, all that is left for Yoo's theory of the war clause is that it gives Congress the power to provide a "courtesy to the enemy"—hardly a persuasive refutation of the clear language by the framers quoted above.

Yoo's evidence does not undermine the conclusion that the framers intended Congress to take responsibility for the decision to send the nation into war, but in some sense, arguments against his theory are academic. Modern practice is closer to Yoo's view than to the framers' vision. Beginning with the Korean War, presidents have routinely involved the nation in military conflicts without waiting for Congress to authorize their initiatives. Yoo notes that, whereas the nation has been involved in approximately 125 military conflicts, Congress has declared war only five times. Were the framers lacking in practical judgment when they gave Congress this power?

Yoo claims that, since 9/11, it is all the more essential that the nation be able to act swiftly and without hesitation, even preemptively, to protect itself. We can't afford to wait around for Congress to figure out what it wants to do. The War on Terror does not permit democratic deliberation, at least not in advance. And, as Yoo repeatedly insists, Congress remains free to cut off funds for any military action that it does not like.

But there is as good reason today as there was when the Constitution was drafted to give Congress the power to authorize military activities. As the framers accurately predicted, presidents have proven much more eager than Congress to involve the nation in wars. It is easier for one person to make up his mind than for a majority of two houses of Congress to agree on a war policy.

Presidents also tend to benefit from war more than do members of Congress—by increasing their short-term popularity, by acquiring broader powers over both the civilian economy and the armed forces, and, sometimes, by the historical recognition later accorded them. Moreover, as the Vietnam War illustrated, even when a war becomes extremely unpopular, it is not easy to cut off funds for the troops.

It is true, as Yoo observes, that, since Harry Truman, presidents of both parties have generally resisted the view that they need congressional authorization to commit forces to military conflict. But this attitude is in fact a relatively recent development. Although formal declarations of war have been rare, Yoo fails to note that presidents have generally sought congressional authorization for military actions. Until the Korean War, presidents either openly acknowledged that congressional authorization was necessary or offered rationales for why a particular military initiative was an exception to that rule. Thus, the view that Yoo promotes as "original" has in fact been advanced only during the last fifty years, and only by self-interested executives.

This originalist view is particularly disputed by Congress, as can be seen in the 1973 War Powers Resolution, which sought to reaffirm and restore Congress's constitutional role in deciding on whether to go to war, and also in the legislative debates that inevitably take place when presidents talk of going to war. As the war in Iraq has painfully underscored, the decision to go to war, especially a war initiated by the president without broad international support, can have disastrous consequences, and extricating the country from such a war can be extremely difficult. Were Congress to be eliminated from the initial decision-making process, as Yoo would prefer, the result would almost certainly be even more wars and more quagmires such as the one in Iraq. On this issue, the framers were persuasive, and it is Yoo who has failed to understand both the checks on executive power they imposed and the reasons they did so.

Treaties

Yoo's interpretation of the treaty power, like his view of the war power, departs dramatically from the text of the Constitution and its traditional understanding. The Constitution's Supremacy Clause explicitly provides that "all Treaties made, or which shall be made, under the Authority of the United States, shall be the supreme Law of the Land; and the Judges in every State shall be bound thereby."

On the strength of that clause, and statements made about treaties at the time of the framing, it has long been accepted that treaties have the force of law in the United States, create binding obligations, and may be enforced by courts. Indeed, the Supreme Court long ago stated that treaties are "to be regarded . . . as equivalent to an act of the legislature."

In the modern era, Congress often specifies when ratifying a treaty that it should not be enforceable in court until further legislation is enacted. And even without such directives, courts sometimes find treaties not to be judicially enforceable; the U.S. Court of Appeals for the Washington, D.C., Circuit did so recently in rejecting a Guantánamo detainee's claim that his pending trial in a military tribunal violated the Geneva Conventions.

Yoo would go further, however, insisting on a presumption against judicial enforcement unless Congress clearly specifies otherwise. On this view, treaties lack the force of law and become mere political promises, having about as much force as campaign rhetoric. And he further claims that the president has unilateral authority to interpret, reinterpret, and terminate treaties, effectively rendering presidents above the law when it comes to treaties.

To support these revisionist views, Yoo relies heavily and repeatedly on a rigid dichotomy between foreign affairs—which he sees, in the British tradition, as the executive's domain—and domestic matters—which he sees as the province of the legislature. But as we have seen, the Constitution's framers explicitly rejected such a rigid division, giving Congress and the Senate substantial power over functions that the British saw as executive in nature, including the power to make war and treaties, and expressly assigning the judiciary the responsibility to enforce treaties as the "Law of the Land."

If anything, Yoo's historical evidence is even thinner with respect to the treaty power and the Supremacy Clause than it is with respect to the clause on declaring war. As Jack Rakove, one of the foremost historians of the federal period, has concluded, the framers "were virtually of one mind when it came to giving treaties the status of law." As other historians have pointed out, one of the principal incentives for convening the Constitutional Convention was the embarrassing refusal of state governments to enforce treaties. The Supremacy Clause solved that problem in as direct a way as possible—by making treaties the "Law of the Land," enforceable in courts and binding on government and citizenry alike. That treaties were not thought to need further implementing is underscored by the framers' unanimous decision to omit treaty enforcement from Congress's enumerated powers, "as being superfluous since treaties were to be 'laws.'" Yoo's account turns that conclusion on its head; his reading would render superfluous the Supremacy Clause's assertion that treaties are laws. If treaties had domestic force only when implemented by a subsequent statute, as Yoo maintains, then the statute itself would have the status of the "Law of the Land," not the treaty.

Yoo is no more convincing with respect to presidential interpretation of treaties. He maintains that, because foreign policy is an executive prerogative, the executive must be able to reinterpret and terminate treaties unilaterally. But although the Constitution plainly envisioned the president as the principal negotiator of treaties, it gave clear responsibilities for treaties to the other branches; all treaties must be approved by two-thirds of the Senate, and once ratified, treaties become "law" enforceable by the courts. The president must certainly be able to interpret treaties to "execute" the laws, just as he must be able to interpret statutes for that purpose, but there is no reason why his interpretations of treaties should be any more binding on courts or the legislature than his interpretations of statutes.

The Rule of Law

Yoo's views on the war and treaty powers share two features. First, they both depart radically from the text of the Constitution. He would reduce the power to "declare War" to a mere formality, a courtesy to the enemy, and he would render entirely superfluous the Supremacy Clause's provision that treaties are the "Law of the Land." It is ironic that a president who proclaims his faith in "strict construction" of the Constitution would have found Yoo's interpretations so persuasive, for Yoo is anything but a strict constructionist. One of the arguments most often made in defense of "originalism" is that interpretations emphasizing a "living" or evolving Constitution are too open-ended and, accordingly, permit judges to stray too far from the text. Yoo unwittingly demonstrates that his brand of originalism is just as vulnerable to that criticism as other approaches, if not more so. He not only departs from the text but contradicts the principles that underlie it.

Second, and more significantly, all of Yoo's departures from the text of the Constitution point in one direction—toward eliminating legal checks on presidential power over foreign affairs. He is candid about this and defends his theory on the grounds that it preserves "flexibility" for the executive in foreign affairs. But the specific "flexibility" he seeks to preserve is the flexibility to involve the nation in war without congressional approval and to ignore and violate international commitments with impunity. As Carlos Vazquez, a professor of law at Georgetown, has argued in response to Yoo, "flexibility has its benefits, but so does precommitment." The Constitution committed the nation to a legal regime that would make it difficult to go to war and that would provide reliable enforcement of international obligations. Yoo would dispense with both in the name of letting the president have his way.

Even if Yoo is wrong about the original understanding in 1787, is he wrong about 2005? As the subtitle of his book indicates, his argument rests not just on revisionist history but also on arguments about what is practically necessary in a twenty-first-century world threatened by terrorism and weapons of mass destruction. He contends that these developments demand that the president have the leeway to insulate his foreign policy decisions both from the will of Congress and from the demands of international law. Here it is worth reviewing the positions Yoo advocated while in the executive branch and since, and their consequences in the War on Terror.

At every turn, Yoo has sought to exploit the "flexibility" he finds in the Constitution to advocate an approach to the War on Terror in which legal limits are either interpreted away or rejected outright. Just two weeks after the September 11 attacks, Yoo sent an extensive memo to Tim Flanigan, deputy White House counsel, arguing that the president had unilateral authority to use military force not only against the terrorists responsible for the September 11 attacks but against terrorists anywhere on the globe, with or without congressional authorization.

Yoo followed that opinion with a series of memos in January 2002 maintaining, against the strong objections of the State Department, that the Geneva Conventions should not be applied to any detainees captured in the conflict in Afghanistan. Yoo argued that the president could unilaterally suspend the conventions, that al Qaeda was not party to the treaty, that Afghanistan was a "failed state" and therefore the president could ignore the fact that it had signed the conventions, and that the Taliban had failed to adhere to the requirements of the Geneva Conventions regarding the conduct of war and therefore deserved no protection. Nor, he argued, was the president bound by customary international law, which insists on humane treatment for all wartime detainees. Relying on Yoo's reasoning, the Bush administration claimed that it could capture and detain any person whom the president said was a member or supporter of al Qaeda or the Taliban and could categorically deny all detainees the protections of the Geneva Conventions, including restrictions on inhumane interrogation practices and allowing a hearing to permit them to challenge their status.

Echoing Yoo, Alberto Gonzales, then White House counsel, argued that one of the principal reasons for denying detainees protection under the Geneva Conventions was to "preserve flexibility" and make it easier to "quickly obtain information from captured terrorists and their sponsors." When CIA officials reportedly raised concerns that the methods they were using to interrogate high-level al Qaeda detainees—such as waterboarding—might subject them to criminal liability, Yoo was again consulted. In response, he drafted the August 1, 2002, torture memo, signed by his superior, Jay Bybee, and delivered to Gonzales. In that memo, Yoo "interpreted" the criminal and international law bans on torture in as narrow and legalistic a way as possible; his evident purpose was to allow government officials to use as much coercion as possible in interrogations.

Yoo wrote that threats of death are permissible if they do not threaten "imminent death" and that drugs designed to disrupt the personality may be administered as long as they do not "penetrate to the core of an individual's ability to perceive the world around him." He said that the law prohibiting torture did not prevent interrogators from inflicting mental harm as long as it was not "prolonged." Physical pain could be inflicted as long as it was less severe than the pain associated with "serious physical injury, such as organ failure, impairment of bodily function, or even death."

Even this interpretation did not preserve enough executive "flexibility" for Yoo. In a separate section of the memo, he argued that, if these loopholes were not sufficient, the president was free to order outright torture. Any law limiting the president's authority to order torture during wartime, the memo claimed, would "violate the Constitution's sole vesting of the Commander-in-Chief authority in the President."

Since leaving the Justice Department, Yoo has also defended the practice of "extraordinary renditions," in which the United States has kidnapped numerous "suspects" in the War on Terror and "rendered" them to third countries with records of torturing detainees. He has argued that the federal courts have no right to review actions by the president that are said to violate the War Powers Clause. And he has defended the practice of targeted assassinations, otherwise known as "summary executions." In short, the flexibility Yoo advocates allows the administration to lock up human beings indefinitely without charges or hearings, to subject them to brutally coercive interrogation tactics, to send them to other countries with a record of doing worse, to assassinate persons it describes as the enemy without trial, and to keep the courts from interfering with all such actions.

Has such flexibility actually aided the United States in dealing with terrorism? In all likelihood, the policies and attitudes Yoo has advanced have made the country less secure. The abuses at Guantánamo and Abu Ghraib have become international embarrassments for the United States and, by many accounts, have helped to recruit young people to join al Qaeda. The United States has squandered the sympathy it had on September 12, 2001, and we now find ourselves in a world perhaps more hostile than ever before.

With respect to detainees, thanks to Yoo, the United States is now in an untenable bind: on the one hand, it has become increasingly unacceptable for the United States to hold hundreds of prisoners indefinitely without trying them; on the other hand, our coercive and inhumane interrogation tactics have effectively granted many of the prisoners immunity from trial. Because the evidence we might use against them is tainted by their mistreatment, trials would likely turn into occasions for exposing American brutal interrogation tactics. This predicament was entirely avoidable. Had we given alleged al Qaeda detainees the fair hearings required by the Geneva Conventions at the outset, and had we conducted humane interrogations at Guantánamo, Abu Ghraib, Camp Mercury, and elsewhere, few would have objected to holding some detainees for the duration of the military conflict, and we could have tried those responsible for war crimes. What has been so objectionable to many in the United States and abroad is the government's refusal to accept even the limited constraints of the laws of war.

The consequences of Yoo's vaunted "flexibility" have been self-destructive for the United States—we have turned a world in which international law was on our side into one in which we see it as our enemy. The Pentagon's National Defense Strategy, issued in March 2005, states, "Our strength as a nation state will continue to be challenged by those who employ a strategy of the weak, using international fora, judicial processes, and terrorism."

The proposition that judicial processes—the very essence of the rule of law—are to be dismissed as a strategy of the weak, akin to terrorism, suggests the continuing strength of Yoo's influence. When the rule of law is seen simply as a device used by terrorists, something has gone perilously wrong. Michael Ignatieff has written that "it is the very nature of a democracy that it not only does, but should, fight with one hand tied behind its back. It is also in the nature of democracy that it prevails against its enemies precisely because it does." Yoo persuaded the Bush administration to untie its hand and abandon the constraints of the rule of law. Perhaps that is why we are not prevailing.

CHAPTER 3

The Absent Congress

GARY HART

Upon entering office, every member of Congress, both in the House of Representatives and Senate, takes an oath of office. This oath requires a congressional member to "support and defend the Constitution of the United States." Between the 2001 and 2006 elections, the Republican majority and, on occasion, too many Democrats overwhelmingly behaved as if they had taken an oath to "support and defend the president."

Article I of the Constitution establishes the authority and duties of Congress. It is not the first article by accident. The powers of Congress to oversee the activities of the executive branch are nowhere explicitly enumerated in the Constitution. They are, instead, inherent in and implied by all the other legislative powers of Congress specifically enumerated in Article I, section 8, including the authority to enact laws, to raise revenues and appropriate funds, to raise and support an army and navy, to declare war, to impeach the president and other executive officers, and a variety of other duties. To guarantee that the laws of the United States, and that these various other powers, are being faithfully executed requires knowledge of executive branch activities, largely obtained through congressional hearings, inquiry into the methods of statutory enforcement, monitoring the proper conduct of administrators, and accounting for the expenditure of taxpayer dollars.

The constant and vigilant review of the branch of government that administers the laws is a necessary corollary of Congress's other enumerated powers. Congressional oversight activity of the executive branch is absolutely crucial to the proper functioning of a constitutional democracy. It is the principal way the administrative branch is held accountable.

The Constitution defines congressional authority broadly, to include the power "to make all laws which shall be necessary and proper for carrying into execution the foregoing powers, and all other powers vested by this Constitution of the United States, or in any Department or Officer thereof." In 1789, the oversight principle was confirmed by Congress when it created the Department of the Treasury and required it to report directly to Congress on all expenditures and accounts. Several Supreme Court decisions have confirmed this oversight responsibility. One of the Court's most explicit decisions concluded as follows:

> The power of the Congress to conduct investigations is inherent in the legislative process. That power is broad. It encompasses inquiries concerning the administration of existing laws as well as proposed or possibly needed statutes. It includes surveys of defects in our social, economic, or political system for the purpose of enabling the Congress to remedy them. It comprehends probes into departments of the Federal Government to expose corruption, inefficiency, or waste. (*Watkins v. United States*, 354 U.S. 178 [1957])

Oversight is defined in the dictionary as "supervision," "superintendence," "direction," and "protection," and its synonyms include "responsibility" and "accountability." It is Congress's responsibility to hold the executive accountable both to Congress and to the American people. John Stuart Mill held that "the proper office of a representative assembly is to watch and control the government." In *Federalist No. 51*, James Madison articulated his ideal of checks and balances as "subordinate distribution of power, where the constant aim is to divide and arrange the several offices in such a manner that each may be a check on the other." In an 1885 essay, *Congressional Government*, Woodrow Wilson placed oversight on a plane with legislating itself as the principal duty of the Congress: "Quite as important as legislation is vigilant oversight of administration."

In a Congressional Research Service report for Congress, the purposes of oversight are detailed. They include improving "the efficiency, economy, and effectiveness of governmental operations"; evaluating programs and performance; preventing inadequate administration, as well as waste, abuse, arbitrary conduct, and illegal or unconstitutional behavior; protecting civil liberties and constitutional rights; informing the public; collecting information for future legislation or for improving existing legislation; and preventing encroachment by the executive on legislative authority and prerogative.

Congressional oversight is principally conducted through hearings. Except in cases involving national security, these hearings are open to the public. They thus serve two purposes: they demonstrate congressional vigilance, and, through the media, they educate the people about their public business.

Despite overwhelming concurrence regarding congressional responsibility for oversight of the executive, for all intents and purposes Congress has failed to perform its oversight function for the past six years. Thus, by omission, Congress has violated its oath of office. But the issue before the nation goes beyond the blatant failure of Congress to carry out its oversight responsibilities; it extends to the purposeful and willful obstruction of those responsibilities.

The failure of Congress to hold the Bush administration accountable has invited a wholesale abuse of executive authority. The period from 2001 until 2007 has been historic by any measure. The Congresses of the early twenty-first century have not been burdened by the Cold War, but these Congresses have presided over a new age marked most vividly by jihadist attacks on the homeland of the United States. In September 2001, President Bush focused the energies of both the government and the nation on a War on Terrorism. Legislatively, this declaration has produced an open-ended war resolution authorizing the use of large-scale military force in Afghanistan and Iraq, Patriot Acts I and II, and statutory authority to ignore international law and Geneva Conventions in the treatment of prisoners in those wars. Administratively, the Bush administration has undertaken massive surreptitious wiretapping and surveillance of U.S. citizens, the elaborate scrutiny of domestic and international financial transactions, the operation of a far-flung secret prison system, and the rendition of suspects to countries notable for resorting to torture.

Neither the Bush legislative nor administrative agendas resulting from 9/11 have been placed under the constitutional scrutiny of Congress through its oversight responsibilities. As the nation's founders fully appreciated, an executive operating without the restraints of congressional oversight and, therefore, public scrutiny, especially in times of national threat, is an executive tempted toward the abuse of power and excessive zeal in unilateral actions.

Congressional oversight is not instituted as a way to harass the executive branch or as a barrier to the conduct of its constitutional duties. Indeed, if Congress were to abuse its authority through excessive zeal in this regard, its members would be severely penalized by the people at the polls. Reasonable balance and latitude and prudent judgment on both sides is required. But with the virtual abdication of congressional oversight responsibility in the early years of the twenty-first century, the central instruments for the proper functioning of democratic governance—accountability and responsibility—have been sacrificed.

Historians will find it exceptional that President George W. Bush has operated for one and a half presidential terms with so little restraint. His own Republican supporters in Congress have willingly provided him with the status of monarch. And the Democratic minority opposition party, in too many cases and with a few important exceptions, permitted itself to be cowed into silence by methods of political intimidation. Those with the courage to resist unwise, and quite possibly unconstitutional, legislation and to criticize unilateral governance by presidential fiat have been met with charges of undermining national security and even condoning terrorist actions. Thus, the majority has willingly sacrificed its constitutional responsibilities, and too many in the minority largely allowed themselves to be intimidated into silence.

It was not until 2006, almost four years after the unilateral and unprovoked invasion of Iraq, that President Bush accepted responsibility for his conduct of the war. He did so out of response to pressure from the public, not because of pressure from Congress. Few of his administration's other actions have been accounted for either to Congress or to the people.

If Congress were now to begin carrying out its constitutional duties, its oversight activities would continue nonstop for months simply to catch up to the current hour. With regard to the war in Iraq alone, many questions abound. Who is responsible for the failure of intelligence regarding the alleged presence of weapons of mass destruction, alleged ties between Saddam Hussein and al Qaeda, and Iraq's alleged intent to attack the United States? How much has the war cost, and where have the tens of billions of dollars for occupation and reconstruction gone? Why has Iraqi reconstruction failed, and can it ever be satisfactorily achieved? Did the administration massively waste taxpayer dollars via no-bid contracts with politically favored construction companies? Why was protective equipment not made available to American troops when the insurgency began in 2003? Why were Department of State plans for reconstruction totally ignored? And the list of unanswered, and largely unasked, questions goes on.

In a Special Investigations Division report on January 17, 2006, by the Committee on Government Reform's minority staff of the House of Representatives, this conclusion was presented: "During the last five years, the Republican-controlled Congress has failed to meet this constitutional oversight responsibility. On issue after issue, the Congress has failed to conduct meaningful investigations of significant allegations of wrongdoing by the Bush Administration. [T]his approach stands in stark contrast to the breadth and intrusiveness of congressional investigations of the [previous] Clinton Administration."

This report cites at least fifteen instances of this congressional dereliction, having to do both with the war in Iraq and domestic political abuses. First among these were the repeated statements made by administration officials before the invasion of Iraq regarding Iraq's production of chemical, biological, and nuclear weapons and its ties to al Qaeda. Republican congressional leaders refused repeated requests by opposition Democrats and the press to investigate these misstatements. When no weapons of mass destruction were discovered in Iraq, and when no ties between Iraq and al Qaeda could be verified, those same congressional leaders suggested that the president and the administration had been given poor intelligence on both subjects. However, demands for hearings on whether intelligence had been poor or had been intentionally manipulated were similarly rejected. Congress blatantly refused to determine who should be held accountable for promoting false reasons for undertaking an unprecedented preemptive war resulting in almost 25,000 American casualties and hundreds of thousands of Iraqi casualties.

One of the results of the wars in Iraq and Afghanistan was the creation of a series of prisons for "detainees," many of whom were noncombatants, and the abuse of those prisoners at Abu Graib, Guantánamo, Bagram, and a number of other locations still not disclosed. There has been no serious congressional assessment of responsibility for these abuses and those accountable for them, despite statements by former senior administration officials that the policies regarding treatment of prisoners originated in the offices of Vice President Dick Cheney and former Secretary of Defense Donald Rumsfeld.

In addition, the Intelligence Identity Protection Act of 1982 was violated by at least two senior Bush administration officials in the public disclosure of the identity of Valerie Plame, a covert CIA officer. This legislation, passed in the wake of disclosure of high-level intelligence operatives in the 1970s that resulted in at least one death, was designed to protect those developing the nation's most crucial intelligence in an undercover and often dangerous manner. No congressional hearings or investigations have been held to determine responsibility for this serious violation of federal law.

Similarly, the Foreign Intelligence Surveillance Act (FISA) of 1978 was violated by a secret presidential order in 2002 authorizing the National Security Agency to conduct virtually unlimited wiretapping of and eavesdropping on the telecommunications of American citizens without obtaining a judicial warrant, as required by FISA. More importantly, this order violated the Fourth Amendment to the Constitution protecting American citizens from unreasonable searches and seizures except where authorized by warrants based upon probable cause. Though a select number of members of Congress were briefed on the program, even after its public disclosure Congress refused to investigate whether this massive and intrusive program was both necessary and legal. Few rights in a democracy are more sacred than the right of a citizen and his or her property to be free from arbitrary state intrusion. Congress seemed unencumbered by concerns for constitutional rights.

Tens of billions of dollars have been spent on the reconstruction of Iraq, in a number of cases on contracts awarded without competitive bidding to the Halliburton Corporation, whose former chief executive officer was Vice President Dick Cheney. There have been a considerable number of published reports documenting misperformance, nonperformance, and waste and abuse in those, and other, contracts. Despite repeated requests from minority House and Senate members, Republican congressional leaders refused to explore the role Vice President Cheney played in the issuance of those contracts or the serious malfeasance in their performance.

Overall, between 2002 and 2007, Congress virtually abdicated its constitutional responsibility to investigate the facts leading up to the war in Iraq, its conduct, and the occupation chaos in its aftermath. In contrast to this blatant partisanship, during the height of World War II, a Democratic senator, Harry Truman, conducted public hearings on defense contractor fraud and abuse under a Democratic president, Franklin Roosevelt. And Democratic senators similarly conducted hearings on the conduct of the war in Vietnam being carried out by a Democratic president, Lyndon Johnson; by revealing that the war was going nowhere, those hearings contributed to its eventual conclusion. It is, thus, nothing short of unconscionable for early twenty-first-century Congresses to abdicate their responsibilities in order to protect their partisan interests. History will judge this dereliction of duty harshly.

But rank partisanship on the part of Congress during the early years of the twenty-first century is not confined to the war in Iraq. Most notably, the disaster in the Gulf Coast area brought on by Hurricane Katrina represented a classic case study in government mismanagement and ineffectiveness. Though efforts were made to assign responsibility to middle-level officials in the Federal Emergency Management Agency, when the scope of federal bungling and mismanagement were revealed, ample evidence existed that high-level White House officials were implicated in the failed federal response to this historic disaster. Yet the House of Representatives minority report concludes that congressional majority leadership "failed to obtain the most relevant evidence of the White House role in the failed federal response to Hurricane Katrina."

In the early months of the Bush administration in 2001, Vice President Cheney met with energy industry officials, all of whom had vital commercial interests in the outcome, to discuss formulation of a national energy plan. "The White House energy plan that resulted from the task force's work," according to the House minority report, "contained dozens of specific recommendations from top energy industry campaign contributors such as Enron." The House, and subsequently the Senate, under control of President Bush's party refused requests to conduct oversight hearings on the identity of the energy officials and the coincidence of their companies' contribution to the 2000 election campaign and the provisions of the energy plan from which they benefited.

By all accounts, there have been multiple and massive conflicts of interest in a variety of federal agencies by industry officials appointed to administrative and regulatory positions directly related to the companies and industries they previously represented, and to which they subsequently returned. These conflicts included the deputy secretary of the Department of the Interior, who dealt with issues of great concern to companies for which he had previously lobbied; the chief Medicare official, who left office to join pharmaceutical interests directly affected by drug legislation he drafted; the president's chief political advisor, who met with representatives of companies in which he held stock; and the chairman of the Defense Policy Board, who received a high six-figure fee from a company seeking Defense Department approval of a very lucrative project in China. In these and dozens of similar cases, Congress has repeatedly refused to conduct public hearings on blatant conflict of interest charges.

Additionally, according to the House minority report, "Administration officials have repeatedly distorted and suppressed scientific evidence for political purposes." They "have manipulated scientific advisory committees by appointing members based on political considerations as opposed to expertise, interfered with the conduct of federally-funded research in order to bias the outcome, and distorted scientific findings when communicating them to Congress and the public." Almost to the same degree, individuals with intense religious biases have been carefully selected for appointment to administrative posts, boards and commissions, and other positions of trust to ensure that a favored set of religious "values" relating to reproductive rights, stem cell research, and other divisive social issues is promoted. And prominent conservative religious figures have been routinely consulted on national policies and the administration of public laws. Yet neither in cases of scientific ignorance nor in those of religious bias has Congress examined whether the results amounted to purposeful perversion of the public trust and the public interest.

In key cases of voter manipulation in Texas and Georgia, the Department of Justice has refused to enforce the Voting Rights Act of 1965. Congress refused to call the Justice Department to account, despite the resignation of career professionals in the department in protest. And in numerous cases of alleged waste, fraud, and abuse of contracts granted by the Department of Homeland Security, Congress has also refused to carry out its constitutionally mandated duty to see that the laws of the nation are faithfully executed.

The list of reported instances of administration neglect, mismanagement, and manipulation seems almost unlimited. But whether it is the failure to enforce laws and regulations protecting the public from mercury contamination, farm pollution, and carcinogens in the air or the influence of tobacco industry lobbyists on tobacco-related legislation, the response remains the same: no congressional oversight, no administration accountability.

Even more questions arise as to unilateral, often surreptitious, actions taken by the executive branch. Why is the administration violating the Fourth Amendment to the Constitution and the Federal Intelligence Surveillance Act by refusing to submit wiretapping authorizations to special secure courts? What statutory authority does the president have to render suspects to foreign countries to be tortured? Where are U.S. prisons outside the United States located, and who is operating them? How long will "detainees" and "unlawful combatants" be detained at Guantánamo and elsewhere without due process of law?

Most of all, by what authority does the president claim to be above the laws and Constitution of the United States? And overshadowing all else is this question: Was the invasion and occupation of Iraq genuinely required for U.S. national security, and, if so, why?

Absent a demonstration of candor and openness heretofore not evidenced by the Bush administration, the only constitutional process by which these questions, and a host of others, will be answered is via congressional oversight, with administration witnesses subjected to straightforward questions under oath and under the bright light of public scrutiny. This process is what America's founders assumed would be required to guarantee democratic accountability.

What possible justification might be given, history will surely ask, for Congress to be so submissive, abeyant, and acquiescent? It is difficult to know how anyone elected to represent a constituency either in the House or Senate justifies setting aside his or her constitutional duties in favor of putative party loyalty. Few if any of those who have achieved distinction in congressional service over the years have placed party before duty, the common good, and the national interest. Schoolchildren know that the oath of office trumps party loyalty any day of the week. The Congresses of the past six years, however, defy even this elementary school knowledge.

Lockstep party loyalty, especially when the lives of Americans are at stake, reveals a fundamental misunderstanding and misinterpretation of the nature of representative government. One is not elected to the House or Senate to represent a party; one is elected to represent an entire constituency, including those of other parties or no party. And one is elected to uphold the national interest and the common good. To surrender one's independence of judgment in the interest of party loyalty is to sacrifice personal integrity and sacred honor and to violate one's solemn oath of office.

From the performance or, better, nonperformance of recent Congresses, it is possible only to conclude that some groupthink or mass psychology has been at work. If so, then good men and women are not suborned by a system of partisan orthodoxy once elected; rather, potential candidates are preselected for their rigid commitment to that orthodoxy before being admitted to the ranks of nominated candidates. By this ritual, the *select* become qualified to enter among the *elect* by surrendering their personal judgment on a prescribed list of social issues such as abortion, of economic issues such as tax cuts for the wealthy, and of foreign policy issues such as unconditional permission for the president of their party to use military force as he sees fit. And on these and many related issues, from these carefully preselected party loyalists, there would be no dissent.

If this process seems foreign to democratic traditions, it is understandable, for this process has more in common with a sophisticated form of authoritarianism than with liberal democracy. An acquiescent Congress, partisan in an almost robotic sense, is anathema to the U.S. Constitution. But that is exactly the Congress we have had. To understand how far America has come down this road, it is necessary only to remember once again a Democratically controlled Senate holding a Democratic White House accountable for the tragedy of Vietnam.

Even the minority Democrats, unable to block administration actions and proposed legislation, cannot escape criticism. The role of the opposition party is to question, to force daylight into dark corners, and, particularly in the case of the Senate, to use the rules to force attention if not also disclosure; that is, if necessary, to shame the press into doing its job. Take the case of Iraq. Democrats were forced to vote on a resolution authorizing the Bush administration to use force in Iraq, ostensibly after all other diplomatic options were exhausted. More than half of the Democrats in the Senate and almost half in the House approved the resolution. But they failed to use the occasion to demand full disclosure. What other major democratic powers were going to join us? How long would we be there? How much would it cost? And what were the projected casualties? These are eminently reasonable questions to ask before voting to go to war. And it is eminently reasonable to demand answers before blind approval is given. In retrospect, of course, the Bush administration was not about to answer these questions honestly, either because its representatives did not know the answers or they did not want to be on record giving false answers and then, subsequently, be held to account. But refusal to answer the ultimate questions regarding war and peace provides extraordinarily strong grounds upon which to deny an approving vote.

Once again, the fear factor seemed to dominate. We were at war against terrorism, according to the president. A nation traumatized by bloody-minded violence against three thousand of its innocent citizens overwhelmingly supported the president in this war. To dissent, even to question, was an invitation to be branded as weak, vacillating, and timid. Given the lack of more solid national security credentials, too many Democrats took the easy course and gave the executive branch free rein. And some continued to do so even after the stated basis for the invasion of Iraq proved false, after the liberated nation turned against its liberators, and after America found itself deeply enmeshed in a bloody, violent, and interminable insurgency.

The pattern of unchallenged abuse of executive power under the Bush administration is so widespread and so endemic that it cannot be justified on any traditional constitutional grounds, including, as with the case of Iraq, the ultimate excuse for the concentration of power—national security. The only conceivable argument that can explain this concentration of power, and its almost inevitable abuse, is a premise called the theory of the "unitary presidency." This theory traces its roots to Watergate and the impeachment of President Richard Nixon. Republican veterans of this period, including most notably Dick Cheney and Donald Rumsfeld, emerged from the experience convinced that the application of checks and balances and of congressional oversight authority had so weakened the nation as to require reassertion of unilateral presidential powers, including some not granted in the Constitution. This dubious theory found intellectual roots in the Federalist Society and similar conservative organizations.

The theory seems to rest upon the proposition that Article II united the administrative authority of the Constitution in the person of the president; therefore, any action taken by anyone in the executive branch traces its authority to that unitary principle. Any action, taken by any officer of any agency or department of the executive branch, is taken in the name of the president and therefore is authorized by the Article II conference of exclusive executive power.

Adherents of this theory cite portions of the early constitutional debates that argued for a "unitary" executive. But those debates involved a contest between two plans: the Virginia Plan, which insisted on a single occupant in the presidency, and the New Jersey Plan, which proposed an executive council wherein executive authority would be shared. Nowhere in the constitutional debate was it suggested that a president cannot be held accountable, be questioned by Congress, or be responsible to the legislative branch for the administration of the nation's laws.

Though past administrations have at various times sought to assert extraordinary authority, usually in times of war or national emergency, none has gone as far as the second Bush presidency in claiming the power to obey portions of laws with which it concurs and to ignore or violate portions of laws that restrict its powers. These claims, mostly contained in "signing statements" accompanying more than five hundred acts of Congress, amount to an unconstitutional exercise of a line-item veto. They have been accomplished without citing the veto authority in the Constitution and amount to a simple declaration of intent not to obey the law.

The "unitary presidency" theory essentially means that the president can do whatever he deems to be in the national interest (in Nixon's famous formulation, "if the president does it, it is not illegal") without accounting for it to the Congress and the

American people. The attacks of 9/11 merely provided the occasion and the excuse to put this bizarre and unconstitutional theory into practice. Secret prisons would be created. In violation of international law and the Geneva Conventions, torture of "detainees" would be permitted. The ancient right of habeas corpus would be unilaterally suspended. The Fourth Amendment guarantee of the security of person and property would be trampled. The oversight of both courts and Congress, and thus the whole Madisonian concept of checks and balances, would be summarily dismissed.

By themselves, these and many more abuses of power by the executive would represent a dark period of American history and an even darker cloud over the American Constitution. This cloud loomed even darker, however, when it was accompanied by a virtually complete dereliction of duty by Congress.

In this way, the majority Republicans surrendered their individual judgments and identities even before walking through the doors of the House of Representatives and the Senate, and too many minority Democrats were cowed into submission. This is hardly a prescription for an Article I Congress constitutionally required to hold the executive branch of government accountable for its faithful execution of the laws of the United States.

Confronted with the possibility that such congressional abdication might occur, the nation's founders would no doubt have gritted their collective teeth and allowed for its conceivability. They would have found the possibility highly unlikely, however, given what they knew of the independence of the American character, the good judgment and common sense of the American people, and the inherent resistance of Americans to one-party rule, especially to a party of lockstep automatons.

But even that scenario, they surely believed, could not last long. The abdication of personal judgment, integrity, and honor, not to mention constitutional duty, would, sooner or later, have to be corrected. That process of correction finally began with the congressional election of 2006. The degree to which a change in the partisan balance of power in the House of Representatives and the Senate also represents a reassertion by the new Congress of its constitutional authority remains to be seen.

If the American people want one-party rule, or even one narrow wing of one party rigidly enforcing its own internal discipline on itself, they can surely choose to have it. But it will in no case be the kind of checked-and-balanced form of liberal democratic government brilliantly devised by James Madison and others. It will be an absolutist autocracy that obeys only its own rules, admits only an orthodox membership, creates its own coded language, treats disagreement as heresy, brooks no dissent from within or without, demonizes its opponents, and listens only to its own counsel. In terms of the acquisition of power, it may be successful, but it will not be democracy. And it will, inevitably, be corrupt.

And corrupt, indeed, the recent Congresses became. Corrupt in the modern sense, and corrupt in the classic sense. Today we think of corruption as granting favors in return for financial rewards. Given the embrace by congressional members of privileged special interests, the corruption of Abramoff, Cunningham, Ney, and quite possibly others to follow was as predictable as the sunrise. The concentration of power in the hands of the orthodox few led to the incorporation of the lobbying and fundraising system into the process of governance and the narrow corridors of power. Its code name was "the K Street project," and it forced all campaign money through the hands, and all access through the doors, of those lobbyists admitted to the brotherhood of the orthodox. It was an invitation to venality as chilling as an unavoidable train crash.

But corruption has also occurred in the classic sense as defined by the ancient republicans, that is, placing one's personal or special interest ahead of the common good. To the Athenians and early Romans, this kind of corruption was what they feared the most. It was the destroyer of republics. Given the trading of favors for campaign contributions and the explosion of "ear-markings" for special interest projects, by the standards of the classic republic, the American republic is massively corrupt.

Our founders repeatedly concerned themselves with the corruption of the American republic, for they knew that a corrupt Congress was an emasculated Congress. They certainly did not seek a Congress that quickly, unquestioningly, and quietly approved all executive actions and failed in its oversight responsibilities. Instead, they feared the concentration of power in the hands of the one or the few, especially when the few were not elected. They would be appalled at the concentration of power in the current executive, the enthusiastic embrace of a lobbying and campaign finance system designed to perpetuate that concentrated power, and the sight of a Congress that acquiesced in it all.

If our elected representatives do not protect the American people from an executive branch operating outside the rule of law, who will? If members of the House of Representatives and the Senate choose repeatedly and consistently to abdicate the responsibilities they took an oath to uphold, our last resort rests in the courts. It is no accident that those promoting a theory such as "the unitary presidency" would also want a compliant

Congress that will approve judges who agree with this theory and with a social agenda that will justify any measures in its achievement.

There is every reason to believe that history will judge the early years of the twenty-first century in America with astonishment and alarm. Fear eliminated dissent and deliberation. Concentration of power in the presidency was fear's requirement. Pre-Enlightenment attitudes toward tolerance, inquiry, and liberal thought in domestic matters joined unilateral and imperial preventive warfare in global affairs. Unquestioning loyalty was the requirement to approach the throne of power.

The bulwark of the people's rights since the Magna Carta—representative government—failed in its duty and failed absolutely.

CHAPTER 4

More Secrets, Less Security

JOHN D. PODESTA

Consider the following three documents:

- *A 1962 telegram from the U.S. ambassador to Yugoslavia, George F. Kennan, featuring a translated newspaper article on China's nuclear weapons program.*

- *An intelligence estimate from 1950, written days before Chinese forces crossed into North Korea, predicting that Chinese involvement was "not probable."*

- *A 1950s-era document on the "Feasibility of Participating in Exchange Program with USSR to Study Highway Transportation in the USSR."*

In addition to these three, thousands of similar documents—some seemingly harmless, others potentially embarrassing for the government—have been reclassified due to a secret government program designed to remove historical documents from public view. In fact, according to a February 2006 report by the National Security Archive at George Washington University,

9,500 documents totaling 55,500 pages, some dating as far back as World War II, have been reclassified and withdrawn from public circulation. The study found that eight of the reclassified documents had actually been published as part of the State Department's official history series or made available on the CIA's own database. Taken at face value, perhaps the study's findings could be considered comical, akin to the Soviet Union's penchant for airbrushing out photos of politburo members who had fallen out of favor; however, they are emblematic of a much more serious and alarming trend toward excessive government secrecy.

Upon taking office, President George W. Bush made his penchant for secrecy well known. Early in 2001, the president ordered the National Archives to postpone the release of approximately 68,000 pages of previously restricted presidential records from the Reagan administration. Later that year, he issued an executive order fundamentally reinterpreting the 1978 Presidential Records Act, which requires most records to be released within twelve years after a president leaves office. Under the Bush order, any current or future president can now block the release of any presidential record, perhaps indefinitely.

In the wake of the attacks of September 11, 2001, and the ensuing War on Terror, the Bush administration used the banner of national security to expand the veil of secrecy that began to envelop the federal government shortly after his first inauguration. Examples include:

- a memo issued in 2001 by then Attorney General John Ashcroft, which radically changed the Justice Department's interpretation of the Freedom of Information Act (FOIA) by urging agencies to withhold documents if any possible legal reason existed and thus reversing the previous presumption of disclosure;

- the secret detention of thousands of suspected terrorists, without charge or representation, in facilities located from Guantánamo Bay to Baghdad, where torture and illegal treatment has been documented;
- a memo issued in 2002 by then Chief of Staff Andrew Card, which ordered the immediate reexamination of all public documents posted on the Internet and resulted in the removal of thousands of documents vital to public safety;
- the revelation that the president secretly authorized a National Security Agency program to eavesdrop on domestic phone calls and e-mails without obtaining a wiretapping warrant from the secret Foreign Intelligence Surveillance Court; and
- a 2003 pact made between the National Academy of Sciences (NAS) and the government to censor scientific articles that could compromise national security. The pact, drafted with the help of administration officials, was made after the administration warned the NAS that, if scientific journals did not voluntarily censor, the government would mandate it.

The extent to which the administration has sought to expand government secrecy is not limited to the restriction or withholding of information from public scrutiny. Congress has also been unwillingly left in the dark. For instance, in an April 2006 hearing of the House Judiciary Committee on the Department of Justice, Attorney General Alberto R. Gonzales, the sole witness, consistently dodged a wide range of questions. According to transcripts, he repeatedly responded to the committee members' questions by simply asserting that the information they sought was classified and could not be presented, despite the fact that committee members have security clearances. After many hours and multiple attempts to elicit informative responses, the committee chairman, Representative James Sensenbrenner (R-WI), rhetorically asked the attorney general, "How can we discharge our oversight responsibilities if every time we ask a pointed question we are told that the answer is classified?" Following the hearing, Sensenbrenner remarked, "I am really concerned that the Judiciary Committee has been kind of put in the trash heap."

Adding to congressional frustration is the lack of efficacy of a special panel created to reduce excessive secrecy in government. The Public Interest Declassification Board was established into law in 2000, following a 1997 recommendation from the Moynihan Secrecy Commission, named for its chair, the late Senator Daniel Patrick Moynihan. The board was set up, according to statute, "to promote the fullest possible public access to a thorough, accurate, and reliable documentary record of significant U.S. national security decisions and . . . activities." But the administration did not appoint any members until September 2004, and no funds were appropriated for it until 2005. Moreover, a provision buried within the 2004 intelligence overhaul law enacted by Congress changed the board's charter, adding two seemingly contradictory provisions. As a result of the conflicting provisions, the board's chair told Congress in the fall of 2006 that he could not act except at the request of the president, thus rendering the panel "toothless" for all intents and purposes.

The press has also become an unwitting target of the administration's attempts to restrict access to information in the name of national security. Specifically, the White House is on the verge of creating an Official Secrets Act through its pursuit of individuals who leak information and its threats to prosecute journalists. For instance, after the *New York Times* first revealed the existence of the president's domestic surveillance program, Attorney General Alberto Gonzales hinted that there was a "possibility" that journalists could be prosecuted under the 1917 Espionage Act for publishing classified information. A federal judge in Alexandria, Virginia, accepted the Justice Department's sweeping interpretation of the eighty-nine-year-old law; if this ruling is allowed to stand by the higher courts, every national security journalist and researcher in America could be threatened with prison time. The Bush administration has aggressively invoked the Espionage Act to suppress information rather than to protect national security. For example, in late 2006 the statute was invoked by federal prosecutors to issue a criminal grand jury subpoena, ordering the American Civil Liberties Union to turn over a three-and-a-half-page document that apparently contained no classified information but may have been "mildly embarrassing" for the federal government. If federal prosecutors in New York had not decided to drop the subpoena recently, the ACLU case would have marked the first time in history that a criminal grand jury subpoena was used to recoup leaked material.

Every administration is forced to contend with the terrible consequences of national security leaks, but how an administration chooses to handle them and what it does to prevent them varies and has important consequences. It almost goes without saying that unauthorized disclosures can be extraordinarily harmful to our national security interests and that far too many such disclosures occur. They damage intelligence relationships abroad, compromise intelligence gathering, jeopardize lives, and increase the threat of terrorism. Additionally, it is generally agreed that information must be closely held to protect national security and to engage in effective diplomacy. Often the greater concern is in protecting the method by which information was obtained rather than in protecting the actual content. For example, when disclosures of classified information mention satellite photos or intercepted phone conversations, other nations or organizations often take heed and better conceal their activities.

The need for clandestine actions today is clear; we face an enemy who is neither easily seen nor deterred and resolved to take American lives. However, this legitimate need for operational security has been used by the Bush administration to make broad policies that hide information from public and congressional scrutiny. Its actions in this regard can be attributed to its embrace of the unitary executive theory—a theory that attributes to the executive branch almost unlimited power over government officials and government operations. The president has acted on this theory, expanding executive power and the veil of secrecy over the federal government, at the expense of our system of checks and balances and the security of the American people.

Contrast this view with that of the administration that came before it. For instance, President Bill Clinton vetoed the 2001 Intelligence Authorization Act that contained the so-called Official Secrets Act provision, which would have made any "unauthorized" disclosure of classified information a felony. In stark contrast to the current administration, President Clinton's veto resulted from an intrinsic understanding of the best way to encourage respect for our most important secrets: to set clear standards, demand through administrative enforcement that they be respected, and perhaps most importantly, return secrecy to a limited but necessary role, ultimately reducing the number of secrets overall.

The Threats of Secrecy

James Madison, known as the Father of the Constitution and the recognized author of the Bill of Rights, said that "a popular government without popular information or the means of acquiring it is but a prologue to farce or tragedy or perhaps both." More than five years after the attacks of 9/11, this principle of openness that Madison put forward to the newly formed republic is itself under attack, as we find ourselves living in an unstable, uncertain, and warring world. There is no question that excessive secrecy threatens the pillars of American democracy, but in the post–9/11 world, excessive secrecy also directly threatens our national security interests. Perhaps no point illustrates this better than the findings of the bipartisan 9/11 Commission.

Among its conclusions, the commission found that the way in which the United States conducted counterterrorist operations was unnecessarily complicated, confusing, overly expensive, and secretive. Secrecy in this instance prevented different military, law enforcement, and intelligence officials from sharing relevant information and mounting a singular, effective defense. To address this concern, the commission recommended that the overall amount of money appropriated for national intelligence and its agencies be made public and that Congress pass a separate appropriations act for intelligence. If implemented, this recommendation would force the administration to defend the broad allocations of the tens of billions of dollars that are spent. Without the disclosure of even broad categorical amounts, the commission concluded that it would be difficult to "judge priorities or foster accountability."

Additionally, the commission revealed an even more devastating consequence of excessive secrecy. The final report referred to an interrogation in which the hijackers' bankroller stated that, if the organizers had known that the so-called twentieth hijacker, Zacarias Moussaoui, had been arrested at his Minnesota flight school on immigration charges, the attackers probably would have aborted the mission for fear that Moussaoui would have blown their cover. The commission concluded that only "publicity" could have derailed the attacks.

Not only did the administration fail to heed the commission's warnings about the tragic effects of excessive secrecy on national security, but it actually delayed the release of the commission's findings. As soon as the commission's legal mandate expired, heavy-handed declassification practices were applied. As a result, release of the final staff report on threats to civil aviation were delayed, and the version finally made public contains numerous redactions, some of which needlessly seek to shield information already released by other agencies.

Another example illustrates how excessive secrecy exacerbates the potential for physical harm to the American public. According to a May 2006 report by the New Jersey Work Environment Council (WEC), a chemical catastrophe at any one of six New Jersey facilities could seriously injure or kill nearly one million people living in the area. New Jersey is home to 110 facilities that have the potential to harm thousands of residents in the event of an accidental or terrorism-related worst-case chemical release. A worst-case chemical release from the most hazardous of these facilities, the Kuehne Chemical Company located in Hudson County, could harm up to 12 million people in New Jersey and New York City.

Since 9/11, much of the information regarding facilities using or storing specific, extraordinarily hazardous chemicals has been withdrawn from the Internet and is now only available to facility workers and the public at large in public reading rooms. Facilities' risk management plans were among the first documents to be taken off the Internet. Not surprisingly, then, when the WEC conducted a survey of sixty-five emergency responders and health officers, it found an alarming lack of understanding about toxic risks in New Jersey communities. When asked whether "the majority of residents know what steps to take to protect themselves (e.g., evacuation) if there is a chemical accident in your municipality," fifty-five of the sixty-five respondents (85 percent) said "no."

Risk management plans, along with other data available under federal and state right-to-know laws, were intended to improve the safety of and help protect workplaces and communities not only from terrorism but from accidents. Public safety—and national security interests broadly—are not served by covering up our vulnerabilities. As Sidney J. Casperson, former director of New Jersey's Office of Counterterrorism, said: "The terrorists already know what's out here. The only question is whether we will find a way to protect these targets before they find a way to attack them." As we near the sixth anniversary of the 9/11 attacks, our country is still without meaningful chemical security regulation, leaving the protection of some of our most dangerous plants in the hands of the industry and leaving local communities with little idea of the possible threats brewing in their own backyards.

Whether by accident or terrorist attack, numerous high-level chemical and research facilities around the country have already endured deadly events that have endangered workers and residents in surrounding communities. But rather than arming the public with the information necessary to possibly prevent and protect their families from such incidents, the administration and federal agencies have hidden it.

Consider that the Bush administration has begun building a 60,000-square-foot biodefense laboratory known as the National Biodefense Analysis and Countermeasures Center (NBACC) at a military base in Fort Detrick, Maryland. Once construction is completed, scientists at the NBACC will produce, experiment with, and store some of the world's deadliest bacteria and viruses, including anthrax, Ebola, and common viruses capable of becoming incurable and unstoppable.

The massive NBACC compound will be designated as highly restricted space. Few federal facilities, including nuclear labs, operate under such secrecy. As noted by the *Washington Post*, secrecy has become a defining characteristic of U.S. biodefense policy as implemented by the Department of Homeland Security (DHS), which created the NBACC. Since DHS's inception, the government has been given broad authority to conduct tests of pathogens and the methods of dissemination that could be used in a bioterrorist attack. With minimal oversight and excessive secrecy, the risks posed to the residents in the areas surrounding Fort Detrick increase exponentially. This is especially frightening considering that Fort Detrick is no stranger to deadly incidents—the anthrax spores used in the September 2001 mail attacks were traced back to Fort Detrick.

In addition to exacerbating the potential for physical harm to the public, there is another national security concern posed by the excessive secrecy of the NBACC. Arms-control experts argue that the compound's excessive secrecy might fuel interna-

tional suspicions, leading other countries to pursue secret biological research of their own. Already, the world may be entering into a bioweapons arms race: in the past five years,
numerous governments, including some in the developing
world—India, China, and Cuba among them—have begun
building high-security labs for studying the most lethal bacteria
and viruses. Such actions threaten the enforcement of the Biological and Toxin Weapons Convention (BWC) Treaty, which
was the first internationally binding agreement banning an entire class of weapons of mass destruction, a key element in preventing weapons proliferation. Whether the work at NBACC is
legal or not under the BWC, there is no question that without
transparency the ability of the United States to prevent the proliferation of bioweapons by some of the world's most hostile
regimes—like Iran and North Korea—is significantly undermined, rendering it difficult to leverage diplomatic credibility to
achieve a peaceful resolution.

To protect the American people, clearly the government
must protect the principle of openness. However, the Bush administration has decidedly gone the other way. National security has become the blanket excuse to hide potentially
embarrassing and politically harmful information from the
public. Perhaps the most insidious means by which the administration has covered up its own incompetence is its invocation
of the state secrets privilege. The privilege stems from the 1953
case *United States v. Reynolds,* a suit brought by the relatives of
passengers killed in a mysterious crash of a B–29 airplane in
1948. The relatives sued the government, hoping to gain access
to the plane's accident reports, which they hoped might tell
them why the plane went down, killing their loved ones. These
hopes were dashed, however, when the government successfully

claimed that it possessed a privilege to withhold documents that contained "state secrets." Access to the plane's history was blocked, and the modern state secrets privilege was born.

Decades later, the government declassified the documents. It was revealed that the plane had a history of mechanical failures and accidents. Moreover, the air force had not complied with maintenance directives for the plane, including preventive maintenance orders on the engine, which caught fire and resulted in the deaths of the passengers. In the wake of the *Reynolds* case, the courts began to defer to the government's assertion of privilege as long as it could establish a "reasonable danger" in disclosure. Such deference usually comes with little scrutiny. Even so, previous administrations rarely invoked the state secrets privilege; in the time between the *Reynolds* case and 9/11, nine presidents claimed the privilege a collective total of just fifty-five times. In the five years since the attacks, the Bush administration has already invoked the privilege twenty-two times.

Two cases highlight how the administration has used the Cold War–era privilege to cover up its mistakes or incompetence rather than protect our nation's security. Khaled El-Masri alleged that the government had kidnapped and tortured him in a case of mistaken identity. In the six months of his captivity, his wife and children, believing him to be dead, left their home and moved to Lebanon. Upon his release, El-Masri sued the CIA for his capture and treatment, but the government succeeded in having his case dismissed by invoking the state secrets privilege, claiming that national security would be harmed even by simple admission or denial of his charges. With the aid of the American Civil Liberties Union, El-Masri took his case to the Fourth Circuit Court of Appeals, whose decision on whether the case could proceed was still pending at the time of this writing. In the second instance, Sibel Edmonds, a Turkish translator for the FBI, reported a number of whistleblower allegations ranging from the dispatch of translators without the requisite language skills to Guantánamo Bay to the assignment of relatives of surveillance targets to translate wiretap transcripts. Dismissed after her attempt to bring these incidents to the attention of her supervisors, she sued the government. The government succeeded in its state secrets privilege claim; the district court dismissed the case without any consideration of whether the information needed to vindicate or refute Ms. Edmonds's allegations would truly damage national security. With the dismissal of the Edmonds case, the administration succeeded in preventing potentially damaging information from coming to light and left Edmonds with no legal recourse.

In addition to its frequent invocation of the state secrets privilege, the administration's tendency toward excessive secrecy has led agencies to simply withhold potentially embarrassing information, as noted by Congressman Henry Waxman (D-CA) in a 2005 hearing of the House Committee on Government Reform:

- The State Department withheld unclassified conclusions by the agency's inspector general that the CIA was involved in preparing a grossly inaccurate global terrorism report.
- Over the objections of chief U.S. weapons inspector Charles A. Duelfer, the CIA directed Duelfer to conceal the unclassified names of U.S. companies that conducted business with Saddam Hussein under the Oil for Food program.
- The State Department concealed unclassified information about the role of John Bolton, then under secretary of state

for arms control, in the creation of a fact sheet that falsely claimed that Iraq sought uranium from Niger.

These examples point to a larger problem stemming from the administration's presumption of secrecy: massive overclassification. Since 2002, the number of classification actions undertaken annually nearly doubled. In 2004, the government reached an all-time high of 15.6 million classification actions, and in 2005, it posted a second all-time high of 14.2 million actions. Overclassification comes at great cost to transparency, but it also comes at great cost to our national treasury: for every dollar the federal government spent in 2005 releasing old secrets, it spent $134 creating new ones. The costs are not merely financial but also involve human resources. A virtual bureaucratic army is charged with simply rearranging the growing mountain of "national secrets" rather than working to protect the nation's security.

The ability of agencies to withhold more and more information is a direct result of a new brand of classification. Since the Truman administration, the classification system has been governed by presidential executive orders that set relatively uniform rules across federal agencies, and only a limited number of authorized personnel are permitted to designate information as classified pursuant to that presidential authority. The executive order also establishes guidelines on how information must be declassified.

In contrast, during the Bush administration, a new breed of classification systems has emerged lacking even minimal rules or monitoring. For example, the designation "restricted but unclassified" is governed by a rapidly evolving patchwork of disparate agency regulations and directives. Practically any federal employee has the authority to designate documents "sensitive but unclassified," or SBU. There are no uniform rules about when or how to remove these designations, and there are few checks in place to prevent abuses. As a result of the slippery labeling and loose legal framework governing the withholding of information, both Congress and the American people are left with little idea how frequently information is being withheld, what type of information is being held, the accuracy of the information, and how that information factors into policy decisions that directly concern their own safety. Furthermore, the flagrant abuse of the classification system hurts national security by watering down the very system being abused. As the late Supreme Court Justice Potter Stewart noted, when everything is classified, nothing remains classified.

A Framework for Fewer Secrets, Greater Security

Given the administration's prolonged assault on open government in the name of national security, the Congress must seize upon the opportunity to take a fresh look at how our government decides what information should be kept secret and how those secrets should be preserved. Building on the work of the 9/11 Commission and the Moynihan Secrecy Commission, Congress should conduct a top-to-bottom review of U.S. secrecy policy and consider reforms that will better protect our security, restore checks and balances, and facilitate democratic decision making.

In conducting that review, Congress would be wise to start with three lines of inquiry:

Does the information fall within a class that should presumptively be kept secret? Operational plans, troop movements, human source identities, technological methods of surveillance, and advanced weapons designs must continue to command the highest level of protection.

Does the information's important public value outweigh any risk of harm from public disclosure? For example, in the Clinton administration, the White House worked with the EPA and the FBI on a disclosure regime for information in EPA's toxic release inventory, including emergency evacuation plans. The public was able to receive important public safety information that the FBI had concluded was of no unique value to terrorists. Likewise, under the leadership of Vice President Gore, overhead images from the CORONA, ARGON, and LANYARD intelligence satellite missions, as well as underseas military data, were declassified. The declassified material has since proven to be very valuable to the environmental community's efforts to study and stop the advance of climate change.

Does releasing the information educate the public about security vulnerabilities that, if known, can be corrected by individuals or public action? Justice Louis Brandeis said that sunlight is the best of disinfectants. When applied to the security arena, the principle put forward by Brandeis means that flaws in our national security can be corrected by placing them out in the open—they are thus exposed, addressed, and corrected. History demonstrates that hiding our nation's security vulnerabilities is not an effective strategy.

After considering these three lines of inquiry, the Congress should consider taking the following steps to protect open government and our nation's security:

- Enact a framework statute that creates clear, uniform, legal guidelines to govern the process of classification and declassification of government information.
- Establish a statutory presumption of disclosure unless the government demonstrates that the benefits of secrecy outweigh its costs.
- Require automatic declassification after an appropriate interval unless the government certifies that there is a continued need for secrecy.
- Require agencies to make periodic reports to Congress on their classification and declassification policies and practices.
- Enact reforms to bolster the independence of the Public Interest Declassification Board and empower it to get on with the work of declassifying secrets whose useful life has expired.
- Make public the top line of the annual intelligence budget, as recommended by the 9/11 Commission and the 1996 Commission on the Roles and Capabilities of the United States Intelligence Community.
- Enact legislation, such as that proposed by Senators Patrick Leahy (D-VT) and John Cornyn (R-TX), to require lawmakers to clearly identify and explain new FOIA exemptions, close loopholes in the statute, and help ensure that requests are answered in a timely way.
- Consider statutory provisions that would provide meaningful judicial review of the government's assertion of

the state secrets privilege by directing the courts to weigh the harms and benefits of public disclosure.

Such measures would enhance accountability and increase public confidence, thus helping to ensure that government secrecy is employed only when truly necessary and that information that truly needs to be kept secret is properly protected. The fact that our country has yet to formulate workable, sustainable policies or regulations governing secrecy is a testament to the difficulty and complexity of the task itself. However, as the country continues to face new and varied threats from both inside its borders and beyond, it is imperative that we take on this challenge to protect ourselves and our way of life. Abraham Lincoln, military leader and former president, made the argument succinctly: "If given the truth, the American people can be depended upon to meet any national crisis. The great point is to bring them the real facts."

CHAPTER 5

The Media and Bush's Wars

PETER OSNOS

There is an inherent tension between governments wanting to control the portrayal of events and journalists determined to report what is really happening. In 1734, John Peter Zenger, a printer and editor in New York City, was indicted, tried, and acquitted on charges of sedition and libel against Governor William Cosby of the New York Colony. The jurors accepted the defense's contention that Zenger's articles were not libelous because they were based on facts. There has been a direct line from the fulminations of the colonial regime to the administration of George W. Bush that is intent—at a minimum—on threatening journalists for revealing what the government doesn't think the public has a right to know. Recognizing that this struggle between authorities and the Fourth Estate is an embedded feature of American life doesn't mean, however, that the press ultimately prevails, as Zenger did. The Bush administration's attempts since 9/11 to intimidate and punish the media, or at least to manipulate and mislead it, represent one of the most concerted assaults on the First Amendment since it was written by our revered forefathers.

"Bush's War against the Press" was the headline on a memorable column by James C. Goodale in the *New York Law Journal* after the 2004 election. Goodale was vice-chairman of The New York Times Company during the *Pentagon Papers* case of 1971. He has been at the law firm of Debevoise and Plimpton for many years specializing in media law. Goodale's list of Bush administration actions include officially sanctioned wiretapping of reporters' phones, demands for documents, possible indictments, and a plan to turn the Espionage Act of 1917 into a British-style official secrets act designed to restrict what can be reported in the press. Goodale calls these actions "chilling" and adds that it is hard to believe that they are coincidental. Regardless of whether or not the president has mandated a concerted strategy to restrain reporting of the government's activities, particularly in the national security area, there is no doubt that Bush has been prepared to use every means available (including those of dubious legality) to limit disclosure of any information the White House chooses to protect.

History clearly shows that when government at any level tries to supervise what is disclosed about what it is doing the goals are usually about official convenience rather than the public good. National security is too often used as a shield to permit tactics that in hindsight have invariably turned out to be excessive. We already know that the attacks on New York and Washington in 2001, culminating a period during which al Qaeda's tentacles had reached throughout South Asia, the Middle East, and Africa, became a pretext for the Bush administration to pursue policies at home and abroad that justified restrictions of civil liberties in ways that are astonishing for their boldness. The War on Terror is now enshrined as one of America's greatest tests of freedom in the face of perceived threats from an enemy abroad, with possible fellow-travelers at home.

It is possible to isolate almost any period in time as an illustration of the struggle between governments and the press. The modern era in defining relations between officials and their monitors probably began, however, with the combination of foreign and domestic upheavals known as Vietnam and Watergate. John F. Kennedy was as sophisticated about reporters' needs and as friendly with them as any president has ever been, yet, in retrospect, many of our contemporary issues were initially framed during his thousand-day administration. The *New York Times* was persuaded to downplay the Bay of Pigs preparations, a Pentagon spokesman asserted that dissembling to the press was part of his job, the president's sexual escapades were studiously overlooked, and the FBI and the president's brother, the attorney general, used wiretaps and other forms of sleuthing to keep track of critics and dissidents in the name of protecting the national interest.

But it was Lyndon Johnson and his anguish over the Vietnam War and Richard M. Nixon's toxic brew of political paranoia symbolized by Watergate that truly set the terms for the modern relationship between White Houses and the media. Another critical determinant was the vast prevalence of network television, which magnified and glamorized the role of the press as never before. Although Johnson and his advisers, particularly Defense Secretary Robert S. McNamara, recognized that the war in Vietnam was not leading to a defeat of the North Vietnamese and Vietcong, they insisted that it was. Inevitably, as reporters described what they were witnessing and underscored the contrast between the official version of the war and the unmistakable reality on the ground, trust on all sides gradually broke down. The more the administration insisted on the reliability of their version of events, the more reporters felt it necessary to refute them. That dynamic was ingrained on both sides, and to this day, journalists assume that whatever the government says is suspect, very often with good reason.

The concept of retaliation against the media was turned into policy by the Nixon administration. The public voice of Nixon's antipathy toward the press was Vice President Spiro Agnew. In a book to be published in 2007 called *Very Strange Bedfellows* about this most dysfunctional of political alliances, the writer, Jules Witcover, who was with the *Washington Post* at the time, recreates the era. Agnew was tasked to take on the *New York Times*, the *Washington Post*, and the television networks in particular, and he hurled insults that were often personal. He called the *Post*'s cartoonist, Herblock, who had famously awarded Nixon a clean shave on inauguration day, "that master of sick invective. . . ." With some speechmaking skill of his own and the assistance of wordsmiths such as Pat Buchanan and William Safire (both of whom, of course, later became celebrated commentators themselves), Agnew proclaimed his right to assail the press. In a diary entry quoted by Witcover, Nixon's chief of staff, H. R. Haldeman, warned on the eve of a 1969 Agnew speech in Montgomery, Alabama, "Huge problem late today as [Press Secretary Ron] Ziegler tells me of VP's speech for tomorrow night, a real blast, not just at TV, now he takes on newspapers, a lot of individuals and the kids again. Pretty rough and really goes too far. Problem is Agnew is determined to give it." Haldeman, as tough an operative as Nixon had around him, actually had to restrain, by his own account, Agnew's vituperation.

The speech as given remained harsh and specific, concluding, "I do not seek to intimidate the press, the networks or anyone else from speaking out. But the time for blind acceptance of their opinions is past. And the time for naïve belief in their neutrality is gone." The notion that the press was an adversary to be singled out and attacked became a routine feature of the Nixon administration, clearly instigated by the president.

While primarily rhetorical at the outset, the idea that the press can and should be bullied and, where possible, disciplined became as much a part of administration political strategy as its attitude toward Democrats, the civil rights movement, and war protestors. Because of the enduring battles over the *Pentagon Papers* and, later, the Watergate break-in and cover-up, this period has an almost mythic glow in the media. The outcomes invariably favored the press, and with the collapse of Nixon's power (Agnew himself was an ignominious sideshow), it was possible to assume that a dynamic, aggressive, intrepid media would forever prevail over governments in the pursuit of truth.

As it was in so many other ways, September 11, 2001, became the de facto start of the new century in relations between the White House and the press. What will likely be known in history as the era between 11/9 (November 9, 1989, the day the Berlin Wall came down) and 9/11 will be seen as an interregnum characterized domestically by the president, his intern, and the piercing shrillness surrounding impeachment, which contrived to largely obscure the emergence of many of the profound ideological, religious, and nationalistic issues that dominate our discourse today. The spectacle in Washington and the sanction it gave to the tabloidization of so much coverage was the major media story of the time. When the events of that period settle into history, Bill Clinton's fecklessness will have to be balanced with the media's own focus on tackiness and the cynical gamesmanship of the sort practiced by Newt Gingrich at the expense, it is fair to argue, of exploring issues that turned out to be far more important.

No one will claim that the wars in Iraq and Afghanistan and the vast assortment of conflicts that arise from theocratic extremism and rage of other kinds are not very serious. The threats of nuclear confrontation that were the most dangerous feature of the Cold War have subsided, and it is tempting now to say that they may have been exaggerated, except perhaps for the Cuban Missile Crisis of 1962. But the consequences of terrorism directed from caves, back alleys, and mosques, as well as from government ministries, have the potential to be vastly disruptive. The possibility of weapons of mass destruction being unleashed by a fervent lunatic is a real one. The scale of today's dangers are not figments of anyone's imagination, even though, as is the case, the administration of George W. Bush finds the dangers compatible with its portrayal of its role as the protector of a nation at great risk and, therefore, within its rights to curtail the civil liberties that are an American bedrock.

The Bush administration has been less rhetorically disposed to attack the media than the Nixon administration was. Vice President Dick Cheney can be as blunt an instrument as Agnew, but he uses less public bluster. Nonetheless, Cheney is acerbic. "The press," he said about coverage of the Iraq war, "is, with all due respect—there are exceptions—oftentimes lazy, often simply reports what someone else in the press says without doing their homework." Bush, Cheney, and ousted Defense Secretary Donald Rumsfeld (the latter pair tracing their political sensibilities to Nixon's time) have sought to assert maximum control over all elements of their landscape, and wherever possible, they demonize their adversary. Rumsfeld's assessment of Iraq media coverage (which is deeply ironic given the chaos that has ensued in the conflict) verged on defamation: "Interestingly, all of the exaggerations seem to be on one side. . . . The steady stream of errors all seem to be of a nature to inflame the situation and give heart to the terrorists and to discourage those who hope for success in Iraq."

We have to assume that the administration takes its tone from the president, with political adviser Karl Rove in "the architect" role, as Bush characterized it, at least until the election defeats in 2006. What we don't know is whether, in their Oval Office and telephone chatter, this team uses the same furious, defensive, and obscene language as the Nixon people did. But when it comes to the media, their demeanor and, in many respects, their actions reflect contempt veering all the way to enmity.

A number of factors have combined to make the clash between this administration and the media particularly nasty. The media has become steadily more omnipresent as technology expands, while the widely disparate standards and speed of information make the whole process of information feel almost chaotic. The ricochet of action and reaction means that reflection is at a minimum, and what remains are impressions of conflict rather than specific arguments that support the respective sides. The war in Iraq has been covered extensively, and the mistakes made by the administration have been documented relentlessly in books by Seymour Hersh, Thomas B. Ricks, Bob Woodward, and others. The newspapers, magazines, and broadcast outlets reporting from Iraq are severely constrained in what they can do because of the level of violence. There has never been a war in which the media's potential for reporting has been so undermined by a collapse of the security situation. Yet for all the limitations and cutbacks of staff, the portrait that has emerged from the battlefronts since the aftermath of the 2003 invasion is unmistakably of a situation that has gone terribly wrong.

But the administration succeeded for a very long time in deflecting the obvious conclusion that its blunders were responsible for the debacle. They adopted the mantra that they are engaged in a Global War on Terror that they are winning and that democracy is the goal. For months, polls showed that a majority of the American public did not agree with the administration's boasts of accomplishment. Despite casualties in the tens of thousands, expenditures in the hundreds of billions, and the refutation of administration claims of progress against the Iraqi insurgencies, al Qaeda, and the Taliban, however, the White House was still not in anything like the crisis brought about by the impeachment proceedings that Bill Clinton faced a decade ago over Monica Lewinsky. In the tests of strength between the media and the government over what has been really happening, it is hard to score on the side of the press, as with Vietnam and Watergate, for example. The revelations about Abu Ghraib, Guantánamo, CIA secret prisons, torture, and the denial of fundamental rights have been portrayed somehow as necessary in the global war against jihadists. And no matter how vividly all these situations have been described, the administration proved largely impervious to pressure. One egregious attack on the press came from Paul Wolfowitz when he was deputy secretary of defense in 2004, who said, "Part of our problem is a lot of the press are afraid to travel very much so they sit in Baghdad and they publish rumors." He later apologized, but his statement is testament to the attitude of a man history will doubtless judge as directly responsible for a catastrophe.

For all the media's commitment and resources, one of the most enduring aspects of events since 9/11 has been a widespread sense that the preparations for war, particularly in Iraq, were poorly covered. The annals of media history contain a litany of mistaken or phony stories: the blowing up of the USS *Maine* in 1898 that led to the Spanish-American War; Walter

Duranty's Pulitzer Prize–winning dispatches from Russia in the 1930s that dramatically misled readers about Joseph Stalin's tyrannical rule; the timid acceptance of Senator Joseph McCarthy's anticommunist ravings in the 1950s. To that list will surely be added coverage of the administration's internal debate over Iraq's weapons of mass destruction and over Iraqi alliances with terrorists in the region.

History will have a field day with our misbegotten war in Iraq. An immense American intelligence apparatus and its strategic allies in places like Britain and Israel simply failed to accurately assess what Saddam Hussein had done with his weapons in the aftermath of the Persian Gulf War of 1991. Richard Butler, the Australian diplomat who headed up the U.N. weapons inspectors until they were expelled by Saddam in 1998, wrote a book called *The Greatest Threat: Iraq, Weapons of Mass Destruction and the Crisis of Global Security*. If anything, Republicans said at the time, Butler underestimated the problem, and they faulted the United Nations and the Clinton administration for not being sufficiently tough on the Iraqi regime.

Could the press, then, have written stories that showed that weapons of mass destruction were not a significant threat? Judith Miller, the *New York Times* reporter who has been pilloried by her professional peers for stories that were substantially wrong, has said in her defense that a reporter is only as effective as the information he or she gets from sources. To be fair to Miller and to the media overall, no one—not one single person in a position to know—asserted flatly between 2001 and 2003 that Saddam Hussein no longer had an arsenal any more dangerous than his traditional weaponry. It was possible, however, to find those who were skeptical of the amount of weapons of mass destruction and others who were doubtful that Saddam was the source of international terrorism as alleged by the Bush administration. Walter Pincus, a wonderful investigative reporter for the *Washington Post*, now in his seventies, wrote stories based on his sources' skepticism, but they were underplayed, as the paper has since acknowledged. The Knight-Ridder Washington bureau did an excellent job also. But in our argumentative age, those sorts of stories were merely seen as predictable nay-saying from people with an anti-Bush bias rather than dry-eyed technocratic judgments. Hans Blix, the U.N. weapons inspector at the time, could have done the world a service by being less Delphic in his skepticism about the presence of weapons of mass destruction. But, again, to be fair, how could he or anyone else be absolutely sure there were none?

By far, the most persuasive case that the prevailing certainty was that there were weapons of mass destruction in Iraq was a top-level marine officer's rueful, private acknowledgment three years after the war started that his troops had been trained to the point of perfection to encounter chemical and biological weapons in their invasion, but that the term "insurgency" was nowhere in the military vocabulary about Iraq. In other words, the greatest military in the history of the world sent its troops to battle prepared for the wrong war. No wonder they have been stymied. But, reflecting the way today's media-driven world operates, the Bush administration has always focused as much on the perception of what is happening as on the facts on the ground. Any reporting that cast doubt on the White House's strategy was easy to belittle as politically motivated. The media is perceived as essentially an extension of ideological differences in politics rather than as the arbiter of truth.

A generation ago, when Agnew attacked the media as tilting toward the liberal side, it was actually, on the whole (think

Cronkite, Huntley-Brinkley, Reston, Lippmann), moderate at most. Over time the notion that the press had to compensate for a natural bias toward the left has had the effect of making it timid. "Bending over backward to be fair" is sometimes the equivalent of suspending critical opinion. Over time, the vociferous and unapologetic right-wing media, the *Wall Street Journal* editorial page, FOX News, and the *Weekly Standard*, among others, has refined a tone that is disciplined, militant, and very penetrating. The moderate press is often muted in its effort to be fairminded and is tepid by comparison to its adversaries on the right. There are commentators on the liberal or what is now called "progressive" side, for example Al Franken and Michael Moore, but their invective does not contain the menacing messages used by the right—for example, the argument that to disagree with the administration is to support terrorism and appeasement.

When, after holding the story for a year, the *New York Times* was preparing to publish its blockbuster on domestic wiretapping by the National Security Agency, President Bush told the *Times* publisher and editor that, if something dreadful happened in the aftermath of publication, they personally would have "blood on their hands," according to reports of the meeting. The *Times* went ahead with the story but was subjected to widespread condemnation from Republicans. In May 2006, Attorney General Alberto Gonzales said on ABC's *This Week* that he would seek indictment of the press if he could show, as Paragraph 798 of the U.S. Code requires, that publication "will surely result in direct, immediate and irreparable damage to our Nation or its people." In its relationship with the media, like it has done in so many other ways in determining the rules of American justice, the Bush administration has decided that a

War on Terror permits sharply restricting the fundamental principles of liberty in our society. By framing its policies as a defense of the country in wartime, the Bush White House has shifted the rules of engagement in the traditional tussles with the media to a conflict with much higher stakes.

During World War II, the press was inarguably supportive of the life-and-death struggle with fascism. During the Cold War, the press was wary of being perceived as "soft on communism." Today, criticism or skepticism of the administration's goals in Iraq, Afghanistan, and elsewhere in the global struggle is suggested to be as unwarranted and dangerous as it would have been to question the U.S. determination to defeat Nazis and Soviets. From the moment of the 9/11 attacks through the early months of the Iraq War, the balance of belief was heavily on the administration's side. The media's role in that period was, thus, considered in retrospect to be lacking in toughness. But, just as we now know that the intelligence on weapons of mass destruction was all wrong, we are also learning in a torrent of revelations from journalists who have found their voice and the needed information for making a strong case that the White House and Pentagon provided disastrously inadequate leadership in the war effort. The Bush-Cheney-Rumsfeld domination of policy and tactical execution looks now to be one of the worst episodes of incompetence in our modern history.

A massive military apparatus (and a nation that fervently wants to hold its soldiers in high regard) has been degraded by mistakes in planning for the post-invasion period. The press on the ground in Iraq and their counterparts at the Pentagon gave the war effort the benefit of the doubt for about a year, until the bloody uprising in Fallujah and the revelations of abuse at Abu Ghraib made it obvious that things in Iraq were not going the way they had been intended. For a while, as noted earlier, the administration's response was to drag out the old Vietnam-era chestnuts about how the press was missing the story by concentrating on the negative. And reporters, acutely conscious of the risks of being "unfair," went to significant lengths to keep their stories balanced. Finally, however, the scale of violence in the war zones, and a worsening situation in Afghanistan as well, brought about a consensus even among the war's strongest supporters in the political arena and media: the wars probably could not be won by any conventional metric of victory, and the best that could be obtained was an orderly withdrawal that gave the peoples of the respective countries a chance to settle their own differences.

The Bush administration still confronts the media as siding with the enemy, but it has become increasingly difficult to make the press a scapegoat. As the stories about detainee abuses and the use of surveillance at home have multiplied, the White House spokesmen have tended to adopt the position that they are, on the whole, recycled material and already known. The president's tone has become more strident as his poll numbers have declined, and journalists, including Bob Woodward whose first two books about the war were considered pro-Bush, have come out firmly with the view that the post–9/11 war effort occurred in the wrong places, with the wrong deployment of troops, and without the sort of popular alliance at home and abroad necessary for success.

So where does that actually leave the media in its tug-of-war with the White House and the substantial security machine at its disposal? Much is being written and said about the explosion of information resources in the age of round-the-clock broadcast and Web news. There is so much commentary and opinion to choose from that it is possible to overlook that the indispensable material comes from reporters at the serious echelons of radio and television and from those who write for the best newspapers and magazines and are turning out an unprecedented number of revealing books. It is hard to denounce books like Thomas B. Ricks's *Fiasco*, which is based on unassailable accounts from scores of military and civilian experts. The evidence of failure is now too strong for the administration to get away with insults, warnings, and threats.

But there are long-term consequences of the relentless assertion by political leaders that the press is irresponsible and wrong-headed. The contorted saga of the leak that revealed Valerie Plame as a CIA official in retaliation for her husband's article in the *Times* about how the White House had exaggerated Saddam's efforts to develop nuclear weaponry ended badly for the press. Judy Miller went to jail for refusing to reveal the name of her source about Plame, even though she never actually wrote the article. Instead of emerging as a martyr for the rights of the press, however, Miller's case ended with a Supreme Court judgment that had the net effect of making it harder in the future for reporters to protect the names of their sources. Even some of the most ardent supporters of media rights in the legal community concluded that the Plame case did the press more harm than good.

Philip Meyer, the Knight Professor at the University of North Carolina, recently wrote about a study by two professors at the University of Connecticut. They surveyed high school students in 2004 and 2006 and made a disturbing discovery. Most of the students knew that the Constitution's First Amendment guaranteed freedom of religion, speech, and press, as well as the right to peaceably assemble and to petition the government for a redress of grievances. Among almost 15,000 students surveyed in 2006, 55 percent thought the First Amendment went too far in granting rights, according to Meyer, a swing from a majority support for those rights in 2004. Meyer wrote that the researchers, Kenneth Dautrich and David Yalof, who have studied attitudes toward the First Amendment for many years, believe that the reason for the change in views is the current debate over liberty versus national security.

The Bush administration's expansive view of its power in wartime and the public's complicated feelings about what the media does have combined to create an atmosphere in which it is easier to attack the "nattering nabobs of negativism" (in Spiro Agnew's famous phrase) as a source of problems rather than as a solution. But publishers, reporters, and editors do have one very powerful act at their disposal that will withstand any attacks; that is, to seek out the facts and report them with precision. The best stories do not need to be embellished with flourishes of rhetoric. Truth speaks for itself.

PART II

Americans Under Watch

CHAPTER 6

The Patriot Act and the Surveillance Society

STEPHEN J. SCHULHOFER

On March 9, 2006, after much delay and heated accusations between Republicans and Democrats, Congress reauthorized the USA Patriot Act—the famous (or infamous) grab bag of law enforcement and intelligence-gathering powers originally approved by Congress immediately after the attacks of September 11, 2001. Despite the passage of five years and countless working hours of experience implementing its provisions, the bitter reauthorization debate unfolded in virtually complete darkness. The administration insisted that the new powers be preserved intact—indeed, that anything less would invite disaster. Yet the administration provided almost none of the concrete details necessary to assess the provisions or to understand their impact. In the end, the act's most controversial powers were approved with little or no change, and nearly all were made permanent.

The elections of November 2006, which shifted control of both the Senate and House of Representatives from the Republican Party to the Democrats, clearly signaled public dissatisfaction with the Iraq War but also a more general skepticism about unchecked executive authority and a hunger for responsible oversight. It remains to be seen whether Congress will accept that mandate or allow itself to be pushed back into the quiescent role it played during the past five years. Despite the meager results of the recent reauthorization debate, there is still time to correct some of the Patriot Act's worst flaws if Congress is willing to insist on obtaining essential information, make it public where possible, and enact new legislation that reins in unnecessary powers and establishes effective safeguards against abuse.

As enacted on October 26, 2001, the original USA Patriot Act represented for many Americans the epitome of mindless overreaction, a tragically misguided grant of law enforcement power that will end by destroying our liberties in order to save them. Those reactions, though not baseless, are easy for the act's defenders to refute. As they accurately point out, the act is filled with innocuous technical correctives, well-justified responses to new communications technologies, and even a few provisions creating useful new safeguards for civil liberties. Of the act's 161 distinct provisions, most are in no way controversial or problematic. Among the provisions that really do enhance law enforcement power, many are narrow and carefully tailored, enough so that few experts see in them any legitimate basis for concern.*

That said, the Patriot Act also includes provisions that seem technical but, once understood, have alarming implications. Many of its new surveillance powers are far broader than neces-

---

*For a thorough discussion, examining each of the act's major provisions in detail, see Stephen J. Schulhofer, *Rethinking the Patriot Act* (The Century Foundation, 2005).

sary. Some bear no relation to the terrorist threat at all. And even where a grant of new intelligence-gathering authority can be justified, the Patriot Act fails to ensure that executive branch officials remain accountable for the ways their broad new powers are used.

The absence of effective oversight is no minor detail. This deficiency is dangerous. It not only heightens the risk of over-reaching and abuse, but it also undermines the counterterrorism effort itself. As members of the 9/11 Commission unanimously warned: "The American public has vested enormous authority in the U.S. government. . . . This shift of power and authority to the government calls for an enhanced system of checks and balances to protect the precious liberties that are vital to our way of life." Yet the Patriot Act, as originally written, paid scant attention to this concern, and subsequent amendments have compounded the problem, expanding several of the act's most problematic provisions while doing little to require effective oversight.

Ultimately, therefore, the Patriot Act does deserve much of its dark reputation. Yet legitimate criticism and public uneasiness about the act have been swamped by skillfully manipulated fears of a new terrorist attack. And in some areas where the Patriot Act retains significant safeguards, the Bush administration has simply by-passed existing laws to engage in secret surveillance on its own terms, with no accountability whatsoever. These actions have generated criticism, to be sure, but much of the public has been favorable or indifferent to them, indicating again the absence of widespread appreciation that these unnecessary shortcuts are dangerous to both our civil liberties *and* our security.

Before focusing on the dangers, however, it is worthwhile first to acknowledge the places where the Patriot Act made constructive, well-justified changes in American surveillance law.

Legitimate, Uncontroversial Fixes

The laws that govern wiretapping and electronic surveillance are a dense web of technically detailed statutes enacted at different times and amended frequently, on an ad hoc basis, in response to particular problems. The resulting edifice, as it stood before September 11, 2001, was a largely workable framework that nonetheless suffered from important gaps, inconsistencies, and anachronisms.

So-called "roving" surveillance is one example. Ordinary warrants authorize tapping conversations from a particular phone, but occasionally an individual who fears surveillance will change phones frequently to defeat the government's surveillance efforts. As a result, domestic law enforcement statutes were amended to authorize surveillance of a suspect wherever he may be (rather than restricting surveillance to a particular telephone), although only when a judge finds that the suspect has taken evasive action that thwarts ordinary surveillance tactics. Such "roving" surveillance is broader, and potentially more subject to abuse, than wiretapping of a single phone, and it therefore has its critics. Nonetheless, when confined to suspects who switch phones frequently for purposes of evasion, the technique seems well justified on balance, and Congress has permitted it for many years in ordinary drug distribution and racketeering investigations. As a result of a quirk in the statutory structure, however, roving surveillance was not available in foreign intelligence investigations, an area where the government is ordinarily afforded more leeway. The Patriot Act justifiably fixed that illogical gap by authorizing roving surveillance, under the same conditions, in foreign intelligence investigations as well.

Technological change made some pre–9/11 statutory requirements obsolete or needlessly complicated. For example, the law required one kind of warrant to seize unopened e-mail messages stored on a server and a different, more cumbersome kind of warrant to seize unopened audio messages stored in a voice mail system. There was never a significant reason to treat the two types of messages differently, and recent innovations complicated the picture by blurring the differences between them. The Patriot Act dismantled this statutory obstacle course by eliminating the distinction and permitting a single type of warrant for both sorts of messages. In similar fashion, the Patriot Act justifiably eliminated the increasingly artificial lines that distinguished the legal rules applicable to customer records held by telephone companies from those held by Internet service providers and cable service providers.

Before 9/11, search warrants were, with rare exceptions, valid only within the judicial district where the judge who issued the order sat. In an investigation of national scope, agents had to prepare separate warrant applications for each district in which a search or surveillance was required. The process was cumbersome and to no purpose. Also, Internet technology was rapidly compounding the difficulties, because magistrates in Silicon Valley, where many Internet service providers are located, were swamped with large numbers of surveillance applications unrelated to any local criminal activity. The Patriot Act, again with ample justification, fixed this problem by authorizing a judge in any district connected to the investigation to issue warrants of nationwide scope.

Dangerous Powers

Mixed among these easily defended corrective measures are many provisions that are partially justifiable but dangerously overbroad.

Private Records

Prior to 9/11, investigators normally could gain access to personal documents and records only by serving a subpoena, a procedure that affords substantial judicial safeguards to the person affected. A person or institution that receives a subpoena can challenge it in court. Additional safeguards are in place to protect individuals whose private records are held by someone else, such as clients whose financial records are held by their banks and students whose educational records are held by their schools or colleges. In these situations, statutes require the bank or college to notify the affected individual so that this person also has an opportunity to challenge the subpoena in court. Exceptions to these requirements were allowed in foreign intelligence and national security investigations, but only under narrow, carefully guarded circumstances.

The Patriot Act dramatically expanded the scope of these foreign intelligence and national security exceptions, placing highly sensitive personal records at risk, with few significant safeguards. One technique used to accomplish that revolutionary change was the National Security Letter (NSL). This device, an order issued by an FBI official (not a judge), requires certain business firms to give government agents access to particular kinds of financial data and telephone records for customers under investigation. Before 9/11, the FBI could issue an NSL only when it had specific facts indicating that the customer was a foreign agent. But the Patriot Act relaxed this restriction, requiring the FBI official to certify only that the records were "sought for an authorized investigation [of] international terrorism." In addition, the Patriot Act broadened the kinds of records subject to this type of inspection without judicial review, so that the NSL can now reach the records of real estate agents, car dealers, and any other business "whose cash transactions have a high degree of usefulness in criminal, tax, or regulatory matters." And the law imposes a "gag order" that forbids the firm receiving the NSL from informing anyone that it was required to make disclosures to the FBI.

The privacy of personal records has also been attacked in a much more comprehensive manner through the document-disclosure authority available under the Foreign Intelligence Surveillance Act (FISA). A FISA demand for the disclosure of documents requires a court order, a safeguard unavailable for NSLs, but the scope of this authority and its potential for abuse is far greater. Prior to 9/11, a judge of the Foreign Intelligence Surveillance Court could issue an order giving investigators access to certain kinds of "business records." This FISA order was limited in two notable ways. First, to get such an order, investigators were required to certify that they had specific facts indicating that the records pertained to the agent of a foreign power or a member of an international terrorist group. Second, the only records available for inspection in this way were the records of specific travel-related businesses—for example, airlines, railroads, car rental companies, and hotels (but not restaurants).

Section 215 of the Patriot Act eliminated the requirement that the records pertain to a foreign agent; instead FBI investigators were only required to certify that the records were "sought for an authorized investigation." In other words, investigators were merely required to self-certify that they were acting in good faith. And Section 215 eliminated all restrictions on the kinds of records that could be obtained. As amended, FISA now allows investigators to obtain access to the records of any business, as well as all records, documents, and any other "tangible things" held by any person or entity, including libraries, bookstores, hospitals, HMOs, charities, political parties, and religious associations, including any church, synagogue, or mosque. And FISA directives, like the NSLs, carry a "gag order": the organization is prohibited from ever informing anyone that records and documents were disclosed.

These sweeping powers open our most personal records to unrestricted government scrutiny. They also strike at the heart of political and religious liberty, undermining the shelter of privacy required for the associational activities of minority groups and dissenters of all stripes. No legitimate investigative need can justify making these powers available against persons not suspected of potential terrorist activity and in the absence of any objective facts supporting such a concern. In fact, the Justice Department has defended these powers by claiming (incorrectly) that "the law only applies to agents of a foreign power or a member of a terrorist organization." As that defense inadvertently acknowledges, there is no valid reason for granting these dangerous powers in other circumstances. A top priority for the new Congress should be an effort to rein in these powers of access to sensitive private information.

Foreign Intelligence Surveillance

Because wiretaps and other electronic surveillance can sweep up vast amounts of information, much of it irrelevant to any legitimate inquiry, this investigative technique is subject to special statutory restrictions and safeguards. The most important of these statutory regimes, generally known as "Title III," governs the gathering of evidence for criminal prosecutions, and it imposes strict limits on the initiation, duration, and subsequent use of electronic surveillance, all subject to close judicial oversight. In foreign intelligence surveillance, however, government agents focus not on gathering evidence for use in criminal cases but rather on gathering information for intelligence analysis and the prevention of attacks. For that reason, this type of surveillance traditionally has been allowed more leeway. FISA—the statutory regime that regulates it—permits surveillance on a less specific standard of suspicion, and it allows surveillance to continue for longer periods of time, with less judicial oversight. In addition, the persons targeted under FISA (unlike those targeted under Title III) normally are never notified that they have been subjected to surveillance. As a result, the government actions remain secret indefinitely, and the checks on potential overreaching and abuse are thus far weaker than they are in the case of surveillance conducted under the authority of Title III.

Those differences predated 9/11, but the Patriot Act included one amendment that greatly multiplied their importance. Before 9/11, the more flexible FISA regime was available only when foreign intelligence gathering was the primary purpose of the investigation. Criminal prosecutors were not permitted to invoke the loose FISA regime on their own initiative, and the possibility of later utilizing the results of FISA surveillance in a criminal case could be, at most, an incidental or subsidiary purpose of the investigation. The Patriot Act, however, made the FISA regime available whenever foreign intelligence gathering was merely "a significant purpose" of the inquiry, with the result that *criminal prosecution* could now be the primary purpose. And criminal prosecutors are now permitted even to "direct and control" the deployment of FISA tools when they are investigating any crimes that have a national security or foreign intelligence dimension.

To be sure, the Patriot Act amendment was prompted by a legitimate concern, because FISA had been interpreted, and indeed misinterpreted, to impose an overly rigid barrier (the so-called "wall") between intelligence analysts and criminal investigators. But in dismantling the wall, the Patriot Act went much too far in the other direction, leaving prosecutors free to make virtually unrestricted use of FISA's secret, relatively unsupervised procedures. Congress could easily, as a minimum first step, correct this situation by requiring that oversight committees be kept apprised of prosecutorial use of FISA and that, absent exceptional circumstances, prosecutors no longer be free to "direct and control" FISA surveillance.

Sneak and Peek

When police search a business or residence, they ordinarily must give the property owner a copy of the search warrant so that the owner knows the exact scope of the officer's authority and what, if anything, he is permitted to seize. Notification of this sort is essential for assuring that government officials remain within the law and remain accountable when they exercise the power to forcibly enter and search our homes. In rare situations where secrecy is essential to the law enforcement objective (for example, when officers have court approval to plant a microphone or video camera), courts can permit a completely surreptitious entry and search. The so-called "sneak and peek" is carried out when the owner is away from the premises, and no copy of the warrant is left behind; instead, courts permit the police to postpone giving the required notice of the search until some time (usually a week) has passed. Delayed notice prevents contemporaneous observation of how the search is carried out but at least permits a relatively prompt check on overreaching or abuse.

The Patriot Act relaxed the requirements for a sneak-and-peek search and permitted the required notice to be delayed for a longer period—indeed, for any "reasonable" period of time. The diluted safeguards surrounding the sneak and peek so alarmed many civil liberties groups and libertarian conservatives that a bill prohibiting all delayed-notice searches passed the House by a lopsided majority in 2003, and many believed that this overbroad Patriot Act provision would not survive. Adding to the unease about the sneak-and-peek power is the fact, rarely noticed, that this new law enforcement authority is not a counterterrorism measure at all. The Patriot Act provision expanding sneak-and-peek powers is available for investigation of *any* crime. Moreover, it is not needed for terrorism cases because, in that area, an even broader sneak-and-peek authority is available under FISA, which permits sneak and peeks not with *delayed* notice but with *no* notice, ever.

In fact, the Patriot Act expanded the foreign intelligence sneak and peek as well. It doubled (from forty-five to ninety days) the period of time during which a U.S. citizen can be subjected to repeated sneak and peeks under FISA, and it eliminated the requirement that these FISA searches be used only when foreign intelligence gathering is the investigator's primary purpose. As a result of the Patriot Act amendments, criminal prosecutors can now initiate and control the use of this loosely regulated, never-give-notice search.

Despite the broad sneak-and-peek power available in terrorism cases and intense criticism of the Patriot Act provision expanding sneak and peeks in the investigation of ordinary domestic crime, the domestic sneak-and-peek authority ultimately survived with only modest, cosmetic changes. The 2006 amendments to the Patriot Act (the "USA Patriot Act Improvement and Reauthorization Act") set the initial period of delayed notice at thirty days and allowed courts to authorize further delay for an unlimited number of additional periods of ninety days each. That sweeping, surreptitious law enforcement power is both dangerously broad and completely unnecessary as a tool to combat international terrorism. In ordinary criminal cases—those not connected to international terrorism—the maximum period of delay should be much more limited; for example, as was the practice prior to 9/11, the initial delay ordinarily should not exceed seven days, with further extensions only at fourteen-day intervals.

Internet Surveillance

American surveillance laws set a very low standard for court orders that authorize law enforcement officials to monitor only the telephone numbers (but not the content) of a suspect's incoming and outgoing calls. Officials must certify that the information sought is considered relevant to an ongoing investigation, but they need not present any facts indicating an objective basis for suspicion, much less probable cause. Before 9/11, however, the law was unclear as to whether comparable surveillance of e-mail (monitoring origin and destination addresses) was subject to the same regime, was more strictly regulated, or was not regulated at all.

The Patriot Act solved this puzzle by providing that e-mail and Internet addresses (specifically, "routing, addressing, and signaling information") will be subject to surveillance under the same low standard applicable to phone numbers. Although this approach is superficially logical, it ignores the fact that routing identifiers for e-mail and Internet browsing (such as Web site URLs) convey much more sensitive information than does the number of an incoming or outgoing phone call. The new Patriot Act authority therefore poses a serious threat to the privacy of online communication and research. And the threat is not one that the dangers of terrorism in any way require us to accept, because the new Patriot Act authority is available in the investigation of any crime, no matter how trivial.

The Erosion of Accountability

While granting dangerous, unnecessarily broad surveillance powers, the Patriot Act failed to put adequate oversight mechanisms in place, and in some instances it even took steps to dilute the oversight safeguards that were previously available.

The treatment of private records is one example. The expanded NSLs can be issued by an FBI official with no judicial approval or oversight at all. Although FISA document-production orders must be issued by a FISA judge, the Patriot Act eliminated the requirement that officials seeking the order certify that they are targeting a foreign agent or terrorism suspect and that they have specific, objective facts supporting their suspicions. Instead, they now are required to certify only that the records are "sought for an authorized investigation." As a result, the Patriot Act for all practical purposes eliminated any significant opportunity for a judicial role in restraining or overseeing the way that these orders are employed.

The Patriot Act did create a few additional possibilities for congressional oversight. It required the attorney general semi-annually to inform the House and Senate Judiciary Committees of the number of FISA document-production orders sought, granted, and denied. It also preserved the longstanding requirement of an annual report on the number of FISA electronic surveillance orders sought, granted, and denied. But the act did not require disclosure of any of the details that would have made either of these reports useful, such as the kinds of locations where electronic surveillance occurred, the average duration of surveillance, the number of times document-production orders were sought from libraries, political groups, or religious organizations, and the number of times electronic surveillance and document searches produced relevant information rather than fruitless intrusions on presumably innocent individuals.* With respect to NSLs, moreover, the Patriot Act did not require any reports at all.

Subsequent legislation has modestly enhanced the available oversight tools, but much more vigorous measures remain needed. The Intelligence Reform Act of 2004 requires the Jus-

*FISA and the Patriot Act also require the attorney general semiannually to "fully inform" the House and Senate Intelligence Committees about the use of electronic surveillance and document-production orders, presumably on a classified basis.

tice Department to provide slightly more information about FISA electronic surveillance, but it still permits the department to withhold many details that are in no way sensitive and that are routinely disclosed with respect to criminal investigations under Title III. The 2004 act, responding to a recommendation of the 9/11 Commission, also created a Civil Liberties Oversight Board in the executive office of the president. But although the 9/11 Commission (and the Senate bill implementing its proposal) contemplated a board with features designed to guarantee its independence and ability to investigate, the final version of the legislation stripped away these features and created a board with no independence whatsoever and with only the most limited ability to gather information about matters within its responsibility.

Congress again made efforts to redress this imbalance in the 2006 legislation reauthorizing the Patriot Act. The reauthorization act requires somewhat more detail in the reports made available to Congress, including information on the number of electronic surveillance orders that produced evidence for criminal prosecutions and, for the first time, disclosure of the number of NSLs issued. The gag orders that apply to NSLs and FISA document demands have been relaxed to the modest extent of permitting the recipient of the order to consult an attorney. There are now limited possibilities for seeking judicial permission to lift the gag order entirely, but this judicial power is subject to a unilateral veto by the attorney general—a prime example of the kind of constraints on oversight that the new Congress should remove. With respect to FISA document demands, investigators are now required to show "reasonable grounds" to believe that the items sought are relevant to an authorized investigation, restoring at least a slender basis for some judicial oversight. In addition, the Justice Department is now required to disclose to Congress the number of document demands granted and denied that pertain to library records, book sales, firearms sales, tax returns, educational records, and medical records—but *not* the number that pertain to political and religious organizations. Finally, the reauthorization act requires the inspector general of the Department of Justice to audit and report to Congress on the effectiveness and use of NSLs and FISA document demands.

These are unquestionably constructive—and long overdue—steps in the direction of meaningful accountability. They pose no risk of impeding legitimate national security measures; to the contrary, they can only serve to enhance the prospects for keeping our counterterrorism activity well focused, minimizing waste, misdirected effort, and abuse of individual rights. But there is a great deal more that urgently needs to be done—for example, requiring full disclosure of all the circumstances surrounding demands for sensitive private records, granting the courts discretion to lift document "gag orders" in situations no longer justifying secrecy, and creating a full-time Civil Liberties Oversight Board with subpoena power and protection against arbitrary removal by the president. Only with safeguards such as these can we ensure that judicial, congressional, and public oversight will be well informed and effective. It remains to be seen, moreover, whether Congress and the public will succeed in forcing the executive branch to comply even with the modest reporting and disclosure obligations now in effect. Prior to the 2006 reauthorization act, when disclosure requirements were even less significant than they are now, members of the Senate Judiciary Committee nonetheless were driven to complain repeatedly that "[r]eports required by statute to be filed are months late or we never get them at all." And administration resistance to oversight has taken far more serious forms as well.

Defiance of the Law

Shortly after 9/11, the National Security Agency (NSA) began conducting warrantless electronic surveillance of international calls in which one of the parties was inside the United States. President Bush formally authorized the program in October 2001, at about the same time that the Patriot Act, with its many proposed amendments to FISA, was working its way through Congress. Yet neither then nor later did the administration seek legislation authorizing the program, which became public only when news of its existence was anonymously leaked to reporters and published in the *New York Times*.

For more than a year after that disclosure, the administration insisted on its right to continue conducting such surveillance without the FISA court approval and without revealing any information about the requirements and limits of the program. Indeed, the administration insisted that its ability to proceed outside the FISA framework was an indispensable tool in the struggle against terrorism. Then in January 2007, in what was either an abrupt about-face or an astute tactical retreat, the administration announced that the original surveillance program would be terminated and that the kind of surveillance conducted under that program "will now be conducted subject to the approval of the Foreign Intelligence Surveillance Court."

As described by Attorney General Gonzales in a letter to the Senate Judiciary Committee, the new approach permits surveillance only when there is "probable cause to believe that one of the communicants is a member or agent of al Qaeda or an associated terrorist organization"—a prerequisite that sounds identical to the prerequisite that had been in place under FISA all along. Yet the administration continues to withhold specifics about what this requirement means and whether in particular its "probable cause" determination is made wholesale for a broad group of cases or is delegated to Justice Department officials, rather than remaining a matter for a FISA judge to assess independently on a case-by-case basis. The secrecy that continues to surround the program, together with the administration's track record of pushing law enforcement powers far beyond the boundaries publicly revealed and its continued insistence that surveillance outside the FISA framework was and is perfectly legal, all suggest that concerns about the wisdom and legality of the program have yet to be met.

As in the case of the original NSA surveillance initiative, important information about the new program remains unknown, including the prerequisites for conducting surveillance; the degree of *individual* suspicion (if any) that must attach to persons targeted; whether, in addition to targeting individuals, the surveillance also sweeps in a wide range of data on a deliberately indiscriminate basis; what limits (if any) apply to the distribution and use of information collected; and what sort of checks and oversight (if any) are in place to guard against abuse. Congress should no longer be willing to tolerate continued secrecy in these matters. No one, of course, seeks public disclosure of operational details, such as the names of suspects targeted or the technical capabilities of the equipment used. But there is no legitimate national security justification for continuing to withhold from Congress and the public the broad outlines of the program's threshold requirements and limitations.

In addition to these concerns regarding the new framework, the controversy surrounding the original NSA surveillance program remains relevant and important because the administration insists that the president has the power to conduct surveillance outside the FISA system whenever he judges necessary. The original NSA program was carried out for more than five years without FISA court approval, other clandestine surveillance programs may still be operational, and the administration claims the legal authority to put new ones into place at will. Yet the original NSA program was unquestionably illegal. FISA states explicitly that its procedures and those of Title III are the "exclusive means" by which electronic surveillance may be conducted. And FISA does not overlook the need for flexibility in unusual situations. It permits the attorney general to conduct warrantless surveillance for up to seventy-two hours under emergency circumstances, provided that the FISA court is notified and that a warrant is subsequently sought. It permits warrantless surveillance for a period not to exceed fifteen days in the event of a formal congressional declaration of war. Obviously, the original NSA program did not qualify under either of these emergency provisions; the fact that it did not meet their requirements makes doubly clear that the NSA program was in conflict with FISA. Indeed, Attorney General Alberto Gonzales conceded, in briefing the press on the program, that "[t]he Foreign Intelligence Surveillance Act requires a court order before engaging in this kind of surveillance that I've just discussed."

To defend its position that the NSA program was not illegal, despite its admitted conflict with FISA, the administration has argued that the Authorization to Use Military Force (AUMF), a congressional resolution enacted a week after 9/11, overrides statutory restrictions in effect before its passage. The AUMF grants the president the authority "to use all necessary and appropriate force against those nations, organizations or persons he determines planned, authorized, committed, or aided the terrorist attacks that occurred on September 11, 2001, or harbored such organizations or persons, in order to prevent any future acts of international terrorism." The administration contends that this endorsement for the use of "force" was not limited to the deployment of military force in its conventional sense but rather gave the president discretion to ignore at will any laws that normally restrict specific governmental actions, even within the United States.

This strained argument was expressly rejected by the Supreme Court in June 2006 in *Hamdan v. Rumsfeld.* The Supreme Court has long held that new legislation should be interpreted as repealing an earlier statute only when there is "overwhelming evidence" that Congress intended to do so. Applying this well-settled principle in the *Hamdan* case, the Court held that the broad general language of the AUMF cannot be read to override legislation regulating specific aspects of military operations. The *Hamdan* ruling rejected the administration's claim that AUMF allowed the president to bypass statutes governing the manner in which enemy fighters captured on a foreign battlefield can be tried. The notion that the vague terms of the AUMF permit the president to bypass FISA's rules governing surveillance of individuals within the United States is even more far-fetched. As the Court expressly held in *Hamdan,* "[T]here is nothing in the text or legislative history of the AUMF even hinting that Congress intended to expand or alter the authorization set forth in [a specific statute]. . . . 'Repeals by implication are not favored.'" It was reasonably clear before *Hamdan,* and is now clear beyond any possible doubt, that the original NSA program violated existing law.

The violation, moreover, was inexcusable. FISA has been amended many times since 9/11. The administration could have sought congressional approval for further legal changes if they are indeed justified by the circumstances.

The administration's remaining defense of the original NSA program is that existing law, no matter what it says, cannot restrict the president's actions in military matters because the Constitution designates the president as "commander-in-chief" of the armed forces. The first point to notice here is that, *if* the administration's arguments were valid, then the elasticity of concepts like "war," "battlefield," and "military affairs" would in effect give the president carte blanche to ignore thousands of pages of domestic legislation, along with most of the principles and safeguards that we identify with the rule of law.

Fortunately, the administration's argument is not plausible, even in theory. The Constitution does not give the president sole responsibility for managing military affairs. It makes this crucial point clear in Article I, Section 8, by giving explicitly to *Congress*, not to the president, the power to "make Rules for the Government and Regulation of the land and naval Forces." When President Truman, during the Korean War, seized the steel mills to end a labor dispute that threatened to block production of military supplies, the Court held that Truman's authority as commander-in-chief did not include a power to seize property needed for the war effort, in the absence of legislation affirmatively granting such power. This principle of course applies even more strongly when Congress has not merely remained silent on the subject but has expressly prohibited the executive action, as it has in the case of FISA. Thus, even if electronic surveillance is considered a tool of military operations, the Constitution makes clear that the president cannot deploy it however he pleases in the face of congressional legislation to the contrary. The "commander-in-chief" clause was intended to place the military under civilian control; it cannot be converted, by the administration's inverted logic, into a vehicle for placing civilians under military control.

Many intelligence specialists nonetheless argue that FISA's requirements are no longer suited to modern technology and the needs of an effective counterterrorism effort. And, they add, it matters little in the end whether those requirements are updated by executive order or by Congress. Much of the public seems sympathetic to this contention. Yet, the first point—that FISA might be outdated—has never been demonstrated, or even explained with any specificity. And the second point—that updates can just as well be made by the president as by Congress—is wrong in the most fundamental and disturbing way.

The NSA initiative is a scandal not only because of its impact on privacy but, more importantly, because the original program and its still-mysterious successor both represent a direct assault on our constitutional structure and our commitment to the separation of powers. The framers of the Constitution deliberately chose *not* to give the president the power to rule by decree, even under emergency circumstances. Precisely because reasonable people can disagree about the kind of electronic surveillance that should be permissible and the kind of oversight safeguards that are necessary, the judgment about whether and how to change the law must be made through democratic deliberation in Congress, as our Constitution specifies. It should not be made through unilateral decisions taken in secret by the president and his inner circle of advisors. Even if one knew exactly what the original and new NSA programs entail (none of us in the general public does), and even if one thought those details were all perfectly appropriate, the programs' most dangerous feature would remain—the claim that, because we are "at war," the president can unilaterally change laws and disregard laws at will.

What We've Lost

For the American public, the 9/11 attacks triggered widespread and wholly understandable feelings of insecurity. Americans normally suspicious of government instinctively relaxed their ordinary impulse to limit official powers and ensure close control of their exercise. Political leaders, predictably, exploited the fear and fanned it for their own partisan purposes. Much of the public has been readily persuaded by insistent claims, from the president, vice president, and others, that the executive branch must have sweeping new powers and freedom from bothersome oversight if it is to prevent future attacks of even greater magnitude. The result, paradoxically, is that accountability has been dramatically reduced at the very moment when it is needed more than ever. Even in the face of repeated, irrefutable evidence of executive branch capacity for catastrophic mismanagement, ranging from the response to Hurricane Katrina to the planning and execution of the occupation in Iraq, many citizens remain all too ready to believe that legislative and judicial oversight of counterterrorism powers will somehow make them ineffective.

The truth is just the reverse. In law enforcement and intelligence gathering, as elsewhere, unchecked powers are dangerous and counterproductive, permitting "mission creep" and the squandering of scarce energy and resources. The challenge of international terrorism, far from diminishing the need for accountability, makes unchecked executive powers unusually dangerous. For many Americans, the absence of effective oversight may not arouse personal anxiety or objections, but for immigrants, minority groups, and others whose support is crucial to a successful counterterrorism strategy, secret powers provoke suspicion or animosity and undermine the perceived legitimacy and fairness of every step our officials seek to take. As surveillance powers grow, secrecy and lack of accountability diminish the trust of these outsiders and chill cooperation at the very points where law enforcement authorities need it most.

As Benjamin Franklin warned, those who would sacrifice their liberty for security will in the end find that they have lost both. Franklin could not have foreseen the challenges of the twenty-first century, but his insight remains applicable, perhaps more so now than before. Unless Americans can recover their ability to face danger with self-confidence and a willingness to match strong military and law enforcement powers with equally strong safeguards, our world is likely to become increasingly dangerous. The quest for security will be ceaseless but futile.

CHAPTER 7

The Espionage Industrial Complex

PATRICK RADDEN KEEFE

O n the evening of September 13, 2001, a Florida busi-
nessman named Hank Asher stood up after supper
and set out to catch the 9/11 hijackers. Asher was a
colorful figure, a onetime drug runner who flew cocaine by the
kilo from Colombia to the Bahamas in the 1980s before rein-
venting himself in the 1990s as a successful technology entre-
preneur. His latest venture, a company called Seisint, had
amassed an extensive trove of data on some 450 million people,
and he spent that evening formulating algorithms to sift
through these files and identify possible terrorists.

Asher knew the hijackers were likely Muslim foreign nationals who had entered the United States within the last two years,
so he focused on that profile. Each individual the program
flagged was assigned a score, indicating the probability that he
or she was involved in the attacks on the World Trade Center
and the Pentagon. Asher worked through the night and eventually produced a list of 1,200 suspicious individuals, which he
forwarded to the FBI. He didn't realize it at the time, but five of
the hijackers were on that list.

Hank Asher's program didn't just generate names. It culled
surprisingly comprehensive dossiers from all that public and

private data: bank and automotive records, credit histories, even digital photographs. By September 16, the FBI had visited Asher, wanting to know more about his magic program, soon dubbed the Multistate Anti-Terrorism Information Exchange, or Matrix.* Asher was eager to make the technology available and pointed out that, as other states contributed records to the system, Matrix would have an ever-widening scope. Various state agencies agreed to share their data, and soon the program could access 20 billion pieces of information. Through some mysterious alchemy, Matrix churned property taxes and parking tickets and assigned to each individual a "terrorist quotient," which indicated the likelihood that he or she was in fact a violent jihadist.

Florida governor Jeb Bush became an early fan of the system, and in January 2003 he brought Hank Asher to the White House, where Asher demonstrated the system for Vice President Dick Cheney in the Roosevelt Room. Cheney was impressed, and Matrix soon received $12 million in development money from the federal government.

Desperate to avert further terrorist attacks, various state and local authorities across the country quickly signed up for the program. What Asher was really peddling was a beautiful idea: actionable intelligence at the touch of a button. With Matrix, police officers and federal agents could pluck suspects from the

---

*From Darpa's Total Information Awareness to the FBI's Carnivore, the authors of invasive data mining and surveillance programs have betrayed a curious tendency to insist that their inventions are benign and harmless to the citizenry while bestowing them with unmistakably menacing names. Echoing as it did the popular *Matrix* film trilogy, which transpires in a paranoid near-future dystopia in which humans are subjugated by machines, the chosen acronym in this instance was no exception.

citizenry at large without learning Arabic, without expending any shoe leather, without so much as leaving their desks.

Asher was a millionaire many times over by the time he devised Matrix, and he initially made the system available to law enforcement free of charge. But in 2004, as the size of the market for this type of data-mining product became clear, Reed Elsevier, the giant multinational that owns LexisNexis, moved to purchase Seisint, the company Asher had founded in 1998. The purchase price was $775 million. By that time, Asher had resigned from formal management of the company in the face of controversy surrounding his criminal history.* But he personally earned over $250 million from the sale.

It is all too easy, when considering the range of intrusive new surveillance technologies brought to bear by various agencies of the American government in the years since 9/11, to overlook the fact that the real driver behind these technologies is not the government at all but, rather, private inventors and entrepreneurs like Hank Asher. To the extent that the policy community and the public at large express concerns about balancing an aggressive pursuit of foreign adversaries with this nation's traditional values of privacy and civil liberties, that concern often manifests itself in Orwellian caricatures of frighteningly powerful, tech-savvy government agencies. But this kind of oversimplification misses the point and obscures what may ultimately be a more malignant danger. In the years since 9/11,

---

*Appropriately enough, authorities had first discovered Asher's shady past by using his own data-mining technology to run a background search on him.

it has become clear that our federal government tends toward the opposite extreme: our intelligence agencies lag far behind the technological curve and are increasingly obliged to outsource tasks of any technical complexity to a burgeoning community of espionage contractors and innovative entrepreneurs. The result has been the sudden emergence of what might be described as an espionage industrial complex: a rapidly growing technology sector that conjures up ambitious new programs and devices to assist the government in its War on Terrorism.

Forty-six years ago, in the early days of the Cold War, President Dwight Eisenhower warned Americans about the "grave implications" of the "conjunction of an immense military establishment and a large arms industry." The famous speech, delivered as Eisenhower was leaving office, proved remarkably prescient. As a peacetime armaments industry arose to satisfy the country's security needs in a new strategic environment, Eisenhower intuited that the dependence of the government on this profit-driven industry ran a major risk of distorting, in ways large and small, the broader interests of the nation. He cautioned, "Only an alert and knowledgeable citizenry can compel the proper meshing of the huge industrial and military machinery of defense with our peaceful methods and goals, so that security and liberty may prosper together."

Today, at the outset of a new conflict of global scope and indefinite duration, America's defense and intelligence establishments are meshing with another rapidly expanding industry of private sector suppliers. And one suspects that, were Eisenhower to witness this peculiar combination of panicked and technologically naïve officials, optimistic and opportunistic private sector salesmen, and oversight-shy, special-interest-friendly legislators, he might see another perfect storm brewing on the horizon.

This chapter explores the rise of the spy technology industry in the years since 9/11 and the grave implications that the privatization of espionage will have for liberty and security in the twenty-first century. In grappling with the tricky negotiation between liberty and security, we tend to focus almost exclusively on liberty. Most Americans are comfortable with the idea of sacrificing some measure of liberty in exchange for greater security. Reasonable people differ, and differ strongly, about the precise increment of liberty we should be willing to barter away, and it is this question—which rights will we trade for greater safety and for how long—that has dominated debate in the last five years. Much less effort has been expended in quantifying the other element in the equation—security—and in ascertaining whether, *whatever* the price we are willing to pay, be it airport searches, wiretapping, ethnic profiling, or the suspension of habeas corpus, we will really get much safety in exchange.

Even before it was revealed that the National Security Agency (NSA) had enlisted the support of private-sector telephone companies to monitor communications inside the United States, the outsourcing to private companies of espionage innovation and activities was already well under way. The huge government market for new intelligence and security technologies has ceded the debate over what new measures are compatible with the American Constitution and way of life to the technologists, whose first loyalty is to technological innovation and profit maximization, not to constitutional protections or even American security. But even more importantly, perhaps, the boom time for espionage technology has drawn out its fair share of prospectors and sellers of snake oil. As a result, many of the new technologies employed by our government will succeed in jeopardizing our privacy and civil liberties (because they were considered only as an afterthought) while *failing* to make us any safer (because the technologies couldn't quite live up to the salespeople's patter). And because of the intense secrecy surrounding the allocation of contracts in the intelligence community, the "alert and knowledgeable citizenry" upon which Eisenhower calls is seldom even aware of the ill-considered expenditures being made in its name.

Gold Rush

For much of the twentieth century, America's soldiers and spies enjoyed a considerable head start on the private sector when it came to cutting-edge research and development. The eavesdroppers and code breakers at the NSA traditionally prided themselves on being ten years ahead of anything you could buy off the shelf. Even the Internet started life as the Arpanet, a networked communications infrastructure designed by the Pentagon's Advanced Research Projects Agency (ARPA, now known as DARPA) to withstand a nuclear attack. The *Economist* once observed that, without the Pentagon, "Silicon Valley might still be covered with fruit orchards."

As those fruit orchards gave way during the 1980s to the wave of young computer scientists at the vanguard of the personal computer and Internet revolutions, America's intelligence community remained aloof, convinced of its own enduring superiority and suspicious of these civilian and academic upstarts. Insular and smug, America's spies began to fall behind, clinging to their analog-era strengths even as the digital era swept the world around them. Meanwhile, the dot com boom coincided with considerable downsizing within the U.S. intelligence community, and those who were forced out or lured away by the promise of interesting research and windfall initial public offerings (IPOs) contributed to a devastating brain drain.

So it was that, when the American government scrambled in the months and years after 9/11 to prevent another terrorist attack, it was obliged to turn, hat in hand, to the private sector. One former head of the NSA, Ken Minihan, captured the new mood: "Homeland security is too important to be left to the government." As it happened, private technology companies were just as eager to collaborate. Some of this eagerness was surely driven by patriotism. Many, like Asher, happily volunteered their services or reconfigured research they were doing so that it would have a security application. But many others were driven by a coincidence of timing; in the fall of 2001, the bubble had only recently burst on the Internet economy. Venture capital for tech startups had run completely dry; dot com employees were being laid off in droves. For entrepreneurs like Hank Asher and for refugees of the heady "irrational exuberance" of the late nineties, the suddenly emerging demand for homeland security technologies and the U.S. government, in all its desperate largesse, represented a new—and similarly irrational—market. Another boom.

By fiscal year 2007, federal spending on domestic security reached $58.3 billion, up from $16.8 billion in 2001. On top of that figure, states and cities contribute an additional $20 to $30 billion for security each year, and the federal intelligence budget is an estimated $40 billion, roughly half of which goes to private contractors. From biometrics to explosives screening and from data mining to automated translation, government spending is on the rise, and this profligacy is creating one growth industry after another. Each new boomlet spawns the next; some

30 million surveillance cameras scan America's airports, schools, office buildings, and shopping malls, with 2 million new cameras erected each year since 9/11. This hardware alone represents a $3 billion industry. But the cameras generate some 4 billion hours of footage each week. How can authorities possibly sort through it all? The answer is video analysis technologies, which scan video feeds for particular times, locations, clothing, even facial characteristics. Video analysis is itself a nearly $1 billion industry. From the collection of mountains of raw data to the processing of that data, entrepreneurial possibilities arise at each step of the way. By some estimates, the aggregate market for homeland security tops $200 billion today.

This is welcome news for technology startups. Venture capitalists have shifted their attentions from Internet technology companies to anything with a surveillance or security application. "Every fund is seeing how big the trough is and asking, How do I get a piece of that action?" Roger Novak, a Maryland venture capitalist, told *Wired*. "When the IT industry shut down, post-bubble, guess who had all the money? The government."

Interestingly, this national security bubble bears some striking similarities to the dot com bubble that preceded it. Both share a similar cast of characters, from the scientists to the entrepreneurs to the venture capitalists. Both relied for their momentum on a generous dose of old-fashioned optimism, if not credulity, about the infinite possibilities of technological wizardry. And both were characterized by great urgency and haste, a sense during the Internet bubble that everyone should get in on the colossal bonanza while the going was good, and in the current case that anything and everything should be done to secure the country, as soon as possible, and at all costs.

The problem is that, in the marketplace, this type of hysteria is an invitation to bad judgment and impulsive investments. Just as the Internet bubble enabled hucksters of every stripe to throw together a dubious business plan and score an infusion of venture capital, the national security bubble has occasioned a similar invest-first, ask-questions-later approach. Consider the case of Fortress America, a shell company established in 2004 by a number of investors to operate as a self-described "blank check company," an entity the Securities and Exchange Commission describes as "a development stage company that has no specific business plan or purpose." Fortress America was founded by Tom McMillen, a charismatic Rhodes Scholar turned NBA basketball player, turned Democratic congressman from Maryland, turned investment banker, who had more recently run a health care company that went bankrupt in 2001. Fortress America had no assets, no product, no revenue, and no business plan, apart from the vague promise that it would acquire companies in the "homeland security industry." So it was curious when McMillen announced his intention to raise capital through an initial public offering (IPO). "There are ribs that have marinated for longer than this company has," one commentator joked. Nevertheless, in July 2005, just seven months after founding Fortress America, McMillen held his IPO and managed to raise $46.8 million.

So intense is the speculation in new espionage technologies that the CIA has its own venture capital fund. Known as In-Q-Tell ("Q" for the wizened gadget man of James Bond fame), the fund began life in 1999. According to the fund's Web site, it was established because "the CIA determined that it needed a means to engage with young innovative companies that were building cutting edge commercial technologies." Gilman Louie, a former video game executive with a good eye for emerging technologies, was appointed to run In-Q-Tel. He received about 1,000 business plans in the two years before 9/11 and 1,200 in the nine months following the attacks. Whereas a typical venture capital firm might do a dozen major deals a year, In-Q-Tel has been making investments in new technologies roughly every other week, with initial investments ranging from $500,000 to $3 million. To date the company has leveraged more than $1 billion in private-sector funds to support new espionage technologies.

Although In-Q-Tel's mission statement maintains that "the bulk of innovation is occurring in commercial markets, driven by young companies that have little experience, or visibility, with the government," larger, more established defense contractors are moving aggressively into the market as well. Having identified the surging demand and high-profit margins for intelligence technologies, traditional "Beltway Bandit" military hardware and aerospace giants like Boeing, Lockheed Martin, and Northrop Grumman have rapidly expanded their intelligence and security divisions. Raytheon's homeland security division did $38 million of business in 2001 and some $300 million in 2004. The gold rush is so extensive that there is room for both the big, entrenched Washington players and their smaller, startup counterparts. Often the contracts are so large that work trickles down from the former to the latter. When Boeing scored a $2.5 billion contract to secure the Mexican and Canadian borders, surveillance startups took note, knowing that Boeing would be in the market for subcontractors who manufacture remote sensing devices.

Perhaps the most telling confirmation of the investments (and the fortunes) being made in the name of national security was a recent report in the *Washington Post* that, according to 2006 census figures, the suburbs of Loudoun, Fairfax, and Howard counties on the outskirts of Washington, D.C., are now three of the wealthiest jurisdictions in the nation. The article explained that this new concentration of suburban wealth "is a side effect of the enormous flow of federal money into the region through contracts for defense and homeland security work in the five years since the Sept. 11, 2001, attacks, coming after the local technology boom of the 1990s."

Contract Players

As he introduced the Intelligence Authorization Act of 2002, Senator Lindsey Graham (R-SC) declared that the Senate Intelligence Committee, which he chaired, "encourages a symbiotic relationship between the intelligence community and the private sector." On its face, this sentiment seems unassailable. A vigilant intelligence community is vital to maintaining safety and security, and if private-sector technology is more advanced than what agencies can produce in-house, then it is only responsible for our spies to make use of that greater expertise. The problem, as Eisenhower was quick to see, is that the symbiosis, or "meshing," of two separate entities has a way of muddying the respective institutional interests of each.

To see how this plays out, one need look no further than the current state of the military-industrial complex. As the recent Eugene Jarecki documentary *Why We Fight* makes clear, the defense industry relies for its survival on continued government orders for big-ticket weapons systems, whether or not those systems correlate well with America's particular strategic interests. The relationship between the defense industry, the Pentagon, and the Congress has grown so "symbiotic" that the contract process for major defense acquisitions begins to look dangerously rigged. Private firms envision a new product, or a new generation of an existing product, that they market to the Defense Department and the Congress. During the competitive bidding process, the firms are likely to consciously understate the ultimate price tag for the item. As profit-maximizing actors in a competitive marketplace—as salespeople—they are also likely to overestimate the capabilities of the item, to underestimate the likelihood that technical hurdles will stymie the project, and to cite an unrealistically optimistic date by which the item will be delivered. Given the similarly "symbiotic" relationship—to put it politely—that many of our key congressional leaders have with the defense industry, various big-ticket items are approved without much resistance. And as soon as they are approved, the firms in question channel investment and jobs associated with the contract to the relevant congressional districts. Thus, when, as surely as night follows day, the product comes in overdue and overbudget and does not appear to do everything its creators claimed it would, the very elected officials who should be calling foul already have too much at stake. The prevailing wisdom appears to be that it is appropriate to throw good money after bad only when the money is being thrown in the general direction of your constituency.

Perhaps the scenario outlined above seems too neat, too much like a conspiracy theory; our elected officials could not possibly find themselves so deep in the pockets of their defense industrialist donors that they would play fast and loose with taxpayers' money and make gratuitous defense allocations in a time of war. But how else does one reconcile the appalling shortages of relatively low-cost armor for our soldiers' vehicles in Iraq with the purchase orders for new F–22A and F–35 fighter jets from Lockheed and Boeing, at a combined price of roughly $8.1 billion? How does one square the DDG 100 destroyer ($3.4 billion; Northrop Grumman) or the Virginia-class attack submarine ($2.6 billion; General Dynamics, Lockheed, Raytheon) with the infinitesimal likelihood that the United States will be engaged in naval, much less submarine, warfare anytime in the near future? The most vivid illustration of the refined symbiosis of the contract process in the defense context is the B–2 stealth bomber. The most expensive airplane ever built, at $2 billion apiece, the B–2 is manufactured by Northrop Grumman. The United States has twenty-one of them. And lest our elected representatives ever raise an eyebrow or suffer from sticker shock, some part of the B–2 is manufactured in nearly every state in the Union.

Although the vested interests in the intelligence and security industries are not nearly as powerful or entrenched as those in the weapons industry, they are headed in that direction. In fact, the contract process for espionage expenditures is in some respects even more prone to abuse than the process for purchasing weapons. Congress may give a free pass to the arms industry, but the public and the press can, at the very least, scrutinize various expenditures and develop a sense of how much Washington is paying, and for what. The intelligence budget, by contrast, is shrouded in secrecy. Even the aggregate amount that the United States spends on intelligence each year—surely an anodyne figure of no use whatsoever to foreign adversaries—is highly classified. The years since 9/11 have witnessed a 48 percent increase in classified Pentagon spending, and "black" budget items have proliferated. Bidding for particular intelligence contracts is often done in secret, making it exceptionally difficult for anyone outside the contractual exchange itself to exercise oversight. This classification poses no impediment for the contractors themselves, for many of them already have high-level clearance for intelligence matters.

Whereas the advocates for a particular secret project are cleared to make a case for it—no matter how risky the endeavor or how high the cost—there is no opportunity for those who might make a case *against* the project to have a say. The latter role is left largely to members of Congress. But, by their own admission, even those legislators who sit on the congressional intelligence committees often lack all but the most rudimentary grasp of the complex technologies in question. When Senator Jay Rockefeller (D-WV) was first briefed on the NSA's warrantless wiretapping program in 2003, he wrote a letter to Dick Cheney confessing that he was "neither a technician nor an attorney" and that he felt unequipped "to evaluate, much less endorse these activities."

To further complicate matters, intelligence contractors employ an army of lobbyists to make the case in Washington that their technologies are necessary. Lockheed alone spent $47 million on outside lobbying between 1997 and 2004 and hired Joe Allbaugh, who managed the 2000 Bush campaign, to lobby specifically for its expanding intelligence division. In addition to the soft incentives of creating jobs in various constituencies, the major intelligence contractors also channel large amounts of money directly to influential lawmakers. Pat Roberts (R-KS), the chairman of the Senate Intelligence Committee, received nearly half of his political action committee intake for the year 2004 from six intelligence contractors. Beyond legitimate contributions of this sort, the interaction between contractors and the Congress has also been marked by a certain amount of outright graft. In 2005, Representative Randy "Duke" Cunningham (R-CA) admitted accepting millions of dollars in bribes while he served on the House Intelligence Committee for steering work to the defense contractor MZM.

Solidifying the indispensability of the private sector intelligence community is the revolving door through which various high-ranking intelligence officials transition seamlessly to corporate work. It behooves former NSA director Ken Minihan to believe that homeland security is "too important to be left to the government"; he now runs the Security Affairs Support Association, a trade group representing 125 intelligence contractors. William Studeman, another former NSA director, is now vice president of Northrop Grumman; Barbara McNamara, former deputy director of the agency, is on the board of another leading contractor, CACI. Former CIA chief James Woolsey is a vice president of Booz Allen Hamilton, a contractor so woven into the fabric of American espionage that one former deputy director of the CIA referred to the company as "the shadow intelligence community."

All the ingredients for an unhealthy relationship are in place. On the one hand, there is a private-sector industry eager for R&D money and trained to believe that nothing is technologically impossible. On the other hand, there is a defense and intelligence bureaucracy desperate to keep the country safe, dependent on private-sector suppliers for new products and always on the hunt for a technological panacea. Overseeing this collaboration and controlling the purse strings are elected representatives who rely on contractors for campaign contributions and indirect support of the local economies in their constituencies, who do not fully comprehend the particular limits and capabilities of the technologies on offer, and who operate in an environment of such intense secrecy that corruption is an ever-present temptation and rigorous oversight is next to impossible.

Overbudget, Overdue, Oversold

Such coziness can have calamitous results, which often go unnoticed by the public. In 1999, the NSA launched a new classified program, code-named Trailblazer, to modernize its systems for sifting through the vast flows of digital communications it intercepts. When the time came to actually build the new system, the agency turned to the major intelligence contractor Science Applications International Corporation (SAIC). With 43,000 employees nationwide and a slew of former intelligence officials on its board of directors, San Diego–based SAIC is known within the intelligence community as "NSA West." A year after SAIC took on the project, the NSA's inspector general found that "inadequate management and oversight" of private contractors and overpayment for work done had resulted in delays and overruns on Trailblazer. By 2005 it emerged that SAIC had failed to live up to its early promises, neglecting to provide computer experts with the relevant technical expertise to create the complex system. "There's a penchant, particularly in the [information technology] area, to [promise] all kinds of things and not be able to deliver on the project," Gordon Adams, director of Security Policy Studies at George Washington University, told the *Baltimore Sun*. Adams described ambitious technology projects like Trailblazer as "traffic accidents waiting to happen." Within the intelligence community, Trailblazer is better known as a "boondoggle." The system has cost taxpayers a staggering $1.2 billion and to date has not gotten off the ground. Robert Steele, a CIA veteran familiar with the program, declared it "a complete and abject failure."

But just as the vested interests that have aligned in Washington ensure that various big-ticket military expenditures continue, the emergent espionage industrial complex is slowly minimizing the role of oversight and common sense in evaluating how the American government allocates its resources. A glaring but little-known example is a highly classified, "stealth" satellite code-named Misty, the single largest item in the intelligence budget for 2005. Designed to orbit the earth undetected while photographing targets on the ground, Misty was better suited to Cold War objectives like monitoring tank divisions and missile silos than to the contemporary challenges of tracing individual terrorists. Moreover, the notion of spending large amounts of money on a "stealth" satellite was misguided, in principle because America's adversaries assume that the United States has near total omniscience from above, and in practice because Misty's first generation, launched in 1990, was immediately spotted—not by Russian intelligence but by amateur space observers in Canada and Europe. Nevertheless, Lockheed Martin was engaged by the National Reconnaissance Office to develop a new generation of the satellite, and in no time the original conservative cost estimates had swelled to $9.5 billion.

To its credit, the Senate Intelligence Committee vetoed Misty in 2003 and 2004, with members calling it a wasteful misallocation of funds that had not been adequately debated by Congress. But the appropriations committees reinstated the satellite in the budget. This put the senators on the Intelligence Committee in an awkward position. At great pains not to describe the specifics of the secret project, Senator Ron Wyden (D-OR) protested on the Senate floor that an especially large item in the 2005 intelligence budget was about to obtain funding despite the fact that several independent reviews had concluded that other programs could produce the same intelligence at far less cost and technological risk and that the item was, in his words, "unnecessary, ineffective, overbudget, and too expensive." Senator Jay Rockefeller (D-WV) pointed out that the allocation was actually "dangerous to national security," insofar as it diverted such an enormous fraction of the intelligence budget away from more cost-effective areas at a time when the country could hardly afford to fritter that budget away on pork barrel projects. To give a sense of the opportunity costs involved, one official told the *Washington Post* that, for $9.5 billion, "you could build a whole new CIA." But the protest, such as it was, was fruitless. Misty got its funding, Lockheed proceeded with its contract, and Justice Department lawyers launched an investigation of the senators for having the temerity to object.

Conclusion

It has become a commonplace, indeed, a cliché that in the years since September 11, 2001, the American people have been confronted with an agonizing choice between the competing demands of national security and civil liberties. Some optimists on either side of the divide like to suggest that this contest is a false one, that it is possible both to have your cake and eat it. But as the illustrations from this chapter reveal, a serious, less-often discussed possibility exists that, by incrementally diminishing our expectations of privacy and liberty in exchange for a promise of elevated security that ultimately proves illusory, we will end up both unsafe and unfree, neither having our cake nor eating it.

One analysis of the dot com–era's demise immediately preceding 9/11 is that investors too seldom asked of a new e-venture, What will it produce? What will it do? Will it work? As citizens, these are the questions that we must be asking about each new technology being brought to bear in the name of making us safer. When the Bush administration's warrantless wiretapping program was brought to light early in 2006, politicians and pundits wrestled with the difficult legal and constitutional questions involved, and cable news anchors wondered about the state of American privacy. But less often addressed is an equally fundamental question: Does this program work? As it happens, it doesn't. The administration's generic bromides about the utility of the program to the contrary, the *Washington Post* reported that, of the thousands of people whose communications were intercepted by the NSA, the vast majority turned out to be unaffiliated with terrorist groups. The *New York Times* reported that the wiretapping produced so many false or inconsequential leads that within the FBI a new batch of tips from the NSA was jokingly referred to as more "calls to Pizza Hut." Impassioned debate about privacy versus executive power seems rather beside the point in the face of stories like these. If a legally dubious measure was actually making us safer, there might be grounds for an argument in favor of it. If it doesn't make us safer, then debate over how much liberty to give up for it is superfluous, a charade.

To be sure, it is crucial that American citizens and lawmakers guard zealously the various civil rights and protections upon which this country is based. But it is equally important not to lose sight of the nature of the security we are being offered, in all its particulars. Whereas the military-industrial complex is already so entrenched that few in Congress are willing to take issue with the annual menu of billion-dollar items the arms industry decides are indispensable for the country, the espionage industrial complex has not yet taken quite the same hold. Whether the item in question is Hank Asher's Matrix, the NSA's wiretapping program, or the Misty photo reconnaissance satellite, Americans must take a greater interest in the tools being used in the War on Terror. Will they work? Are they worth what we pay for them in dollars, and in liberty?

Naturally some necessary measure of official secrecy will prevent broad public scrutiny of intelligence contracts on a case-by-case basis. But the inability of the citizenry to monitor these matters directly is all the more reason why our elected representatives must be aggressive in their oversight and scrupulously independent of the siren song of direct and indirect incentives. If we fail to ask this of them now, we will soon realize the gravest danger of which Eisenhower warned: "that public policy"—and along with it, the security and liberty of the nation—"could itself become the captive of a scientific-technological elite."

CHAPTER 8

The New Counterterrorism: Investigating Terror, Investigating Muslims

AZIZ HUQ

In May 2006, Deputy Attorney General Paul J. McNulty explained to an audience at the American Enterprise Institute that federal law enforcement strategy post–9/11 had dramatically shifted "from predominantly reaction to one of proactive prevention" and "forward-leaning—preventative—prosecutions." Two months later, Secretary of Homeland Security Michael Chertoff added that the government would "always intervene at the earliest possible opportunity"; to do otherwise, Chertoff contended, "would be playing games with people's lives." These statements reflect the Bush administration's wider National Security Strategy, which places a premium on "preemptive actions to counter a sufficient threat to our national security."

"Preventive" prosecution—where prosecutors use a lesser charge in the absence of evidence of a serious offense—is nothing new. During World War II, Attorney General Frank Murphy declared that "every possible effort is being made to indict any Communist who has violated the criminal laws in any respect."

The sad history of McCarthyism and the Smith Act, nevertheless, might caution against uncritical embrace of this law enforcement paradigm.

Today, however, the Department of Justice draws on a gamut of new investigative and prosecutorial powers for preventative prosecution. Besides augmented surveillance powers granted by the USA Patriot Act, the FBI and partner law enforcement agencies aggressively use physical surveillance, informants, and the suspect-detention powers furnished by the regular criminal law. The substantive criminal law also supplies prosecutors with ample resources, which Congress considerably expanded in 1996 and again in 2001. As a result, federal prosecutors can bring the state's power to bear long before overt acts that make up violent terrorism occur.

In so doing, prosecutors necessarily single out harbingers of a violent intent. Perhaps inevitably, in light of al Qaeda's rationale for the 9/11 attacks, Muslim beliefs and practices themselves have become triggers for investigation and prosecution. Practicing Islam has become a ready ground for suspicion of being a terrorist. Current constitutional law does not wholly prohibit reliance on religion or race to justify investigation or prosecution. Law enforcement authorities generally cannot make intervention decisions *solely* based on race (or religion) consistent with the Constitution, although such factors may be part of the calculus used to justify police intervention. A June 2003 Justice Department regulation, however, exempts "national security and terrorism" matters from the department-wide ban on racial profiling. Even if this regulation were to be repealed, the broad scope of prosecutorial discretion makes it almost impossible to challenge any enforcement decision based on the illicit use of religion or race.

Today, moreover, criminal prosecution is an increasingly important part of counterterrorism strategy. A week before the fifth anniversary of 9/11, the Justice Department celebrated federal prosecutors' success in securing convictions or guilty pleas in 288 "terrorism-related cases." This statistic both understates the extent of criminal law resources devoted to terrorism and exaggerates the impact these resources have. The 288 convictions represent only a fraction of the cases investigated. Indeed, U.S. attorneys have declined to prosecute in 68 percent of terrorism referrals since 9/11. On the other hand, out of 288 cases, only fourteen ended in sentences of twenty years or more. Only another 67 were sentenced to five or more years. Many charges involved lesser immigration or social security offenses. Although the raw data do not disclose whether these cases are properly classified as terrorism related, there is cause for skepticism. A 2005 Justice Department tally of 200 terrorism convictions included twenty Iraqi men convicted in a Pennsylvania truck-licensing scam. These men had, however, already been absolved publicly by the FBI of any connection to terrorism.

America's Muslims

Accurate counts of Muslims in the United States are hard to find, though estimates range from 1.1 million to 7 million. Muslim communities in the United States also vary greatly. The first large wave of Muslim migration came between 1875 and 1912 from the Levant. The repeal of national-origin-based immigration quotas triggered another surge from a broader array of Asian, African, and European countries. Conversion supplements this diversity. Hence, about a third of American Muslims were born in the United States, but many others are noncitizen residents or immigrants. Large Muslim communities now live in New York, Chicago, Detroit, and the Dallas/Fort Worth/ Houston area. These include both Sunni and Shia. They encompass the convert, the pious, and the lapsed. And they allow for no easy stereotypes about the manifold ways of being a Muslim American in 2007.

Islamic doctrines more broadly are also far more complex than first appears. It should not need repeating that the overwhelming majority of Muslims have no interest in or appetite for political violence. The sheer number of Muslims in Europe and the United States, set against the single-digit infrequency of ideological violence, ought to give the lie to any such claim.

It appears, moreover, that the numbers of individuals radicalized to the point of adopting violence as a tactic is somewhat higher in European countries than in the United States. Whether this trend will persist, of course, cannot be accurately predicted, particularly since the causes of such seeming variance remain unclear. European countries vary tremendously in how they integrate or assimilate new immigrant communities, particularly with respect to citizenship policies. Broad-brush distinctions between the United States and Europe on that point cannot provide a complete explanation. Additionally, in Europe more than in the United States, radical groups such as Hizb ut-Tahrir and al-Muhajiroun, both of which argue for a return to the Islamic "caliphate," have found toeholds in the public sphere. The degree of ambient race discrimination against Muslims also differs between European countries and the United States. Yet Muslims in Europe, unlike those in the United States, have formal or quasi-formal institutions that act as political intermediaries with the state. And European Muslims find themselves more often in synch with wider public opinion on contentious foreign policy issues such as the Iraq War than do American Muslims. Given the complexity of these factors, any rush to identify specific distinctions between European and American Muslims must necessarily be tentative.

Like Christianity and Judaism, Islamic scriptures contain rhetorical resources that can be harnessed to justify political violence. Political Islam of the kind that spawned Osama bin Laden, though, has a distinctively modern trajectory. In the twentieth century, it was yoked to the project of creating Islamic states in Egypt, Pakistan, and elsewhere. Only when this project failed did bin Laden and his cohorts reframe their campaign in megalomaniacal global terms. Yet, spectacular attacks, from the August 7, 1998, Nairobi and Dar es Salaam embassy bombings onward, did not persuade all of bin Laden's ideological brethren to adopt his inhumane tactics; the Salafi tradition that birthed Ayman al Zawahiri and bin Laden remains fragmented into politically active and quietist branches. In path-breaking work, Fawaz Gerges has shown that other Islamists and jihadists had decidedly mixed reactions to the 9/11 attacks.

Looking for terrorists by scouring Muslim communities either overseas or at home, therefore, is like looking for needles in a haystack; by any measure, they are few and far between, and their ideological roots are difficult to mechanistically untangle from those who endorse a puritanical—but nonviolent—form of Islam. Studies of terrorist radicalization also reveal a multiplicity of individual root causes, both emotional and societal.

Law enforcement authorities have responded to these problems by directing investigative resources toward entire Muslim communities in ways that breed fear and anxiety, do not leave the nation safer, and tread heavily on the religious liberties and human dignity of American Muslims.

Targeting Muslims

In May 2002, then Attorney General John Ashcroft issued a new set of investigative guidelines ending a twenty-six-year policy that barred FBI agents from infiltrating a religious organization without suspicion of specific criminal activity by the organization or its members. In January 2003, FBI Director Robert Mueller ordered all FBI branch offices to count the number of mosques within their jurisdiction. Mueller's post hoc explanation—that the bureau was planning in the event of hate crimes—was not terribly convincing. Since Mueller's remarks, substantial anecdotal evidence has emerged that places of Muslim worship are directly targeted for FBI investigation. In at least one case reported to Representative John Conyers, the FBI demanded lists of worshippers at a mosque, an investigative tactic long understood to chill legitimate speech and association that is protected by the First Amendment. Mosques were also monitored by surveillance cameras (Lackawanna, New York), subjected to flyovers (Bloomington, Illinois), and subpoenaed for phone records. As early as August 2002, *USA Today* named nine U.S. cities where mosques were under investigation, including Cleveland; Falls Church, Virginia; Fort Lauderdale; Jersey City; and Norman, Oklahoma. It is not unreasonable to think this number is still higher today.

More troubling for many Muslims is the secret introduction of confidential informants into mosques and other religious institutions. Informants collect and share details about the subjects and tone of imams' sermons; they have in some cases collected the license plate details of congregants. Further, in cases in Lodi (in California), Manhattan, Brooklyn, and Miami, informants have played a crucial catalytic role in pushing young and impressionable men toward verbal endorsement of violent action—hence exposing them to criminal prosecution. Paid hundreds of thousands of dollars for their ability to prey on the deeply misguided sentiments of youths, informants not only provide evidence but help create the very conspiracies that justify their salary.

In 2006, Brooklyn Muslims were surprised to learn that at least three informants working for the New York Police Department's Terrorist Interdiction Unit had been attending services regularly at a local mosque, the Islamic Society of Bay Ridge, during the winter of 2003. This fact came to light during the trial of twenty-three-year-old Shahawar Matin Siraj, who was charged with plotting an explosion at the Herald Square subway station. Informants played a key role in Siraj's trial, as well as in his prior conduct. Siraj had met one informant, fifty-year-old Osama Elawoody, in a local Islamic bookstore. Elawoody not only taped conversations with Siraj but also provided a spur to Siraj's conduct. Siraj held odious views, calling bin Laden, for example, "a talented brother and a great planner." But it is far from clear that these opinions would have matured into action without Elawoody's prompting. The older man mentored Siraj on matters political, spiritual, and temporal (such as marriage). Siraj, as his defense lawyer explained, was "not the brightest bulb in the chandelier," at one point asking Elawoody whether atomic weapons were different from nuclear weapons. This did not forestall a jury from later convicting Siraj.

The Siraj case is not the only one to illustrate the thin line separating surveillance from provocation. In Lodi, California, the FBI hired an older informant, Naseem Khan, even though he had previously lied to bureau agents about seeing Ayman al Zawahiri in California. In 2002, Khan met and befriended twenty-three-year-old Hamid Hayat, cultivating Hayat's intolerant, bloodier views and urging Hayat to attend a terrorist training camp in Pakistan. Like Elawoody, Khan received tens of thousands of dollars from the FBI. Like Siraj, Hayat was convicted, although his father—who allegedly knew of his son's intentions—was not.

Informants in the Siraj and Hayat cases played on the religious sensibilities of young men, shepherding them toward increasingly extremist religious views. Such overt state manipulation of religious sentiment is rare—and would be surprising even outside the criminal context. The police's use of informants, moreover, casts shadows on religious and community life for Muslim minorities. It creates the feeling that no one in one's religious community, a space that should be free for debate and reflection, can be trusted. And it undermines other kinds of cooperative trust-building; one liaison with the New York police described the Siraj trial as "a real set back to bridge-building." This is hardly surprising given the animating impulse behind the current use of informants: the belief that Muslims cannot be trusted to manage their own communal religious life.

Nor is the cultivation of informants free from abuse. In a dozen California cases, Muslim immigrants have been threatened with deportation for minor technical visa violations, and asked to become informants to avoid this fate. In one case, a twenty-four-year-old Moroccan was threatened with designation as a person "likely to engage in terrorist activity," a label used only five times after 9/11, unless he became an informant. He could also have been detained for two years or more as his deportation case was litigated. Informants, under these circumstances, are under tremendous pressure to produce results.

Given the pressure placed on informants to provide information, it should not be surprising that they would bend others' religious sentiment toward extremist justifications for violence.

Informants and other forms of information gathering are not the only investigative tactics that have affected Muslims in America disproportionately. Prosecutors have also tested a new species of preventative detention almost uniquely against Muslim suspects. The federal "material witness" statute was enacted to permit temporary detention of witnesses who might otherwise flee, hence facilitating their testimony in a criminal trial. After 9/11, however, it became a vehicle to detain suspects— overwhelmingly Muslims—to allow investigation and the development of probable cause to warrant further detention of the same suspect. Of seventy post–9/11 material witnesses identified in a recent study, forty-two were released without charges, and twenty were charged with offenses unrelated to terrorism.

Use of the material witness statute rose dramatically to public attention when Oregon lawyer Brandon Mayfield was arrested as a material witness in connection with the March 2003 bombings in Spain. The FBI claimed to have matched his fingerprint to one found in Madrid. Mayfield, a Muslim convert, protested his innocence from the beginning. Indeed, Mayfield was released from custody two weeks later when it turned out that the fingerprint match was nothing of the kind—Spanish authorities had told the FBI so from the start. An investigation by the Justice Department's inspector general concluded that Mayfield's faith was "not the sole or primary cause" of the FBI's mistaken decision to detain Mayfield as a material witness—but it had contributed to the failure to rectify it. FBI agents had only a degraded copy of the print. They also failed to request the original when they had the chance to do so. Bureau investigation into Mayfield, nevertheless, yielded evidence that "dispelled" its initial doubts about the print—such as the apparently compelling fact that Mayfield had long visited a local mosque. Religious practice, in the government's eyes, hence became a terrorist "trait."

Mayfield's is not a unique case. In March 2003, Abdullah al Kidd was on his way to Saudi Arabia to work on a doctorate in Islamic studies when he was detained as a material witness. He was not charged. It took sixteen months for federal law enforcement authorities to concede that they could not charge him. In the interim, al Kidd lost his scholarship and his marriage collapsed. In September 2006, a federal judge declined to dismiss al Kidd's civil suit for damages against law enforcement officials based on abusive use of the material witness statute.

One final law enforcement tactic merits mention, even though few authorities candidly admit using it: profiling Muslims. Anecdotal evidence from South Asian and Middle Eastern men in the United States confirms the frequent de facto use of profiling, and commentators such as Paul Sperry of the Hoover Institute and Charles Krauthammer, as well as politicians such as Representative Peter King, have argued for overt profiling.

Racial profiling, whether de facto or de jure, does not work and causes needless damage to human dignity. Although there is some evidence that profiling leads to an initial drop in offending rates, evidence from the terrorism context—including studies from Israel and analyses of screening protocols for air travel—shows that the rate of attack soon picks up. Terrorists simply substitute members of a nonprofiled group for profiled individuals or change their mode of attack. As law professor Barnard Harcourt concludes, "there is no reliable evidence, nor a good theoretical reason to believe that profiling would be effective" as counterterrorism. Moreover, profiling—like any other invidious stereotyping—inflicts considerable harm to the dignity of those profiled. In the United Kingdom, the perception that police use stop-and-search powers granted under Article 44 of the 2000 Terrorism Act in a racially discriminatory fashion against young South Asian men (leading to the phenomenon of "standing while Asian") has been a principal cause of anger and resentment against the police.

Yet profiling will remain "a fact of life," especially for those perceived as Muslims. And as long as politicians like King can garner votes through fear-mongering and by promoting ineffectual tactics that project a sense of strength and determination, it will also remain on the political agenda.

The Prosecution Record

After the 1993 World Trade Center attacks, Congress enacted two "material support" criminal statutes targeting actions that support terrorism. One of these measures focused on material support of a "foreign terrorist organization" but, even as amended in 2004, does not require the defendant to know that his acts will facilitate terrorist activity. The other focuses on knowingly aiding certain terrorist acts. In 1996 and 2001, Congress expanded these prohibitions. The material support provisions are not the sole ways in which prosecutors reach beyond conspiracy liability. Another important law, originally included in the 1917 Espionage Act, criminalizes conspiracies to harm foreign property and persons, and has been invoked in cases involving attendance overseas at alleged terrorist training camps.

Though the material support provisions were seldom used before 9/11, they have been used vigorously since. An early, relatively unproblematic example involved the prosecution of John Walker Lindh, who was captured fighting with the Taliban. Lindh was prosecuted based on his involvement in that group. Subsequent aggressive interpretations of the statute, however, have raised equity concerns. In August 2006, for example, a third-grade teacher from Virginia was sentenced to fifteen years' imprisonment on material support charges. Ali Asad Chandia's sentence rested on favors he did for an acquaintance who worked for a Kashmiri group on the U.S. terrorist list: he picked up the acquaintance at the airport and helped him take boxes to a shipping company. To the local Muslim community, doing favors for a friend hardly seemed consequential. It certainly seemed insufficient to justify fifteen years' imprisonment. "If this is how you deliver justice," protested one Maryland Muslim to the *Washington Post*, "you lose your trust in the justice system."

In another case, federal prosecutors charged a graduate student who volunteered to help manage a Muslim charity's Web site. Although the Web site focused on peaceful causes, buried within it were violent messages written by others. On these grounds, University of Idaho student Sami al-Hussayen was charged with material support for providing "expert advice or assistance." As indicators of terrorist intent, bureau agents focused on al-Hussayen's switch in academic advisors, on his study of computer security systems, and on the fact that his office was housed in a building that had once held a long-defunct nuclear reactor. According to al-Hussayen's lawyer, investigators "focused on people they were suspicious of and set about trying to prove they had committed a crime." The trouble with this approach to policing, of course, is that race and religion will often be the unspoken basis of the initial suspicion.

To many, al-Hussayen was indeed guilty before his trial began. University of Idaho President Robert Hoover appeared with federal officials and pronounced himself "betrayed" by al-Hussayen. Idaho Governor Dirk Kempthorne invoked al-Hussayen's arrest to place new security measures around the state capitol. Yet a jury acquitted al-Hussayen, underscoring the fact that prosecutors never produced evidence that al-Hussayen knew of or approved the messages on the site.

Laws involving financial transactions have also had a significant impact on American Muslim communities since 9/11. The International Emergency Economic Powers Act criminalized transactions with certain entities designated by the Treasury Department's Office of Foreign Asset Control (OFAC). The Patriot Act of 2001 permitted OFAC to freeze assets based not only on wrongdoing but also on mere suspicion of wrongdoing. Major Muslim charities in the United States, including the Global Relief Foundation, Benevolence International, and the Holy Land Foundation, have borne the brunt of OFAC's actions, being targeted without the chance to see and challenge evidence used against them. Although Benevolence International's director pleaded guilty to channeling funds to rebel fighters in Bosnia and Chechnya (strenuously denying any al Qaeda connection), these freezes led to no convictions for domestic terrorism. They did, however, foster the perception among Muslim communities that they are being targeted in the absence of hard evidence of wrongdoing. Further, designations raise the specter of possible material support prosecutions of thousands who give to charities. This perception is reinforced by other prosecutions that clearly impinge on First Amendment speech interests.

Since charitable giving is a religious obligation for Muslims, the assault on Muslim charities strikes directly at their religious practice. In the fearful post–9/11 climate, charitable giving has dropped precipitously even to nondesignated entities. At the time of this writing, the Treasury Department has not issued regulations that provide sufficiently clear "safe harbors" for individuals wanting to give money to Muslim charities.

Preventive prosecutions for material support or financial crimes are further troublesome not merely because investigators rely initially on hunches based on racial and religious bias; these prosecutions rely on a different sort of proof. Absent clear evidence of a violent intent, prosecutors use defendants' religious views to show criminal intent. In the Hayat case, prosecutors introduced a scrap of paper found in Hayat's wallet that said, "Oh Allah, we place you at our throats, and we seek refuge in you from their evil" (translated initially by the prosecution as, "Lord, let us be at their throats, and we ask you to give us refuge from their evil"). In their summation, prosecutors used the note and other evidence to argue that Hayat had "a jihadi heart and a jihadi mind." But it is common in Hayat's native Pakistan to carry such a *tawiz*, a paper with an inscribed prayer, in one's wallet. And Hayat's specific *tawiz* was a traditional supplication found in innumerable prayer books. It is impossible to tell whether Hayat's conviction thus rested on false premises about his religious beliefs.

The Hidden Costs of Preventive Prosecution

The benefits from preventive prosecution seem overstated. Government claims of having foiled incipient plots, to be sure, are often difficult to assess. But in high-profile case after high-profile case, pronouncements of the terrible harms averted soon yield to diminished claims about the threat. Besides the Mayfield and Al-Hussayen arrests, high-profile prosecutions in Tampa, Albany, and Detroit have proved less substantial than first claimed. And in cases such as the Siraj and Hayat prosecutions, it is hard to tell where government provocation ends and actual conspiracies begin.

Preventive prosecution, moreover, seems animated by short-sighted political motives as much as considered law enforcement strategy. Political bosses inevitably pressure prosecutors to secure dramatic arrests and convictions in terrorism cases. After the Hayat prosecutions, for example, President Bush congratulated the FBI on its "win," while John Negroponte lauded the breakup of a network of Islamic extremists. Similarly, FBI Director Robert Mueller invoked al Kidd's detention in congressional testimony, even though al Kidd was never charged. There is thus a premium on visible, short-term public relations success without regard to the underlying facts.

A prosecution from Detroit provides telling evidence of the consequences of political pressures to make early public claims of success. FBI agents arrested Karim Koubriti, Ahmed Hannan, and Farouk Ali-Haimoud soon after 9/11 on accusations of being a "sleeper cell." In June 2003, Koubriti and the alleged leader of the cell, Abdel-Ilah El Mardoudi, were convicted of material support, while Hannan was convicted of document fraud. The convictions collapsed, however, when the court discovered that the prosecution had, in its "zeal to obtain a conviction," omitted or misrepresented evidence to a degree "so prevalent and pervasive" that it likely changed the jury's verdict.

The Justice Department tried to pin blame on the lead prosecutor in Detroit, Richard Convertino. It even charged him criminally. But the Detroit case was driven by imperatives from higher up. Soon after the arrests, then Attorney General John

Ashcroft told the public that these Detroit men were "suspected of having knowledge of the Sept. 11 attacks," a wholly baseless allegation that later was retracted. Senior Justice Department officials in Washington took the lead at every step of the prosecution, from formulating strategy to editing the indictment and planning how the suspects would be incarcerated. They even floated the idea of designating the defendants as "enemy combatants" and moving them out of the criminal justice system. Abuse of prosecutorial powers in the Detroit case, in short, was not exceptional but, instead, indicative of a broader approach to domestic terrorism prosecutions. It was indicative too of how visible accoutrements of government success can become more important than frank threat assessment.

Preventive prosecution burdens Muslim communities in inequitable ways and retards the chance of long-term counterterrorism success. The costs of domestic counterterrorism are not equally distributed across the population. It is easier for politicians and officials to adopt burdensome tactics because they know the majority of the voting public will not feel their weight. Innocent people such as Mayfield and al Kidd are swept in without large public outcry. Communal religious life is sapped by distrust and anxiety. Even when a case encompasses evidence of violent intent, it is fair to ask whether this intent would ever manifest as action absent the intervention of the government. Ironically, at the same time that terrorism prosecutions are seemingly being less than effective, increasing evidence suggests that the diversion of law enforcement resources to terrorism ends is contributing to a rise in violent crime across the nation.

Even those unconcerned with the civil liberties of minorities thus ought to be concerned at these outcomes. Preventive prosecutions and their trappings sow fear and anxiety in Muslim communities. At Brooklyn mosques, for example, "people can recite a list of dubious cases as easily as popular verses of the Koran," including failed prosecutions in Idaho and Tampa, prosecutions revealed to be grounded on prosecutorial misconduct in Detroit, and threats of "enemy combatant" designation in Lackawanna. Yet substantial empirical evidence suggests that respecting individual rights—including the right to be free from racial or religious profiling—yields stronger community relations and better policing results. Law enforcement agencies that have legitimacy—because they act fairly—are more successful in nurturing cooperation and compliance with the rules than ones viewed as unfair.

In the counterterrorism context, this legitimacy has two immediate consequences. First, stronger bonds of trust between communities and law enforcement make coming forward with information easier. Tips from within a community matter—especially when police generally lack the language and cultural skills to work with those communities. Arrests by British police in August 2006 of a group alleged to be preparing to bomb transatlantic flights, for example, flowed from a tip from the community. The cases of an alleged sleeper cell in Lackawanna, New York, whatever its ultimate merits, also began when investigators got a tip from within the local Yemeni community. Similarly, a series of major prosecutions in Virginia began with information from the community.

Second, law enforcement authorities, including the Justice Department and the New York Police Department, have acknowledged the importance of recruiting from within Muslim, Middle Eastern, and South Asian communities. It is difficult to see why Muslim youth would select a law enforcement career if their experience with police and federal authorities is consistently one of humiliation and fear.

Good, effective counterterrorism policing is not impossible. Examples can be found at a local level. In Dearborn, Michigan, a formal dialogue mechanism, the BRIDGES program, eased community–law enforcement relations in the teeth of nakedly discriminatory tactics such as Special Registration. Local FBI agents in Dearborn who participate in BRIDGES proved generally careful and responsive to local concerns, while their superiors in Washington tacked with the political winds. Programs such as BRIDGES, and the intensive (but only partially successful) efforts of British police to build links to Muslim minority communities, show that building stable, trusting relations with Muslim communities, even in a time of terror, is eminently possible. But doing so requires political will to set aside the quick and pyrrhic propaganda victory. At least at a national level, this self-discipline has proved in short supply in the United States.

The future may hold worse news for advocates of smart, effective counterterrorist policing. In the fall of 2006, Congress passed and the president signed the Military Commissions Act of 2006. Ambiguous provisions of the act could be invoked by the government to allow the arrest and detention of noncitizens in the United States as "unlawful enemy combatants." This term is defined to include those who purposefully provide material support to anyone engaged in hostilities against the United States. Under the act, noncitizen, unlawful enemy combatants may be held without any review of the grounds for their detention. They may be tried by military commissions, likely to be convened at the Guantánamo Bay Naval Base. These commissions are authorized to punish material support, as well as ill-defined offenses such as "wrongfully aiding the enemy." The act raises the real danger of a second-class system of detention and criminal justice for some noncitizens in the United States. Inevitably, noncitizens will be shunted into this inferior system when the evidence against them will not stand up in a federal criminal prosecution; yet, these cases are exactly the ones that raise the greatest concerns about government miscalculation and misunderstanding of religious speech and practice. Moreover, the present record of counterterrorist criminal prosecutions leaves no doubt that it will be Muslims who will be principally targeted by this development. It is hard to calculate the fear and distrust this move will create in Muslim minority communities in the United States above and beyond the simmering anxieties fostered today by indiscriminate preventive prosecution tactics.

PART III

Is This Justice?

CHAPTER 9

The Guantánamo Question

STACY SULLIVAN

The charter terminal at the Fort Lauderdale airport is usually full of women in sundresses and men in Hawaiian shirts on their way to Caribbean vacation destinations, so it's not hard to spot the handful of soldiers, military contractors, and lawyers en route to Guantánamo Bay, the American naval base and prison on Cuba's southeastern tip.

None of them want to be going there.

Gitmo, as it is known in military parlance, is a craggy, forty-five-square-mile strip of land that is home to iguanas and banana rats and has warm weather year-round and sweeping views of the Caribbean. The base has townhouse subdivisions, a shopping mall, a golf course, batting cages, and a high school, as well as a McDonald's, Starbucks, Pizza Hut, and a bar called the Windjammer that has karaoke on Wednesday nights. Extracurricular activities include scuba diving, fishing, and sailing. It would feel like a package-tour vacation destination were it not for the five sprawling prison camps the United States built to lock up hundreds of terrorist suspects in the wake of the 9/11 terrorist attacks.

In early 2002, photographs of hooded, jump-suited prisoners locked in Camp X-ray, a crude encampment of open-air chain-link cages, sparked global protests against the United

States for human rights violations. Those images will no doubt remain seared into the minds of generations to come, as will the lurid stories of abuse—many of which have been corroborated by the FBI and military personnel.

The Pentagon has made efforts to clean up Guantánamo. Camp X-ray was shut down long ago and is now overgrown with tropical weeds. In its stead, more units have been constructed, including two state-of-the-art facilities modeled on American prisons in the Midwest. The Pentagon now claims that Gitmo is the most comfortable and legally accountable detention facility it maintains for foreigners. It provides journalists with tours of the base that include a visit to the kitchen for a sampling of the detainee meals, a walk through the pristine detainee medical facilities, and a viewing of hundreds of books in English, Arabic, and Pashto that will soon make up the detainee library.

But the window dressing has done little to improve Gitmo's public image. Evidence of the military's disdain for the detainees is everywhere. Souvenir T-shirts for sale in the base's gift shop read, "The Taliban Towers at Guantánamo Bay—The Caribbean's Newest 5-Star Resort" and "JTF-GTMO Behavioral Modification Specialist." Baby outfits in pink and blue read, "Future Behavioral Modification Specialist." Soldiers speak with contempt about the detainee lawyers, whom they brush off reflexively as "terrorist sympathizers." And although only ten of the more than seven hundred men who have passed through Gitmo have been charged, soldiers on the base speak with certainty that all of the detainees are guilty.

"I believe that no detainee was brought to Gitmo as a result of a mistake," Rear Admiral Harry Harris, Gitmo's commander, told me during my visit to the base. "They were all rounded up on the battlefield waging jihad." Just a few weeks before my visit, Seton Hall Law School released a study, based on the military's own data, that showed that only 5 percent of the men being held at Guantánamo Bay were apprehended by U.S. troops. Many were picked up by Afghans and Pakistanis who often handed their captives over to the United States for bounties of $1,000 and up, and most were nowhere near a battlefield. The detainees were captured in at least fourteen different countries in Africa, Europe, North America, and Asia. The vast majority have never been accused of shooting at or even fighting U.S. or coalition forces. Given those statistics, I asked Admiral Harris, how could he be so sure Gitmo was full of terrorists? "They weren't sent here directly without passing go," Admiral Harris said. "They were sent here by an expert body somewhere in the AO [area of operation]." When I asked him if he knew anything about the expert body in the area of operation, he acknowledged that he did not but that he was certain the process was fair and accurate.

Admiral Harris's answers shed light on the mentality—a mindset of certainty—that has made Guantánamo possible. The founding fathers understood the dangers of certainty and built an elaborate system of checks and balances to safeguard against it. They created a legal system built on the bedrock principle that everyone should be presumed innocent until proven guilty and that everyone has the right to a fair hearing before an impartial judge. The men at Guantánamo have been denied such rights by an administration that clings to its certainty regardless of the facts and, until recently, a Republican Congress that obediently turned presidential assertions into laws—in spite of a Supreme Court that has twice intervened to check presidential power.

Six years of single-party control of the executive and legislative branches of government in which presidential certainty has rarely been questioned has given birth to a human rights debacle that has tarnished the reputation of the United States as a law-abiding nation, alienated our allies, inflamed the Arab world, and given other countries an excuse to mistreat Americans who might be captured abroad in the future. Guantánamo will surely go down in history books, alongside such wartime misadventures as the internment of Japanese Americans during World War II and prosecutions under the Espionage and Sedition acts during World War I, as among the most shameful assaults on civil liberties in American history.

Background/History

Just how terrorist suspects captured in the mountains of Afghanistan came to be locked up on a Caribbean island with which the United States has no diplomatic relations is a peculiar story made possible by Guantánamo's peculiar status. Guantánamo is a sort of diplomatic no-man's land that is firmly under U.S. control, although successive presidential administrations have claimed that Washington is not legally accountable for what happens there. As such, it has served as a convenient holding pen for people the U.S. government wants to keep outside the reach of American law. The United States first occupied Cuba in 1898 during the Spanish-American War. Washington agreed to end its occupation provided that Cuba include in its constitution a guarantee that the United States could indefinitely lease the strip of land that is now the Guantánamo naval base and that the lease could only be terminated with American consent. When Fidel Castro came to power in 1959, the United States insisted that the lease was still valid and simply stayed. Castro did not really have a choice in the matter. Each year, Washington sends Cuba a rent check in the amount of $4,085. Castro never cashes it, but the United States remains.

In the early 1990s, under the first Bush administration, thousands of Haitian refugees who tried to flee the military regime that overthrew the island's democratically elected government were picked up at sea by the U.S. Coast Guard and taken to Guantánamo. Some of the Haitians were granted asylum in the United States, but most were returned to Haiti in what many human rights lawyers claimed was a direct violation of the United Nations Refugee Convention. This convention says that states cannot return people to countries where they might fear for their lives or face persecution. But U.S. authorities held that, since the Haitians had not actually reached the shores of the United States, they technically were not returning them. Things became more complicated when about three hundred of the Haitians who were deemed to have a well-founded fear of persecution tested positive for HIV. Fear of AIDS was so extreme at the time that the Bush administration refused to let HIV-positive refugees into the country and detained them at Guantánamo. His administration's legal rationale was essentially that, again, the Haitians were not entitled to asylum by international law because they had not actually reached the shores of the United States and that, because Guantánamo was not a part of the United States, they did not have legal rights under the U.S. Constitution or federal statutes. They were thus locked up in a leaky barracks and denied access to lawyers and, in some cases, to medical care.

During his campaign for president, Bill Clinton vowed to shut down the camp, but after he took office, he changed his mind. To justify keeping the Haitians locked up at Guantánamo, justice department lawyers recycled the advice from the previous administration. A group of law students and human rights lawyers challenged the administration, and a year later, a federal district court in Brooklyn, New York, rejected Clinton's position, ruling that Guantánamo Bay was under the "complete jurisdiction and control" of the United States and that anyone being held there had to be accorded due process rights guaranteed by the Constitution. Thus, the Haitians at Guantánamo were entitled to constitutional due process, including the right to a lawyer, the right to proper medical care, and the right not to be held indefinitely without charge.

Had this critical decision been allowed to stand, Gitmo as a prison for terrorist suspects might never have come to pass. But the Clinton administration, fearful that it might face a refugee crisis in the Caribbean, did not want to have a court precedent limiting its flexibility in handling it. Having access to a territory outside the law could be extremely useful. The administration thus negotiated with the Haitians' lawyers and agreed to close the camp and let them into the United States if they would allow the government to have the decision vacated—that is, struck from the record.* The refugees' lawyers agreed to the deal because they feared they would lose if the case went to the Supreme Court, which had given indications that it would rule in the administration's favor. As a result, what was clearly a landmark decision, the ruling that Guantá-

---

*The government appealed the decision, but because it had already agreed to close the camp, the court ruled that the case was moot and had it vacated.

namo was under the jurisdiction of U.S. courts, technically no longer existed.

When the second Bush administration needed a place to detain and interrogate terrorist suspects, Guantánamo was thus ideal. According to the administration's logic, the United States was facing an unprecedented threat of terrorism. Better intelligence was essential to prevent future terrorist attacks. The hundreds of al Qaeda and Taliban fighters U.S. forces were said to have captured on the battlefield in Afghanistan likely had information about future attacks, and the United States needed to interrogate them to get this information. These alleged terrorists were reportedly trained to withstand conventional interrogation methods, so new, harsher techniques needed to be introduced. The detainees needed to be isolated from the rest of the world so that they would come to rely completely on their interrogators for their welfare. They could not have access to U.S. or any other courts, which might make them believe that help was on the way and thus undermine the interrogation process. Because the Clinton administration had managed to strike the ruling on the Haitians from the books, the Bush administration could recycle the argument that U.S. law did not apply to Guantánamo.* This point, as White House memos would subsequently show, was critical in the decision to set up an interrogation center and prison at Guantánamo.

There was, of course, also the problem of international law, which strictly prohibits the kind of interrogation techniques the

---

*In arguing their case, lawyers for the Bush administration drew on the language in the Platt Amendment, the original agreement that gave the United States the right to establish a naval base a Guantánamo. It stated that the United States exercised "complete jurisdiction and control" of the base but that Cuba retained "ultimate sovereignty." Because ultimate sovereignty lay with Cuba, they argued, U.S. courts did not have jurisdiction over the base.

White House wanted to implement. According to the Geneva Conventions, captured enemy soldiers from an opposing national army are considered prisoners of war and are immune from prosecution for lawful acts of war. Irregular combatants—those from a guerrilla force or other non-state actor—are also entitled to prisoner-of-war status as long as they wear uniforms or other distinguishing attire,* carry their weapons openly, and conduct their operations in accordance with the laws and customs of war. If there is any doubt as to whether or not the detainees are prisoners of war, the convention states that the detaining authority must grant them prisoner-of-war status until a "competent tribunal" determines otherwise.

The Bush administration—again proclaiming certainty—ignored the requirements of the conventions and simply declared that none of these men were prisoners of war but, rather, "illegal enemy combatants." Legal scholars were immediately critical of the White House's designation, arguing that the detainees were either prisoners of war or persons protected under the Fourth Geneva Convention, who were entitled to the protections of the Geneva Conventions, or criminal suspects who were entitled to hearings in U.S. courts. They claimed there was no such thing as an "illegal enemy combatant." The Bush administration countered that there was; in fact, it had just created the category, along with a justice system to address it.

Had the detainees been designated prisoners of war, the conventions would have required that they be given the same trials that the United States gives its own soldiers. But even if it were

---

*Inhabitants of non-occupied territories who spontaneously take up arms on the approach of the enemy without having had time to form themselves into regular armed units also qualify for prisoner-of-war status as long as they carry their arms openly and follow the laws and customs of war.

determined that the detainees were not eligible for prisoner-of-war status, Geneva would still require that the prisoners be charged and get fair trials in accordance with international standards. The administration, however, announced that it was not bound by such laws and that it planned to try the illegal enemy combatants by military commission.*

The proposed military commissions did not resemble anything close to a fair hearing. The rules allowed detainees to be convicted based on evidence that they could not see or rebut and permitted both hearsay evidence and evidence garnered through coercion. A detainee could be convicted based on evidence gleaned from torturing another person, and the detainee would not have the opportunity to confront his accusers. Moreover, the checks and balances upon which the American system was built—the legislative branch defining crimes, the executive branch prosecuting perpetrators, and the judiciary adjudicating guilt and dispensing punishment—were brushed aside. The Bush administration's military commissions allowed the executive branch to perform all of these functions.

There wasn't much question as to whether or not the military commissions were fair—they clearly violated basic fair trial standards of both the Uniform Code of Military Justice (UCMJ) and the Geneva Conventions—but in the post–9/11 environment, the American public was not particularly concerned about the rights of terrorist suspects. Secretary of Defense Donald Rumsfeld described the Gitmo detainees as the "most dangerous, best-trained, vicious killers on the face of the

---

*The military commissions were set up by Presidential Order No. 1, issued on November 13, 2001. The procedural details, outlining how the commissions would work, were set forth in Military Commission Order No. 1 on March 21, 2002.

earth," and for the most part, Americans did not doubt those claims. As so often is the case when a country has been attacked, the populace rallied around the leadership, which vowed to protect America from future attacks. Groups such as Human Rights Watch and Amnesty International condemned the commission rules, but there was not a public uproar.

Thus, in early 2002, the United States began construction of what would eventually be five sprawling prison camps with capacity for about 1,000 detainees who, it claimed, were beyond the reach of both international law and American law.

The Legal Fight

What was taking place at Guantánamo might never have become public were it not for a small group of death penalty lawyers who had a history of taking on cases nobody else seemed to care about. Among them was Clive Stafford-Smith, a joint American and British national who ran a New Orleans–based organization called Justice in Exile and had spent twenty years defending convicts on death row. His death penalty work stemmed from a belief that everyone, no matter how heinous the crime committed, was entitled to a fair hearing—something the Gitmo detainees never had because Gitmo was a legal black hole.

Breaking through that black hole was difficult because the administration, claiming privacy rights, refused to divulge the names of the men it was holding. Stafford-Smith, however, learned through media reports that there were two Britons and an Australian in Gitmo, so he tracked down their families and obtained what is known in legal parlance as next friend authorizations—letters granting permission for a lawyer to represent the detainees. With the next friend authorizations in hand, Stafford-Smith teamed up with the Center for Constitutional Rights (CCR), a New York–based nonprofit organization that advocates for civil rights. The CCR, whose founding members include notable civil rights lawyers such as the late William Kunstler and whose president, Michael Ratner, had been involved in representing the Haitians detained at Guantánamo a decade earlier, recruited another death penalty lawyer, Joseph Margulies, who had spent years representing convicts on death row in Texas.

Rasul

A CCR team led by Margulies began drafting a petition for writ of habeas corpus on behalf of Shafiq Rasul, Asif Iqbal, and David Hicks, the two Britons and the Australian. Habeas corpus, which translates from Latin to "you should have the body," is a request for a court to order the government either to explain the legal basis for holding someone or to release him. The Great Writ, as it is known, dates back to fourteenth-century England and was considered by the founding fathers as such an important safeguard against illegal imprisonment that they enshrined it in the Constitution and specified that it could only be suspended during insurrection or invasion.

The CCR, which often relies on pro bono work, contacted corporate law firms for assistance but didn't get any takers. At the time, the press was reporting that the detainees in Guantánamo were high-level al Qaeda members who were providing valuable intelligence that might be deflecting terrorist attacks against the country. Defending the rights of terrorists in the post–9/11 environment was not a cause anyone wanted to take on. "It was far too close to September 11 and most people didn't want to know about it," recalled Stafford-Smith.

On February 19, 2002, Margulies filed a petition for a writ of habeas corpus, *Rasul v. Bush,* in the federal district court of Washington, D.C. The government asked the court to dismiss the case on the grounds that U.S. courts did not have jurisdiction over Guantánamo, and the court agreed. The Gitmo lawyers appealed and lost again. By now, a year had passed, and the beleaguered coalition of lawyers had accomplished little. They moved ahead anyway and appealed to the Supreme Court. In November 2003, the Supreme Court agreed to hear the case.

By then, two corporate firms had joined the fledgling coalition. Shearman & Sterling, one of the country's largest and most prestigious firms, had several business clients in Kuwait and had agreed to represent a group of Kuwaiti detainees. The New Jersey–based firm Gibbons, Del Deo, Dolan, Griffinger & Vecchione also offered support through its public interest fellows. Bolstered by the arrival of two corporate law firms—and the manpower, resources, and legitimacy that came along with them—the coalition of lawyers began preparing what would be a stunning lineup of amicus briefs, arguments from people who are not part of the case but who offer legal arguments based on their expertise that can shed light on the future implications of any decision. They included, among others, eighty-five British members of Parliament, former Vietnam prisoners of war, and Fred Korematsu, a Japanese American who had been detained in U.S. internment camps for Japanese Americans during World War II.

As the lawyers prepared for their showdown in the Supreme Court, cracks began to appear in the administration's claims that Guantánamo was holding the worst of the worst. Journalists tracked down several of the detainees who had been released and, apart from discovering that some of them were teenagers and old men, heard credible stories about the physical and psychological abuse that they had endured at Gitmo. Among the most common complaints were the so-called IRFs, five-person Immediate Response Forces, that were employed in theory to subdue uncooperative prisoners. Their stories were backed up by a Kentucky national guardsman who had volunteered to pose as a detainee for an IRF practice exercise in January 2003. He was choked and beaten so badly that he suffered traumatic brain injury and seizures.

By April 2004, when the Supreme Court was scheduled to hear *Rasul*, public sentiment about Guantánamo was changing. British judges and members of Parliament from Washington's staunchest ally had publicly lambasted the Bush administration about Guantánamo. Just a couple of months earlier, the administration had announced charges against two detainees, and the military lawyers appointed to defend them before military commissions accused the president of trying to usurp the judicial system. The courtroom was packed, because the case was to provide the first inkling of how the Supreme Court viewed the administration's sweeping assertions of wartime powers.

During the Supreme Court hearings, the justices posed a question: If the United States could maintain a prison beyond judicial scrutiny, they asked, might it not be possible that the men being held there were being tortured? Government lawyers responded emphatically with a blanket statement: The United

States does not torture. Just days later, however, the Abu Ghraib prisoner abuse story broke.

As the gruesome photos of American soldiers smiling and giving the thumbs-up sign next to naked prisoners in humiliating positions were plastered across newspapers and magazines and shown on television around the world, the press discovered a now infamous series of memos prepared by the Defense Department and administration lawyers. The memos argued that the president was not bound by international treaties prohibiting torture or by a federal anti-torture law because, as commander-in-chief, he could approve any technique deemed necessary to protect the nation's security. They went on to define torture so narrowly—"physical pain . . . equivalent in intensity to the pain accompanying serious physical injury such as organ failure, impairment of bodily function or even death"— that many methods that would normally be thought to constitute torture were permitted.

We may never know how the Abu Ghraib photos or the torture memos affected the justices; but on June 28, 2004, in what was a dramatic rebuke to the administration, the Court ruled that Guantánamo was within the jurisdiction of U.S. courts and that the detainees had the right to challenge the legality of their detention.

With the Supreme Court's decision, what had initially seemed a group of unpatriotic pariahs heralding a doomed cause became a forward-thinking coalition that smart lawyers wanted to be a part of. By then, Stafford-Smith had collected some seventy next friend authorizations. The CCR divided them into groups by nationality and again called on corporate firms to help. This time, some of the country's largest and most prestigious firms began lining up to volunteer their services.

The new guard of corporate lawyers—many of them associates in their twenties and thirties who had been working on cases like accounting fraud and telecommunications deals—now formed the backbone of what came to be known as the Guantánamo Bay Bar Association, and they began filing habeas cases. Just nine days after the Supreme Court ruling, however, the Bush administration, intent on making sure that the detainees would not have access to U.S. courts, announced that the Department of Defense would hold its own hearings—so-called Combatant Status Review Tribunals (CSRTs)—that would allegedly allow the detainees to contest their status as illegal enemy combatants. Although the Supreme Court had ruled that the detainees were entitled to a fair hearing, it left open the possibility that the military, and not U.S. courts, could make this determination. The government maintained that the CSRTs, which were to be presided over by three military officers, rendered hearings in U.S. courts unnecessary. In addition, it pointed out that it had previously created Administrative Review Boards, which allowed the detainees to have their status as enemy combatants reviewed each year—something it argued ensured due process.

The Guantánamo Bay Bar Association countered that the CSRTs were not a viable alternative to U.S. courts but, rather, an obvious effort by the administration to circumvent the rule of law. They did not entitle the detainees to see all of the evidence against them, they permitted evidence obtained through coercion, and they did not allow the detainees to call any witnesses other than fellow detainees. In addition, the CSRTs did not allow the detainees to have lawyers but, instead, allowed a "personal representative"—a military officer who helped the detainees understand the CSRT process but who specifically could not be a lawyer. Similarly, detainees were not allowed to have lawyers and not permitted to know the allegations they had to defend themselves against at their Administrative Review Boards. The lawyers now had to return to court to argue that the CSRTs were not viable alternatives to judicial hearings. Until a decision could be rendered, a federal judge ruled that the lawyers were entitled to meet with their clients at Guantánamo and instructed the government to work out procedures for visitation. By the time the lawyers finished negotiating with the Justice Department over the terms—a process that resulted in a judge ordering a set of procedures after the lawyers and the Department of Justice could not agree—and underwent FBI background checks for security clearance, almost all of the detainees had already had their CSRT hearings. The government had concluded that almost all of the detainees were indeed enemy combatants.*

When the lawyers saw the transcripts of the hearings—as well as other evidence the Pentagon had collected on the men—they were stunned. The majority of detainees were not even accused of holding a weapon or committing a hostile act against the United States. In some cases, the detainees were not even alleged to have been in Afghanistan. In one case, the primary allegation against a detainee was that he had been an acquaintance of a known suicide bomber who had blown himself up in a Turkish synagogue. Notwithstanding the fact that the bombing was said to have taken place after the detainee was

---

*Between July 2004 and March 2005, the Department of Defense conducted 558 CSRTs at Guantánamo. Based on a review of the information known to the Department of Defense at that time, 38 detainees were determined to no longer meet the definition of enemy combatant, and 520 detainees were found to be enemy combatants.

taken into U.S. custody, the detainee's lawyer subsequently discovered that the alleged suicide bomber was alive and well and living in Bremen, Germany. "When I looked at the evidence, I understood how generally feeble the cases were against them," said Joshua Colangelo-Bryan, an associate from the law firm Dorsey & Whitney, which had agreed to represent six Bahrainis. "For me, that was a great illustrative lesson in why we need due process."

In September 2004, the lawyers began visiting Guantánamo—the first civilians apart from the International Committee of the Red Cross and a few delegations from home governments to meet with the detainees. The meetings took place in Camp Echo, an encampment of tiny cells with adjoining meeting rooms. In all cases, the men were shackled to the floor and usually handcuffed. Most of the lawyers were able to contact family members before their visits to garner some information about their clients, and they were able to send the clients letters informing them of the upcoming visits; very few, however, had received letters back.

According to the rules worked out in negotiations with the Department of Justice, the lawyers needed to secure signed statements from the detainees authorizing representation within two visits. Some detainees were hesitant; as the lawyers would subsequently learn, interrogators had at times posed as lawyers and asked the detainees to sign statements. Most said that, until their CSRT hearings, they had not even been told of the allegations against them and did not know why they were in Gitmo. More often than not, the detainees told lurid stories about the abuse and neglect they had undergone in U.S. custody, from soldiers urinating on them and putting their cigarettes out on their skin to IRF teams beating them unconscious.

Some said that they were denied medical treatment for weeks or months. One told his lawyer of having a tonsil that was infected and untreated for so long that he tried to pull it out himself with a piece of thread. Others talked about multiple hunger strikes and suicide attempts.

The lawyers initially had questions about the claims of abuse, but in time, many of these allegations were independently corroborated. In conjunction with the American Civil Liberties Union, the CCR filed a request under the Freedom of Information Act and gained access to a series of e-mail and other documentation that FBI agents had written expressing concern about aggressive interrogation techniques they had witnessed at Gitmo. They described interrogators subjecting detainees to extreme hot and cold temperatures, wrapping them in Israeli flags, depriving them of sleep, forcing them to defecate on themselves, making them watch gay pornography, and forcing them to listen to constant loud music. In addition, a former military intelligence soldier who worked as an interpreter at Gitmo published a book, *Behind the Wire*, describing the abuses he witnessed, many of which matched what the detainees had told their lawyers—including wrapping detainees up in Israeli flags, depriving them of sleep for days at a time, turning the air conditioners up to high in their cells and depriving them of blankets and clothing, and IRF beatings.

The lawyers were not permitted to talk about their visits until after they had submitted their notes to the Justice Department for declassification. Although some of the lawyers reported getting their notes back with allegations of abuse redacted out, most of them got their notes cleared, and they soon began talking to the press. In time, stories began appearing in the media that portrayed Gitmo not as a detention center full of hardened terrorists but, rather, as a prison camp that was mostly full of low-level militants and men simply caught in the wrong place at the wrong time. The administration and the military refused to address specific claims of abuse; instead, they refuted the lawyers' allegations with blanket statements about how they had been duped by terrorists who were trained by al Qaeda training manuals to make allegations of torture. "They're taught to lie, they're taught to allege that they have been tortured, and that's part of the training that they received," said then Secretary of Defense Donald Rumsfeld.

In late January 2005, a federal judge reviewing some of the challenges the lawyers had filed ruled that detainees had the right to due process and that the CSRTs were "fundamentally flawed" and did not satisfy that right. However, another judge, reviewing a separate set of challenges, ruled that the detainees were not entitled to due process rights and, even if they were, the CSRTs were adequate. The question was thus left to the U.S. Court of Appeals to decide. As a result, detainee hearings in U.S. courts would be delayed for months, and there was still the possibility that the appeals court would rule in the government's favor.

Hamdan

As the Guantánamo Bay Bar Association continued collecting next friend authorizations and filed more petitions on behalf of the hundreds of detainees being held without charge, a military lawyer for one of the men who was charged filed a lawsuit challenging the anticipated commission proceedings as illegal under both U.S. and international law. Salim Hamdan, who the government claimed was Osama bin Laden's driver, had been charged with conspiracy to attack civilians and commit acts of terrorism. In addition to arguing that the military commissions were illegal, his lawyers, Lt. Cmdr. Charles Swift and Neal Katyal, argued that conspiracy was not a war crime under international law, and thus not a crime eligible for trial by military commission under U.S. law. The military commission proceedings against Hamdan began in Guantánamo in August 2004 amid allegations that Hamdan was beaten, threatened, and kept in isolation for more than eight months. That November, Judge James Robertson of the U.S. District Court for the District of Columbia (a Clinton appointee who had been active in civil rights) ruled that both the UCMJ and Geneva Conventions were applicable and that the military commissions did not meet the standards of either. He stayed the military commission proceedings.

The government appealed, and on July 15, 2005, the U.S. Court of Appeals for the District of Columbia, in a three-judge panel that included the future Chief Justice John Roberts, ruled in the government's favor. It held that the commissions were authorized by Congress under the Authorization for the Use of Military Force (AUMF) and the UCMJ. It also held that the Geneva Conventions were not judicially enforceable. Hamdan's attorneys petitioned the Supreme Court for a review, and on November 7, 2005, the Court agreed to hear the case.

As the *Hamdan* case was making its way through the courts, Senator John McCain of Arizona, who had been held as a prisoner of war in Vietnam, drafted legislation banning the use of "cruel, inhuman or degrading" treatment by U.S. officials operating anywhere around the world. In what would have seemed surreal only a few years earlier, the administration publicly opposed McCain's amendment, arguing that, although the United

States does not torture, it did not want a bill limiting its options when interrogating terrorist suspects.

On November 2, 2005, the *Washington Post* reported that the Bush administration, reluctant to bring more terrorist suspects to Guantánamo, had tasked the CIA with establishing a covert prison system. These so-called black sites, according to the newspaper, were established in eight countries, including Thailand, Afghanistan, and several others in eastern Europe. Neither the public, foreign officials, nor most members of Congress charged with overseeing covert CIA activities knew about the sites, where suspects were held incommunicado and subjected to interrogation techniques euphemistically described by the president as "alternative" and "tough." The McCain amendment would have jeopardized this program because CIA agents, fearful of criminal prosecution, reportedly said they would not continue the abusive interrogations.

Under public and international pressure, the White House finally agreed not to veto the McCain amendment. But it got something else it wanted. In the last days of 2005, Senator Lindsey Graham of South Carolina introduced an amendment to the defense appropriations bill stripping U.S. courts of jurisdiction over Guantánamo. The Graham-Levin amendment, so named because Senator Carl Levin of Michigan added wording that would ensure that the law would not be retroactive, revoked the detainees' right to file habeas corpus petitions and barred them from ever filing suit in U.S. courts for torture should they ever be released.

With public and media attention focused on McCain's torture ban, the Graham-Levin amendment passed with virtually no debate. The Great Writ has rarely been suspended in American history. Abraham Lincoln suspended it in 1861 during the

Civil War (and it was overturned by the Supreme Court in 1866), and President Ulysses Grant did so again in 1870, although the latter occasion only applied to nine counties in South Carolina as part of a federal civil rights action against the Ku Klux Klan.

In the last days of 2005, lawyers representing Guantánamo detainees in lower courts worked frantically before the Detainee Treatment Act became law to file additional motions for habeas corpus based on next friend authorizations obtained from detainees who already had representation. But in January 2006, the government argued that the act was indeed retroactive and petitioned the Supreme Court to dismiss the *Hamdan* case on the grounds that the Detainee Treatment Act divested Hamdan (and any other Gitmo detainees) of the right to seek habeas corpus in a federal court.

The Supreme Court heard oral arguments from both sides on March 28, 2006. Three months later, on June 29, 2006, the Court ruled 5–3, with Chief Justice John Roberts recusing himself, that the administration did not have the authority to set up the military commissions at Guantánamo Bay because it lacked congressional authorization. It further ruled that the Geneva Conventions standards of humane treatment applied in the conflict with al Qaeda and that the commissions were illegal because they violated fair trial standards of both the UCMJ and the Geneva Conventions.

Perhaps even more importantly, the Court ruled that all detainees held in relation to the War on Terror were legally entitled to humane treatment and may not be subject to "cruel treatment and torture" or "outrages upon personal dignity, in particular, humiliating and degrading treatment." Human rights groups insisted that the ruling called into question the legality of holding detainees incommunicado and the CIA's use of coercive interrogation techniques. The *Hamdan* decision had no direct impact on the continued use of Gitmo as a place to detain terrorist suspects and did not say anything about how long the United States may detain the men without charge. However, it did state that their treatment must conform to the requirements of the Geneva Conventions and reasserted their right to habeas corpus.

The Government's Response

In spite of the Court's ruling, however, the Bush administration remained adamant that the detainees did not have the right to a hearing in U.S. courts. Shortly after the *Hamdan* decision, it announced that it would go to Congress to seek approval for its military commissions. It quickly began pressing Congress not only to pass legislation creating military commissions that were virtually identical to those the Supreme Court had just struck down but also to redefine U.S. obligations under the Geneva Conventions, to exempt CIA personnel from prosecution for abusive interrogation methods, and to bar detainees from bringing any court actions, including petitions for habeas corpus.

With leadership from Senators Lindsey Graham, John Warner, and John McCain, Congress refused to redefine U.S. obligations under Geneva or to exempt CIA personnel from prosecution for war crimes; however, it did give the president some leeway to determine what constitutes torture. On September 28, 2006, Congress passed the Military Commissions Act. The act gave the president authority to proceed with the commissions, although with two important differences: the commission rules now ensure that detainees cannot be convicted based on evidence that they cannot see or rebut, and they can appeal their conviction to a civilian appellate court. The act does, however, allow the commissions to permit the introduction of hearsay and in some circumstances evidence obtained through coercion. It also narrowed the definition of what constitutes a war crime under U.S. law, potentially decriminalizing certain acts of mistreatment against detainees that were previously considered criminal offenses.

Perhaps most egregiously, the Military Commissions Act bars detainees from filing habeas corpus petitions and raising claims of torture or other mistreatment in U.S. courts, and unlike the Detainee Treatment Act of the previous year, it specifically states that these court-stripping provisions are retroactive. If the legislation is allowed to stand, the more than two hundred habeas cases filed on behalf of Gitmo detainees will be summarily dismissed, and the men, if they are ever released, will not be entitled to sue in U.S. courts for the torture and mistreatment they may have endured.

The legislation can be considered a step forward in that it provoked the Bush administration to admit what it had never previously disclosed—that it was holding suspects in secret sites. Just days after the Military Commissions Act passed, the administration announced that it had recently transferred fourteen detainees from secret sites abroad to Guantánamo. The act also ensured that torture remains a crime and thus that it is banned. Immediately after Congress passed it, however, the administration began arguing that the act still permits some of its "enhanced" interrogation techniques, such as extended sleep deprivation, exposure to extreme cold, and waterboarding—

making a detainee believe that he is drowning. Indeed, on October 24, 2006, Vice President Dick Cheney stated in a radio interview that he thought it was a "no-brainer" that the United States "could dunk a terrorist in water" if it would save American lives. The administration claimed the vice president wasn't referring to waterboarding, but it's hard to imagine what else he could have been referring to by "a dunk in the water."

As the administration began using the power granted it by the Military Commissions Act—reconstituting the military commissions at Guantánamo and moving to dismiss the now hundreds of habeas cases filed on behalf of the detainees who have yet to be charged—the Republican Congress that granted it the power to do so was unseated. A day after the defeat, the president announced Rumsfeld's resignation. The departure of Guantánamo's architect no doubt sent a powerful and important message to both our allies and enemies, but the house that Rumsfeld built is still very much intact, and it seems unlikely that the new Congress will tear it down. Although the Democrats came to power on a wave of antiwar sentiment, they are not about to start proposing legislation to uphold the rights of terrorist suspects. The CCR and the hundreds of lawyers now supporting its efforts are now arguing that the Military Commissions Act of 2006 is unconstitutional. If the courts agree, the Democratic Congress is unlikely to devise ways to bypass the ruling, as the previous Congress did. Hence, the detainees at Gitmo could finally have a hearing in a U.S. court, though that process could still take years.

In the meantime, both the administration and the Pentagon continue to insist that this little section of Cuba is holding "the worst of the worst," though it may have quietly concluded that many of the men they are holding are far from that. Behind the scenes, Washington has been quietly negotiating with some of the detainees' home countries for their release—in most cases directly back to their families, not into domestic detention. But this should not be read as an indication that the administration is planning to close Gitmo. "By negotiating to send some of the detainees home, the administration is just trying to get rid of a bunch of people who never should have been there in the first place," said Jim Ross, senior legal advisor at Human Rights Watch who has monitored Gitmo since it was opened. "And nothing is stopping it from holding hundreds more in indefinite detention."

CHAPTER 10

What Now for Detainees?

JOSEPH LELYVELD

A lthough the Bush administration would never put it quite so baldly, in its rush to consolidate its authority after the terrorist attacks of 9/11, it came close to asserting that the U.S. commander-in-chief has the power to declare anyone in the world, of whatever citizenship or location, an "unlawful enemy combatant" and—solely on the basis of that designation—to detain the person indefinitely without charge, beyond reach of any court. According to a list being compiled by Human Rights Watch, alleged terrorists were detained at American behest in Mauritania, Bosnia, Indonesia, the United Arab Emirates, and Yemen, as well as in Afghanistan where most al Qaeda and Taliban suspects were captured. They were then turned over to the United States for transfer to the prison hastily knocked together out of cargo containers in the American military enclave at Guantánamo.*

---

*The impression that normal legal restraints had been suspended showed up elsewhere. Italian magistrates charged agents of the Central Intelligence Agency with a kidnapping on the streets of Milan. In that case, "extraordinary rendition" to Egypt of the captured man appears to have obviated any need for him to be declared a combatant.

The five years since 2001 have not been uneventful for constitutional scholars and lawyers concerned with human rights or for journalists of an investigative bent. Their questions and discovery motions have pried information, including names of many detainees, out of a government committed to secrecy. That information has been used as kindling for a slow-burning debate on coercive interrogation that eventually led Congress—nearly two years after publication of the notorious pictures of naked Iraqis being stacked and taunted at Abu Ghraib prison—to affirm legislatively that existing laws and treaty commitments barring torture and cruel, inhuman, and degrading treatment (sometimes called "torture lite") still bind American interrogators in what has been grandiosely named the Global War on Terror.

By the time of the passage of the Detainee Treatment Act in December 2005, a slim majority on a U.S. Supreme Court with conservative leanings had also made it clear that it wasn't prepared to renounce jurisdiction over all tough issues involving detainees simply because those detainees were, overwhelmingly, aliens imprisoned outside the United States. In *Rasul v. Bush*, the Court held that writs of habeas corpus could be filed in federal courts on behalf of the alien detainees at the Guantánamo Bay detention center. Of course, by 2005, most of the detainees had already been there for more than three years. At the same time, in *Hamdi v. Rumsfeld*, the Court held that an American citizen designated as an "enemy combatant" was still entitled to due process and could not be held in indefinite detention without charge. "A state of war is not a blank check for the President," Justice Sandra Day O'Connor wrote in the *Hamdi* decision. This dictum could be read as a response to the more far-reaching claims made by the president's constitutional advisers, notably by the former deputy attorney general in the Office of Legal Counsel at the Justice Department, John C. Yoo, who had written that any congressional attempt to restrict "the President's plenary power over military operations (including the treatment of prisoners)" would be "constitutionally dubious."

Finally, in 2006 in *Hamdan v. Rumsfeld*, the Supreme Court held that the military commissions the administration had sought to establish at Guantánamo to try detainees were defective on various grounds, including their failure to conform to what's known as Common Article 3 of the Geneva Conventions. The administration, of course, had argued from the start that Geneva had no application to the struggle against a transnational terrorist group such as al Qaeda. One way or another, the White House had now to recast its claims to "plenary powers," though it never stopped making them.* Constitutional scholars and human rights lawyers could congratulate themselves on having set the terms of an ongoing debate.

From the standpoint, however, of hundreds, perhaps thousands, of detainees who have been held now for three, four, or five years by U.S. forces not only at Guantánamo but at assorted prisons in Iraq and at the air force base at Bagram in Afghanistan (and, possibly, at other places borrowed from other governments that have yet to be uncovered or acknowledged),

---

*After the administration reached agreement with Republican holdouts in the Senate on the Military Commissions Act of 2006, it made a point of saying that President Bush had not actually needed congressional approval on issues involving interrogation standards, which the act purported to address. "The President, of course, had the authority to do this under his powers as Commander-in-Chief," Stephen J. Hadley, the national security adviser, said in a press briefing, "but what we wanted to do is have an additional legal framework supported by the Congress." His statement seemed to say that such a "legal framework" was desirable but, in the view of the White House, patently unnecessary.

the fact and prospect of indefinite detention have been fixed and unchanging. Decisions have been handed down, and laws have been passed. Some of these may now be revised by the newly elected Democratic Congress; in particular, the recent Military Commissions Act, which among other things denies alien detainees recourse to the writ of habeas corpus. But the question of indefinite detention itself—which might be construed as a core issue—hangs over our discussions like a far-off thundercloud, darkening a little with each report of another suicide attempt at Guantánamo. From the standpoint of the remaining detainees, nothing much has changed over the years.

The action in the courts has mostly focused on Guantánamo; the census and legal status of the more remote prisons is murkier.* According to the organization Human Rights First, which has attempted to keep count, there were, as of late 2006, 395 prisoners at Guantánamo, an estimated 15,000 at various Iraq locations, and about 500 at Bagram. How many of the prisoners in Iraq and Afghanistan have been held indefinitely for a period of years is uncertain; how many are non-Iraqi and non-Afghan is also a matter of guesswork for those who lack an official need to know.**

---

*Administration lawyers have cited a U.N. Security Council resolution recognizing the United States as an occupying authority in Iraq, passed after the start of the occupation, as the legal basis for the United States to continue holding security detainees in what's now a sovereign Iraq.

**Human Rights First, using government figures, estimates that between 60,000 and 70,000 persons have been detained around the globe at one time or another by the United States since the first frantic efforts in 2001 to sweep up as many likely agents and contacts of terrorist networks as possible. The total ought to include the more than one thousand aliens, mostly Muslim, held in the United States since the first months after the 9/11 attacks on unrelated immigration charges or as so-called "material witnesses," on orders of then Attorney General John Ashcroft.

The argument that combatants—both would-be combatants who have merely been trained as well as those captured on a battlefield—can be held indefinitely in wartime until the end of hostilities isn't in itself novel or controversial. Indeed, it's the very basis of the Geneva Conventions, the rule book for preventive detention, which ensures humane treatment on all sides for those imprisoned for the specific purpose of neutralizing them militarily, of keeping them out of action. The issue is whether the United States has legally been in a state of war since September 18, 2001, when Congress authorized the use of military force against those responsible for the attacks a week earlier, and whether that authorization gave the president authority unilaterally to make up new rules and procedures for the treatment of captured supporters of terrorist movements. Since 2001, the United States has cited those parts of international law that serve its purpose and has shrugged off, disputed, or discounted others. "Customary laws of war," our government has correctly argued, justify holding prisoners indefinitely without charge. At the same time, it has contended that the Geneva Conventions, the modern codification of "the customary laws of war," don't apply because al Qaeda and its offshoots are not parties to them and, all too obviously, have no regard for their standards.

The Global War on Terror may have had a certain ring as a battle cry, or at least some utility from a marketing point of view as a brand name for an ongoing security crisis, but it muddies the detention issue. It seems to imply that we must remain at war, transforming ourselves into a permanent national security state, until terrorism—not any particular organized force but a diffuse phenomenon that has existed for more than a century—has been thoroughly banished from the world. In fact,

Congress did not authorize a War on Terror but, rather, a war on the terrorist perpetrators of the 9/11 attacks and anyone who actively abetted them. The administration sometimes acknowledges as much. "When administration officials refer to the war on terror," John Bellinger, the State Department's legal adviser, recently said, "we are not stating that we are in a legal state of armed conflict with every terrorist organization, everywhere in the world, at all times. . . . We do think we are in a legal state of armed conflict with al-Qaeda."

But even by that somewhat limited definition, how will anyone know when the war is over? Will fighting have ceased in Afghanistan? Will the tribal regions along the border of Pakistan, where Osama bin Laden is allegedly finding refuge, be pacified? What measure could security officials use to certify that there remains no network of "sleeper cells" in the West? If hopeful answers to these questions cannot easily be imagined, what about imagining that anyone in authority could declare in the foreseeable future that this war has ended, or been sufficiently contained, to permit the release of supposed hard-core terrorist detainees at Guantánamo and elsewhere? Put this way, the indefinite detention of combatants in this war seems not just open-ended but truly without limits, a predicament to which the "customary laws of war" do not offer an obvious solution. Supreme Court decisions on detention issues have been handed down, and laws have been passed. But the question of whether we're prepared to imprison terrorist suspects without charge for the rest of their natural lives has yet to be squarely addressed.

The issue was much on the minds of some Supreme Court justices when oral arguments were heard in the *Hamdi* case. Justices O'Connor, Souter, and Breyer repeatedly pressed the government's lawyer to say when it might be appropriate for the courts to hear habeas petitions on behalf of prisoners held for many years in an unending conflict. "Doesn't the Court have some business intervening at some point, if it's the Hundred Years War or something?" an impatient Stephen Breyer demanded. "We recognize the viability of the writ of habeas corpus," Paul D. Clement replied on the government's behalf. "There certainly is a challenge that can be brought to the length of the detention at some point."* When that point would come and how it would be recognized were questions left unanswered. Those questions were obviously still on Justice O'Connor's mind when she wrote the opinion for the Court. The plaintiff, she said, faced "the substantial prospect of perpetual detention." If one accepted the government's reasoning, she went on, "Hamdi's detention could last for the rest of his life."

In the immediate aftermath of the Court's ruling, the government shied away from the challenge of prosecuting the prisoner. Instead, it hastily cooked a deal to put Yaser Esam Hamdi on a plane for Saudi Arabia as a way of avoiding either embarrassment over the weakness of its case against him, having to divulge sensitive intelligence in open court, or both. Suddenly, all Hamdi had to do to be let go was to renounce his U.S. citizenship and agree to be repatriated. Shafiq Rasul, a British

---

*In his oral argument a year later in the *Hamdan* case, Clement suggested at one point that the resolution authorizing the use of military force passed by Congress might imply the power to suspend habeas corpus in particular cases, given the so-called suspension clause in the Constitution. That clause says that Congress can suspend the writ in instances of "invasion" or "insurrection." A suspension of the writ of habeas corpus could be "constitutionally valid," he said, even if Congress "sort of stumbles" on it without the formal invocation of the clause specified in the Constitution. "You are leaving us," Justice Souter retorted, "with the position of the United States that the Congress may validly suspend [the writ] inadvertently."

national, had already been sent back to Britain a few months before the Supreme Court got around to pronouncing on his case. Faced with a choice between a measure of judicial transparency and the freeing of prisoners, the government in each case chose to release these "hard-core, well-trained terrorists" (to repeat Secretary Rumsfeld's sweeping verdict) after holding them without charge for more than three years. The striking ease with which these two, who had become subjects of legal challenges, were let go might, as a matter of logic, have deepened doubts about the justification for holding the many others with no prospect of release.

Subsequently, more than 250 other Guantánamo prisoners were repatriated in what appeared to be a tacit admission that they were no longer a great threat nor of any significant value from an intelligence standpoint, if, indeed, they ever had been. The State Department was reportedly hoping to negotiate the repatriation of another sixty or so Guantánamo prisoners but was running into difficulty getting other governments to agree to its demand for continued surveillance. A similar number was deemed to be potentially chargeable in front of the military commissions established by President Bush, which, after *Hamdan*, were given congressional approval via the Military Commissions Act of 2006. As of this writing, however, only 10 have actually been charged. After subtracting these three groups—those who have actually been released, those the United States is seeking to release, and those who may still be charged—on the order of 250 prisoners at Guantánamo alone remain who, it appears, are considered not eligible for release or charging. The plain inference is that we've no evidence that they've been implicated in past acts of terrorism but still consider them too dangerous to let go. These, then, along with whomever else is locked away in Iraq or Afghanistan or in other places where the United States continues to have some say over their fates, are the indefinitely detained in the War on Terror.

The Guantánamo total is not inconsiderable, but it's notably smaller than the population for which the Pentagon once planned. The number of prisoners at Camp Delta, as the prison there is named, was expected to exceed 2,000 in early Pentagon projections; in late 2002, it topped out at slightly more than 650. The shortfall may represent a change in tactics—a belated recognition that the United States could not conceivably detain every would-be Islamic militant in a world where new ones are appearing daily on the streets of Baghdad and Gaza. Alternatively, it could be the result of a decision simply to lower the profile of Guantánamo itself by making greater use of more remote facilities overseas that are even harder for human rights advocates to penetrate.

Since 9/11, counterterrorism officials must have felt that they were responding to an overwhelming imperative. The key to their thinking for Guantánamo and the Ashcroft roundup of supposedly suspicious aliens was their sense of how impoverished their intelligence sources and leads on the looming but largely faceless enemy were. Above all, they felt, they needed to find the small bits of information that might fill in the picture of what they were confronting, the darkly imagined network. At all times, preventing the next terrorism outrage, within our borders especially, took precedence over finding and punishing those responsible for the last one.

This ordering of priorities was not unreasonable after 9/11, when fears of an imminent second attack weighed heavily. From inside the cocoon of those operating what they conceived of as a new kind of war, it seemed obvious that the threat they were facing demanded a shedding of fussy old constraints, especially those imposed at the end of the Vietnam experience. Any reminder that there were limits on a president's power in these new circumstances—that he couldn't order high-tech phone surveillance without judicial approval, for instance, or coercive interrogations, or, in extremis, even torture and assassinations—served as an imperative to remove roadblocks to the efficient working of the security apparatus. Interrogation was the key to intelligence, they believed, and a freer hand was the key to interrogation. There was a consensus at the top levels of government that the time had come to "take the gloves off." The figure of speech gained currency. The CIA said it needed to assure its agents and interrogators that they would be shielded from charges that they had broken the law. Thus began the process of rationalization and the harvest of legal memoranda about a president's "plenary power."

It was the beginning of what was infamously branded "the new paradigm" in the letter signed by Alberto Gonzales, then the White House counsel, after Secretary of State Colin Powell pushed back against his president's declaration that the Geneva Conventions would not apply to captured jihadists. It's not difficult to deduce what the administration found to be "quaint" (to use the language of the Gonzales letter, which we now know to have been drafted in Vice President Cheney's office) about the Geneva regime. Common Article 3, which governs the treatment of captives in both "international armed conflicts" (between states) and "non-international armed conflicts" (within a given country) forbids "outrages upon personal dignity, in particular humiliating and degrading treatment," as well as "cruel treatment and torture." In other words, the article imposes restraints on interrogators that the authorities felt they needed to ease if they were to have any substantial hope of understanding and tracking their shadowy enemy in a time-effective way. The paucity of reliable intelligence they had starting out is suggested by their eagerness to cast a wide net, engineering detentions that were basically indiscriminate in hopes that, among all the minnows with tiny bits of information that they might unwittingly divulge, there might lurk a few really valuable fish. That goal was apparently what the Ashcroft detentions, on the domestic side, and the original intake at Guantánamo, on the international side, were trying to accomplish. The interrogation imperative is thus inextricably bound up with the refusal to accommodate the Geneva regime as well as the unwillingness to confront the leftovers from this great haul of supposed Islamic radicals—the still unresolved issue of indefinite detention.

Outsiders have absolutely no way of evaluating the intelligence harvest yielded by these efforts. It certainly seems that a huge amount of time was wasted by interrogators of varying experience and judgment on prisoners who knew little or nothing. We have a necessarily incomplete picture of the cruelties perpetrated in the course of this effort, but what we do know about the use of isolation, sensory deprivation, stress positions, loud music, and sexual taunting is enough to be shameful. It also is enough to sow skepticism about the claim that the worst abuses were not systematic but rather the wayward acts of a handful of enlisted men and women. "Outrages upon personal dignity" appear to have been very nearly the norm in the early months, at least until the Abu Ghraib scandal broke in early 2004.

In arguing its case against Geneva, the Bush administration did not take public issue with the humane standards of Common Article 3. Oblivious of contradiction, it managed simultaneously to endorse them and to imply that taking them literally could be at least inconvenient, possibly dangerous. Instead of making a candid case for coercive interrogation, it made legal arguments about the failure of the conventions to foresee and account for the outrages of a terrorist network. Strictly speaking, it contended, the struggle against al Qaeda cannot be an "international armed conflict" because al Qaeda isn't a state; nor is the war a "non-international armed conflict," because it sprawls across the borders of many states. Therefore, government lawyers have argued, there is a lacuna in the conventions. The administration, which places a low value on what's called international humanitarian law, came forward with no proposals on how to fill the lacuna it perceived in the Geneva regime. Instead, claiming a license to set its own standard unilaterally, it charged right through it. It looks as if the legal advisers sought to apply to international humanitarian law their usual conservative precepts about "strict construction" and "the intention of the framers." The fact that al Qaeda wasn't foreseen in 1949, however, hardly negates a larger truth about the conventions: that they were intended, in the judgment of most experts, to be entirely comprehensive, setting minimal standards of humane treatment for illegal as well as legal combatants. No class of warrior was exempted from the minimal legal protections built into Common Article 3, which the United States accepted and taught to several generations of military lawyers.

There is, therefore, a measure of poetic, as well as legal, justice in that military lawyers were among the first to blow the whistle on the free-wheeling interpretations of international law that George W. Bush's lawyers devised. The resistance of the uniformed lawyers had much to do with rousing Congress from its posture of supine acquiescence to the administration's security measures, as did the key Supreme Court decisions on "unlawful enemy combatants." But the legislation a Republican-dominated Congress finally passed—notably the Detainee Treatment Act of 2005 and the Military Commissions Act of 2006—severely limited the scope for challenges in federal courts on behalf of detainees. Habeas petitions on their behalf were explicitly barred once it has been determined that they've been "properly detained." Now that Democrats have narrow control of the Senate Judiciary Committee, its new chairman, Senator Patrick J. Leahy, hopes to overturn what he has called "this sickening habeas provision." Even if he is successful, there are still likely to be roughly 250 prisoners at Guantánamo alone facing indefinite detention without charge. A more carefully written law may make it possible for some among them, in the fullness of time, to challenge their designation as "illegal enemy combatants" and their imprisonment. But so far there has been no sign that Democrats care to wrestle with the premise that it's legitimate to hold prisoners indefinitely without charge, await-ing the end of a war that shows no sign of ending.

The Geneva Conventions could, conceivably, be involved in a constitutional challenge on this point. Indefinite detention, for the duration of a war, is permitted for enemy combatants granted prisoner-of-war status in an armed international con-flict, but there is no provision for indefinite detention in the cases of "protected persons" who have been detained—but not charged—in conflicts that don't meet that standard. Here, too, the Military Commissions Act establishes a roadblock to any challenge, for it grants the president "authority for the United States to interpret the meaning and application for the United States of the Geneva Conventions." The act was Congress's re-sponse to the *Hamdan* ruling, which effectively suspended the military tribunals before they could begin their work on grounds that their procedures fell short of the standards of Common Article 3. It could take at least two years to discover whether the legislation will withstand a judicial test, presumably "on the important question," as Justice Breyer put it during oral arguments in the *Hamdan* case, "of whether Congress can constitutionally deprive this Court of jurisdiction in habeas cases." By then, those Guantánamo prisoners who are not (at least as of now) considered by their keepers eligible for charging or release could be in the eighth year of their detention, with no end in sight.

In principle, many find such a prospect odious. But how many of those who deplore the spectacle of Camp Delta, Abu Ghraïb, and Bagram would call for the immediate and unconditional release of 250 or more prisoners who, though proven guilty of no crime, may have among them an untold number of potential jihadists (angrier and more numerous, in all likelihood, than was the case before they underwent the ardors of coercive interrogation and before they saw their world shrink to a 6.8- by 8-foot cage almost round the clock)?

The experience of other democratic countries offers some perspective on the way the United States has handled the detention of suspected terrorists. Israel, which is in a perpetual state of emergency, at any given time holds Palestinians by the thousands. Military tribunals oversee these cases, but the opportunity to appeal to the Israeli Supreme Court on habeas grounds has never been shut off. Periodically, Israel agrees to large-scale prisoner releases to achieve some political end (to secure the release of Israeli prisoners held by the other side or to advance a negotiation at a time when hostilities appear to have ebbed). In Britain, Tony Blair's government was quick off the mark after 9/11 to get parliamentary approval for the indefinite detention of foreigners suspected of terrorist connections. The provisions of the law, known as the Anti-Terrorism, Crime and Security Act, conflicted with the European Convention's prohibition of arbitrary detention. The government sought to get around that difficulty by formally seeking an exception—a "derogation" as the convention terms it—on grounds that it faced an emergency that "threatens the life of the nation." Nevertheless, the Law Lords in 2004 struck down the part of the terrorism act providing for indefinite detention. (Sixteen persons, by then, had been held under the act.) The following year, in the Prevention of Terrorism Act, Parliament gave the government the power to issue "control orders" to foreign suspects, which would confine them in a form of house arrest, specifying when they could leave their residences or how far they could go.

Not satisfied, the Blair government then sought the right to hold terrorism suspects, including citizens, for ninety days without charge. Labor back benches revolted and succeeded, finally, in whittling the period of detention down; the prime minister had to be satisfied with a maximum preventive detention term of twenty-eight days under the Terrorism Act of 2006, which passed after having been voted down in the House of Commons in its original version.* The use of the preventive detention tool was said to have been effective in foiling the plot to blow up airliners leaving Heathrow in the summer of 2006, prompting Attorney General Gonzales and Michael Chertoff,

---

*Like their U.S. counterparts, British authorities have resorted to immigration law to hold a suspect, at least in one case. An Algerian with supposed al Qaeda ties has been held without charge pending deportation since 2001. He uses the name Abu Doha and is said to have been involved in the plot to bomb the airport in Los Angeles at the time of the millennium. As of this writing, he is still in detention without charge.

the secretary of homeland security, to wonder aloud whether the United States needed a preventive detention law.

The USA Patriot Act had already given the attorney general the power to hold a noncitizen for deportation after certifying that he is a threat to national security. A preventive detention law would presumably expand that power of detention to cover citizens and close off repatriation as an escape route for noncitizens who are under suspicion but have not been charged. In general, however, the Bush administration has not been eager to go the legislative route to seek new detention powers. As we've seen, it preferred to assert that any such powers were inherent in the president's authority as commander-in-chief.

Five years after the 9/11 attacks, that expansion of authority has been partly ratified by Congress. The administration has retreated only on the question of whether Congress has the power to legislate against cruel, inhuman, and degrading treatment of prisoners in interrogations conducted by military interrogators. In 2005, Vice President Cheney personally lobbied on Capitol Hill against any such restrictions, opposing a measure introduced by Senator John McCain. The measure passed and was strengthened in the Military Commissions Act a year later. It carefully barred abuses in military interrogations but, in provisions of telling ambiguity, preserved the president's authority to condone the use of interrogation techniques by the Central Intelligence Agency that he judged to be less than "grave breaches" of Common Article 3. In other words, the prohibition against "outrages upon personal dignity" could be stretched but not completely ignored if the president determined it was necessary to permit small outrages; he was left as the sole judge of what might make such an infraction necessary and tolerable. What was defeated was Secretary Rumsfeld's project of creating within the Pentagon an intelligence apparatus that could compete with the CIA and do anything on the clandestine side that the spy agency was able to do. Not finally defeated, however, was the option of coercive intelligence itself.

Still, much of what happened at Guantánamo and the more remote detention centers in the early years would clearly not be legal under this new law. (Whether it was legal then is an issue that's unlikely ever to be settled, since the law seeks to indemnify interrogators against suits over any abuses they may have committed before its passage.) But, granted that there has been a certain degree of legislative tidying up, hundreds of prisoners are still stranded in a state of indefinite detention without charge. It remains to be seen whether new leadership at the Pentagon, following Donald Rumsfeld's departure, will be willing to address a question that clearly never weighed on the former secretary: the political as well as legal question of how long the system of indefinite detention can be sustained. There may be an intention, if not a plan, to deal with the issue by attrition, allowing the population to dwindle with the aim of phasing out the detention center entirely or using it only for prisoners actually facing charges before military commissions.

Such a plan, however, would not address the prisoners who have yet to be reclassified as NLECS ("no longer enemy combatants"), a status a prisoner so far has been able to earn only in exchange for cooperation with interrogators or a finding that he was never really a threat. With it comes the kind of imprisonment envisioned under Geneva for certified prisoners of war—barracks rather than cages, more recreational time, opportunities to mix with fellow prisoners, more access to information from the outside world. It amounts to a halfway house to release.

Tim Golden, in the *New York Times,* described a short-lived attempt by the military authorities at Guantánamo to make conditions there less severe. The plan involved new cellblocks designed with an eye to encouraging communal exercise and meals, in conditions approaching those afforded traditional prisoners of war. By the time the newest cellblock opened at the end of 2006, however, the military authorities had long since lost faith in the experiment. Following a riot and a mass suicide attempt in 2005 and three successful suicide attempts in June 2006, they clamped down and restored the ban on group activities for detainees. "I don't think there is any such thing as a medium-security terrorist," Rear Admiral Harry B. Brown told the *Times* reporter. In other words, the authorities at Guantánamo were once again operating on the premise Donald Rumsfeld first articulated five years ago—that the detainees were "the worst of the worst."

After the three prisoners successfully committed suicide by hanging themselves from the wire-mesh framework of their cages in June 2006, the commander of the detention center asserted that it was "not an act of desperation but an act of asymmetric warfare committed against us." That's a very convenient way of thinking. Another, less convenient idea would be to grasp the possibility that desperation and a political outlook capable of inspiring "an act of asymmetric warfare" need not be mutually exclusive states of mind. More than forty unsuccessful suicide attempts at Guantánamo, mass hunger strikes, and ordinary common sense argue that the detainees wouldn't be human if they didn't experience desperation after more than five years in the cages. Instead of congratulating ourselves for giving them Korans and allowing them to pray toward Mecca, we might renew the effort to ease the conditions of their day-to-day lives, which are harsher by most measures than conditions on death row in mainland prisons. Even if we assume, for the purpose of discussion, that the military authorities are right in considering the indefinitely detained to be committed jihadists to a man, finding ways to ease the circumstances of their confinement might be seen as an investment in the possibility—however remote it may seem—that they will one day return to their homelands; to put it another way, that we might one day be relieved of the political and moral burden involved in their indefinite detention without charge.

CHAPTER 11

The Secrecy Trump

ANN BEESON

In lawsuits challenging human rights abuses committed in the so-called War on Terror, the government now routinely imposes gag orders on clients and lawyers. It submits secret evidence to support its cases and denies plaintiffs' lawyers any access to the evidence. At the government's request, and sometimes on their own, judges close court hearings to the public and sometimes exclude plaintiffs' counsel. And several federal agencies have invoked the state secrets privilege to dismiss a growing number of cases before they can begin and to deny victims of the government's abuses not just a remedy but even the satisfaction of a day in court. In a number of cases in which I have been directly involved as an ACLU lawyer, the government has used the secrecy card to gag librarians and Internet service providers from discussing FBI demands for records as part of the public debate about the Patriot Act, to fire with impunity a whistleblower who exposed potential espionage within the agency that translates national security wiretaps, to avoid accountability for warrantless wiretaps, and to deprive victims of illegal rendition any legal forum for abuses. As the details about some of these cases reveal, the Bush administration has used secrecy not to protect legitimate national security information but to cover up wrongdoing and abuse.

Since 9/11, the government has argued that secrecy is so essential to our safety that the legality of many of its national security policies and practices—from illegal rendition to wiretapping—cannot be reviewed by anyone. Secrecy has emerged as one of the administration's most powerful tools for stifling public debate, hiding human rights abuses, and thwarting legal challenges to such abuses when they are disclosed. The invocation of secrecy to protect national security has in fact caused some courts to relinquish altogether their role as a check on executive power, as I have witnessed firsthand.

"National Security Letters" and Gag Orders

In 2004, an Internet service provider (ISP) contacted the ACLU for advice because the company had received a National Security Letter (NSL) under the Patriot Act demanding records about one of its customers. Today I remain under a federal gag order that prevents me from disclosing the name of the company, where it is located, and the name of its president or even gender (I will use the pronoun "he" only in the generic sense here). In fact, the gag order prevents me from describing many details about the case that I believe pose no threat whatsoever to national security but would be of immense interest in the ongoing debate about expanded government surveillance powers.

We were not surprised to get the call. Through our Freedom of Information Act litigation, we had already learned that the government was aggressively using NSLs to demand personal records, possibly in lieu of using another Patriot Act provision, section 215, which authorizes broad searches of personal records but first requires a sign-off from a secret court. In contrast to section 215 orders, the FBI can issue NSLs unilaterally. No judge approves the demand, and an FBI agent can use an NSL to demand the records of anyone without first establishing probable cause or even reasonable grounds to believe that the person has done anything wrong. In other words, the FBI can use NSLs to demand personal records about innocent people. The agent need only convince himself that the demand is "relevant to an ongoing terrorism investigation." That standard would be extremely low even if being applied by a judge; with an FBI agent as the only judge, there is no meaningful limitation on the FBI's power to spy on you.

NSLs included a mandatory gag order, which prevented anyone who received an NSL from disclosing to "any person that the [FBI] has sought or obtained access to information or records." Read literally—always the safer course when trying to avoid jail time—the gag order prevented NSL recipients from even consulting their lawyers (unless, of course, you believe that lawyers aren't "persons"). To minimize his risks from the gag order, we told the ISP president—now dubbed John Doe—that we needed to meet with him in person. So began a case that might seem funny, in an Orwellian sort of way, if only it were fictional.

After our meeting, Jameel Jaffer (now deputy director of the ACLU's National Security Program) and I agreed to represent John Doe in a challenge to the NSL he had received, as well as to the constitutionality of the law itself. But to avoid penalties under the gag order, we were forced to file the entire case under seal and to negotiate with the government for permission to disclose even innocuous information about the case. The government made it clear that it was going to play hardball from the beginning. For the first several weeks, government lawyers took the position that the gag prevented us from disclosing even *the mere fact that we had challenged a provision of the Patriot Act in court.*

While negotiating conditions for going public with some facts about the lawsuit, we had several stressful encounters with the tight-lipped attorney assigned by the Justice Department to the case. Some of those encounters still can't be disclosed because of the gag, but one early incident illustrates the thick web of secrecy the government wove around the case. Jameel Jaffer got a call one day from a reporter who appeared to have been tipped off about the case. He revealed nothing, but we felt obligated to inform the government and the court because we had assured them that we would not disclose the case until procedures were negotiated to disclose it without risk. When Jameel called the government lawyer, she demanded the name of the reporter. He rightly refused. She called back moments later to confirm "that he was refusing to disclose the name of the reporter." He confirmed. About fifteen minutes later, Jameel rushed into my office, saying that the security guards in the lobby had called up. "Federal agents are in the lobby for us," he said. We were both convinced that they had come to arrest us. We rushed up and down the halls of the ACLU, asking our colleagues to come with us to witness what would happen in the lobby. We finally went down, colleagues in tow, and found an FBI agent waiting. He handed us an envelope marked "confidential" and then left. It contained the government's letter to the judge complaining about our behavior. The adrenaline rush lasted the rest of the day.

After weeks of fighting in secret, Judge Marrero of the Southern District of New York eventually issued an order that allowed us to tell the public that we had filed a lawsuit and provided procedures that would govern the sealing of all future documents in the case. The irony and absurdity of the government's argument for secrecy was obvious from the headline in the *Washington Post* the day the case became public, "Patriot Act Gags News of Lawsuit about Patriot Act." The headline was nearly identical to a joke headline published by the satirical online newspaper, *The Onion,* shortly after Congress passed the Patriot Act, "Revised Patriot Act Will Make It Illegal to Read Patriot Act."

After the case became public, the government continued to insist that we could not tell the public that we were representing a client who had actually received an NSL—even though every journalist who wrote about the case rightly assumed that we were. A reality check is in order here. We were not trying to disclose the name of the target of a terrorism investigation or any other details about the FBI's demand for information from our client. We merely wanted, first, to explain that the FBI had used an NSL to demand sensitive Internet records and, second, to explain that John Doe had received an NSL and was challenging its legality in court. Yet the government took the position for months that merely disclosing the fact that John Doe had received an NSL—*without even revealing John Doe's name*—would threaten national security.

Our relationship with the opposing counsel deteriorated further. The day after we issued a press release about the weeks-old case, *Doe v. Ashcroft,* the Justice Department attorney called me and accused the ACLU of violating the sealing order—and, by implication, the gag order. When I asked what information we had inadvertently released, she said our press release had included the briefing schedule in the case. Apparently we were threatening national security by telling the public when our briefs were due. From then on, we worried about violating the gag order, and risking prosecution, every time we issued a press release in the case.

The judge's procedures required us to submit documents to the government for redactions before any version could be disclosed to the public; we could then challenge particular redactions as overbroad. Throughout the early phases of the litigation, we continued to battle with the government over redactions, some of which were later lifted by the court. For example, on national security grounds the government tried to censor the fact that our client's business "provides clients with the ability to access the Internet" and that an NSL "is written on FBI letterhead." In a particularly ironic example, the government tried to censor the following quote in one of our briefs, taken directly from a 1972 Supreme Court case holding that the government violated the Constitution when it conducted electronic surveillance for domestic security purposes without a warrant: "The danger to political dissent is acute where the Government attempts to act under so vague a concept as the power to protect 'domestic security.'"

While fighting with the government over redactions, we were also busy preparing our briefs to convince the court that the NSL provision in the Patriot Act was unconstitutional and should be invalidated. Shortly before issuing his decision, Judge Marrero called us into his chambers and asked the government whether it still took the position that the gag order required secrecy about even the mere fact that John Doe had received an NSL. The judge said he wanted to issue a fully public opinion and would be prohibited from doing so if the government stuck to its broad interpretation of the gag provision. It was a no-win situation for the government. It could either insist that the law prevented a federal judge from fully publishing a decision about the constitutionality of that law, or it could change its position. After a day of consultation, the government informed the judge that he could disclose in his opinion the fact that an NSL had been served on John Doe. Months of insistence on secrecy to protect national security evaporated. Needless to say, no harm came from the disclosure.

In an eloquent ruling that recognized the danger that censorship and secrecy pose to a free society, Judge Marrero ultimately invalidated the NSL provision of the Patriot Act, finding that it violated the Constitution. The court wrote,

> Democracy abhors undue secrecy, in recognition that public knowledge secures freedom. Hence, an unlimited government warrant to conceal, effectively a form of secrecy *per se*, has no place in our open society. . . . [A] categorical and uncritical extension of non-disclosure may become the cover for spurious ends that government may then deem too inconvenient, inexpedient, merely embarrassing, or even illicit ever to expose to the light of day. At that point, secrecy's protective shield may serve not as much to secure a safe country as simply to save face.

While this decision was being appealed to the Second Circuit, Congress reauthorized the Patriot Act and amended the NSL provision. The amended law makes it clear that recipients can challenge NSL demands and gag orders in court—a victory undoubtedly influenced by Judge Marrero's opinion. But the gag provision remains unconstitutional. Though the law now permits a legal challenge to any gag order issued with an NSL, it ties the hands of any court from lifting the gag order by requiring the court to accept the government's certification that secrecy is necessary for national security purposes. The appellate court remanded the case to Judge Marrero to consider the constitutionality of the amended law. We recently amended the complaint and filed papers asking the court to invalidate the amended gag order provision, as it did with the prior law. In the meantime, John Doe and his legal team—myself included—remain under the gag order.

State Secrets and Closed Hearings

As the ACLU's first Freedom of Information Act (FOIA) litigation over Patriot Act powers proved, FOIA can be an indispensable tool for fighting government secrecy and exposing abusive practices. We filed subsequent FOIAs on a range of issues, and the government continued to fight compliance by relying on a broad "national security" exemption, claiming again that secrecy was necessary to protect us. But many of our FOIA cases eventually forced the disclosure of important documents about the administration's national security practices, most notably the disclosure of over 100,000 pages of documents about torture policies. In another nationwide FOIA effort launched in 2004, the ACLU filed simultaneous FOIAs in several states on behalf of over 150 political and religious groups to expose FBI spying activities. After 9/11, then Attorney General John Ashcroft relaxed the Justice Department guidelines on domestic spying that were developed in response to the abuses of McCarthy and J. Edgar Hoover. We wanted to know whether the relaxed guidelines would herald a return to the bad old days of FBI spying. The FBI spy files project forced the disclosure of hundreds of pages of documents that confirmed our fears—the FBI is now using its counterterrorism resources to monitor groups like Veterans for Peace, who oppose the war in Iraq, and to place confidential informants inside groups like Greenpeace and People for the Ethical Treatment of Animals.

For the ACLU's 2004 membership conference in San Francisco, I was developing a panel to highlight our work on FBI spying and to show the parallels between spying in the 1970s and spying today. Our state office in northern California managed to put me in touch with Daniel Ellsberg, the whistleblower who became a national hero (or villain, depending on your perspective) when he leaked the *Pentagon Papers* to the media in an attempt to end the Vietnam War. The prosecution of Ellsberg for leaking classified information was thrown out of court when the defense team learned that Nixon's plumbers had broken into Ellsberg's psychiatrist's office in an effort to get information to discredit him.

I first met Dan Ellsberg the evening before the conference began. I expected him to talk about history, but he was full of questions and ideas about how to end the abuses of the current administration. Dan asked me if I had encountered the state secrets privilege in any of our cases. I had no idea what he was talking about. Dan told me that the government had invoked state secrets to dismiss a lawsuit on behalf of a former FBI translator named Sibel Edmonds, who had been fired for reporting serious security breaches and potential espionage with the division responsible for translating counterterrorism wiretaps, including wiretaps authorized as part of the investigation into the 9/11 attacks. Dan was interested in Sibel's case both because she was a national security whistleblower like himself and because the state secrets privilege had been invoked years before in a case that Dan had brought with others to challenge his surveillance by the Nixon administration.

After the ACLU conference, Dan Ellsberg invited me to an event he was planning in Washington, D.C., in October 2005 to encourage other whistleblowers to come forward. Sibel Edmonds spoke eloquently and passionately at the event, and I sought her out afterward to offer the ACLU's help in her case. Having been dismissed in the trial court because of the state secrets privilege, her case was now on appeal. Sibel Edmonds eventually retained us, and we plunged headfirst into the case. We had recently hired a talented young lawyer named Melissa Goodman, and Melissa's detailed research into the state secrets privilege proved invaluable. Though we didn't know it at the time, we would spend the next few years fighting the state secrets privilege, not just in Sibel's case but also in lawsuits challenging illegal rendition and wiretapping without a warrant. Dan Ellsberg had nailed the government's pet legal theory for resisting federal court scrutiny in national security cases.

The state secrets privilege was meant to shield particular, sensitive information, such as the location of troops in battle, from disclosure during litigation. It was never intended to provide blanket immunity for any abuse committed by the government in a War on Terror. Yet the government is now relying on the privilege to dismiss entire lawsuits before discovery even begins and before clients have had the chance to prove their cases with publicly available evidence. Defending clients against this broad use of the state secrets privilege is made even more difficult because the government can file secret declarations to support its claim of the privilege. With no opportunity to counter secret declarations that almost certainly present a one-sided view of the relevant issues and evidence in a case, it is no wonder that the privilege has become the administration's silver bullet for avoiding accountability. If the administration has its way, it will be able to avoid accountability for any human rights abuse—including the detention and torture of American citizens within our own borders—merely by invoking "state secrets" and moving to dismiss the case.

The invocation of the privilege in Sibel's case was particularly strange. The issue in the lawsuit had nothing to do with state secrets or even national security—the legal question was whether the FBI had improperly fired Sibel for exercising her free speech rights. Neither her classified work nor the truth or falsity of her whistleblowing was even relevant in the case. And Sibel already had unclassified evidence of the FBI's motivation for firing her. In fact, after the district court dismissed the case, the inspector general of the Justice Department concluded *in a public report* that the FBI had fired Ms. Edmonds in retaliation for her whistleblowing. The FBI now had to argue that state secrets prevent a federal court from deciding an issue that the Justice Department itself had decided in our favor in a public report. Especially after the inspector general's report became public, we were confident that we could convince the appellate court to allow the case to proceed.

As I prepared for oral argument in the Circuit Court for the District of Columbia in April 2005, we were relieved that the government had not asked for a closed hearing in Sibel's case, as they had in other cases for which they claimed secrecy. Sibel had put together an impressive coalition of national security whistleblowers, many of whom planned to attend the hearing. Because of Sibel's courage and charisma, a large turnout from the press was also expected. At three o'clock in the afternoon the day before the hearing, the clerk's office at the courthouse reached me via cell phone. The judges had just issued an order closing the oral argument to the public. Only counsel and Sibel herself would be allowed to attend. Several major media outlets—including the *New York Times*, the *Washington Post*, and CNN—were so appalled by the courtroom closure that they managed to file a motion to intervene to reopen the hearing within a few hours after we learned of the closure. The next morning, a sizable crowd entered the courtroom. Another case was being argued—publicly, of course—before ours. When Sibel's case was called, the panel of judges granted the media's motion to intervene, but then denied their motion to open the hearing. Sibel was so furious that she almost boycotted her own hearing in protest; I convinced her to stay. The courtroom deputy asked all spectators present to clear the courtroom. Judge Ginsberg, the chief judge of the appeals court, then began the session in the quiet courtroom by praising the quality of our briefs—a sure sign in my experience that we would lose. Given the "necessary secrecy" surrounding the case, he did not think it would be helpful for me to proceed with my prepared argument. After just a few questions, Sibel and our entire legal team were excluded from the courtroom while the judges asked the government lawyers questions in secret for another fifteen minutes. A federal marshal was posted at the courtroom door. Before we left the courtroom, I asked the judges whether I was gagged from telling the public outside what had just happened inside. The court said no.

Again, a reality check is in order. Because the government had never provided me with the secret evidence it had submitted to the court to support dismissal of the case, there was no possibility that I could disclose any secrets during the oral argument—and thus no justification whatsoever for closing the courtroom during our arguments.

Less than two weeks later, the appeals court affirmed the dismissal of Sibel's case but issued no opinion explaining its reasoning. We appealed to the Supreme Court, which declined to take the case. Sibel Edmonds would get no day in court.

Gagged Librarians

While we were fighting Patriot Act provisions in the courts, our legislative office was spearheading efforts to convince Congress not to renew key provisions that were scheduled to expire in 2005. In addition to our inside-the-beltway lobbying, we worked with communities to pass over 400 resolutions opposing the Patriot Act. In response, the administration launched its own powerful public relations campaign, touring the country to convince Americans that giving more power to the FBI would make us all safer. The Patriot Act became a daily issue in the news, and whether or not Patriot Act powers had been used to obtain library records became the defining issue in the debate. Then Attorney General John Ashcroft, in a misogynistic attack that was outrageous even from him, called librarians "hysterical" for even suggesting that library records were at risk. Such was the climate when I got a phone call in August 2005 from a quiet voice in Connecticut.

It was George Christian, executive director of Library Connection, a consortium of twenty-six libraries in Connecticut. Library Connection had received an NSL demanding patron records. We knew that this news—if only it could be told—

would be a lightning rod in the Patriot Act debate. Because the gag order made any conversation risky, Jameel Jaffer and I drove to Hartford to meet with the Library Connection executive committee in person. We couldn't even tell our staff at the ACLU where we were going.

Near Hartford, we met George and three librarians, Peter Chase, Janet Nocek, and Barbara Bailey. A more wholesome group would be hard to imagine. And as one would expect from librarians, they were very well informed. As soon as they had received the NSL, they had researched the provision and learned that the federal judge in our New York case had already ruled that it violated the Constitution. With a long history of protecting patron's privacy, they did not want to comply with an FBI demand that no judge had approved. They also didn't want to keep quiet about it. The librarians retained us to challenge the demand and the gag order in court.

Because the timing was crucial given the Patriot Act debate, we moved quickly for a preliminary injunction that would allow the librarians to tell the world about the FBI demand. As in the New York case, the government stalled for weeks before it would even allow us to go public with the fact that we had filed the lawsuit. The morning of the hearing, we discovered that the government had failed to redact Peter Chase's name in some of the documents—the first sign that they were not very thorough censors. The court was notified and substituted redacted versions of the documents just in time for the hearing. The gag order kept the librarians from attending their own hearing in Bridgeport in person; instead they had to sit in a secure room in the Hartford courthouse and watch the hearing via video conference.

A few weeks later, Judge Janet Hall in the district of Connecticut ruled for the librarians, ordering the FBI to lift the gag order. "The [National Security Letter] statute has the practical effect of silencing those who have the most intimate knowledge of the statute's effect and a strong interest in advocating against the federal government's broad investigative powers," she wrote. Judge Hall specifically rejected the government's argument that lifting the gag order would harm national security. The government had argued, with a straight face, that merely disclosing Library Connection's identity would threaten national security because it could tip off the target of the investigation. Judge Hall wrote that, given the organization's broad reach across the state, the number of people who could be the target was "in the tens, if not hundreds, of thousands." As the court sardonically reasoned in what was then a sealed portion of her opinion, "Ungagging the plaintiffs will reveal that sometime in the unknown past, someone who may or may not have been a cardholder of that unknown library, used an internet service at one of 19 libraries located in various cities and towns in Connecticut." The government immediately appealed to the Second Circuit Court of Appeals and then sought and obtained a stay order to keep the librarians gagged while it pursued the appeal.

A few days after the decision, an industrious reporter, Alison Cowan from the *New York Times*, discovered that the identity of the librarians from Connecticut had been inadvertently disclosed on the court's Web-based docket. Her September 21, 2005, article identified our client as Library Connection in Windsor, Connecticut. Through our own careful review of the public record, we then discovered that the government had neglected to redact identifying information about the librarians in at least three other places in publicly filed documents. The cat was out of the bag.

Just as we had assumed our battle on behalf of Sibel Edmonds would end after the Justice Department itself had concluded that she was fired for blowing the whistle on the FBI, we thought the FBI would drop the gag order once Library Connection's identity became public. We quickly filed a motion asking the appeals court to lift the stay and end the gag order. To our amazement, our motion was denied. Even though major newspapers around the world had published Library Connection's identity, and everyone else in the world could now discuss it, the librarians themselves were still gagged. They could not confirm that they were the ones who had received the NSL nor participate in the Patriot Act debate. They had to avoid answering their phones directly and couldn't even talk to their families about what had happened.

The free speech stakes were so high—each day Congress came closer to reauthorizing the Patriot Act—that we decided to take the issue to the Supreme Court through a rarely used procedure to vacate a stay. All of the documents had to be filed under seal. The government even insisted on fully redacting the copies of the *New York Times* articles we included. The phrases "the genie is out of the bottle" and "the cat is out of the bag" were also censored throughout our brief. The motion was assigned to Justice Ginsburg, and, disappointingly, she eventually upheld the stay. Her opinion could be read as critical of the Second Circuit's prior decision, as she appeared to disagree with its evaluation of the harm caused by the ongoing gag order on the librarians. Nevertheless, her ruling meant that the librarians would remain gagged until after the Second Circuit had decided the case on its merits.

In early 2006, Congress reauthorized the Patriot Act. The Connecticut librarians—who had real knowledge of the negative effects of the law—were excluded from the Patriot Act debate by a Patriot Act gag order. A few weeks later, Justice Department lawyers called me to say that the FBI had decided to drop the gag order. Shortly after that, it also dropped its NSL demand for library records. It was a bitter experience for the librarians, too little, too late. Responding to the FBI's questionable timing, Peter Chase said, "Nothing had changed in the case, so what happened to the threat to national security?" If these four brave citizens had been allowed to speak out earlier, Congress might not have reauthorized provisions of the Patriot Act.

Secret Kidnappings

One of the most pernicious, downright evil secret practices promoted by the Bush administration is the practice of illegal rendition—a team of black-masked CIA agents kidnaps a person and forcefully renders him to a secret CIA prison or to another country, where he is tortured, interrogated, and held indefinitely without charges. The ACLU represents one of the innocent victims of the program, Khaled El-Masri, a long-time Lebanese resident of Germany and father of six. El-Masri was on vacation in Macedonia when he was kidnapped, abused, and rendered to a CIA-run "black site" in Afghanistan. High-level government officials, including Condoleeza Rice, knew that they had nabbed an innocent person within weeks of the kidnapping but left El-Masri in an Afghanistan cell for months longer. After several months of confinement in squalid conditions, he was abandoned on a hill in Albania with no explanation, never having been charged with a crime.

After some labor-intensive research in other countries by Steven Watt, an experienced international lawyer who had recently joined our new ACLU Human Rights Program, we filed a lawsuit on behalf of Mr. El-Masri in early December 2005 in federal court in Virginia. We sued George Tenet, the unidentified CIA agents, and the corporations who own the planes used to render El-Masri. Within weeks, the government revealed its intention to move for dismissal of the case based on the state secrets privilege. Having successfully blocked Sibel Edmonds's suit, the government was now using the privilege to avoid judicial review and accountability for kidnapping and torturing innocent people.

In the meantime, governments in Europe were actively investigating their role in the illegal rendition program generally and in El-Masri's abduction specifically. The European Parliament had already gathered evidence proving many of the key allegations, and the German and Spanish governments were also pursuing inquiries. In stark contrast to the U.S. determination to sweep the whole thing under the rug, Europe was doing the right thing; it was investigating the rendition and was willing to accept responsibility for its role—minor compared to the CIA's—in the abuse.

Ben Wizner, another bright young lawyer and part of the El-Masri legal team, argued the motion. As I had tried to do in Sibel's case before the appellate court, Ben countered the state secrets argument with a catalogue of all publicly available evidence to prove that the CIA kidnapped and abused El-Masri. Unfortunately, Ben also received almost no questions from the judge. Within a week, the court granted the government's motion to dismiss the case. Another judge had let secrecy trump the duty of federal courts to serve as a check on executive abuses. We appealed the dismissal to the Fourth Circuit Court of Appeals.

Secret Wiretaps without a Warrant

Just as we were recovering from the flurry of activity around the filing of the El-Masri case and looking forward to a relatively deadline-free holiday season, the *New York Times* disclosed on December 16, 2005, that the president had authorized the National Security Agency (NSA) to eavesdrop on the phone calls and e-mails of Americans without a warrant. While we had been busy opposing Patriot Act provisions that expanded wiretapping powers under the Foreign Intelligence Surveillance Act (FISA), the president was circumventing even the relaxed FISA warrant procedures. He wasn't even bothering to get approval from the secret FISA court. In other words, he was refusing to follow procedures mandated by federal law. We spent the holiday season preparing to challenge the program in court.

A month later, in Detroit, Michigan, we filed a lawsuit challenging the illegal NSA spying program on behalf of a prominent group of journalists, scholars, and attorneys from around the country who routinely call and e-mail people in the Middle East, South Asia, and Africa. (Our colleagues at the Center for Constitutional Rights filed a similar lawsuit the same day in New York.) Because the government had conceded all the facts necessary to decide the case, we quickly filed a motion for summary judgment, asking the court to declare the program unlawful and to enjoin its use. We argued that the program violated FISA, the separation of powers, and the Fourth and First Amendments to the Constitution. If the president wanted to change the rules, he should have gone to Congress. Not even the president can ignore federal laws and the Constitution, we argued.

Once again, the government moved to dismiss the case based on the state secrets privilege. And it was not just our case they were trying to stop. They claimed that secrecy required dismissal of every case filed against the NSA or the phone companies working with the federal government (several such cases were filed after our initial lawsuit). In other words, the government claimed that secrecy should prevent *any* court from deciding whether the president broke the law. Yet the administration had engaged in a very public campaign in which it had defended its illegal surveillance program in a lengthy white paper, in the newspapers, on television, and even in Web blogs.

As we argued in our legal briefs, the state secrets privilege poses no obstacle to federal court review of NSA spying. No additional facts—let alone secret ones—are needed to prove that the president violated federal law and the Constitution when he authorized the NSA to wiretap Americans without court approval. The president hasn't denied that the NSA program exists; in fact, he has publicly defended the program, claiming that his powers as commander-in-chief during wartime trump laws passed by Congress that expressly prohibit warrantless eavesdropping. Government officials have repeatedly conceded that the program operates entirely without judicial supervision or probable cause.

In August 2006, Judge Anna Diggs Taylor rejected the government's attempt to dismiss our challenge to the NSA program based on state secrets. The court wrote, "The Bush

Administration has repeatedly told the general public that there is a valid basis in law for the [wiretapping program]. . . . Consequently, the court finds Defendants' argument that they cannot defend this case without the use of classified information to be disingenuous and without merit." Judge Taylor had recognized that courts have a duty to scrutinize government secrecy claims to serve as a check on unbridled executive power. Her opinion went on to enjoin the president from wiretapping Americans without a warrant, in violation of federal law. She rejected the administration's argument that the president had "inherent authority" as commander-in-chief to ignore a federal statute. "There are no hereditary kings in America and no powers not created by the Constitution," Judge Taylor wrote. The government has appealed the decision, but we remain hopeful that the courts may have reached their limit in accepting the government's overbroad claims for secrecy.

THOUGH THE ACLU and other groups will continue to fight government claims seeking excessive secrecy, there are reasons to be hopeful. Some judges have reacted with skepticism and refused to accept the government's arguments. Congress may begin to exercise its oversight function, now that the Democrats are in power, and may expose other abuses hidden from public view. Most importantly, many of the victims of the government's secret policies and gag orders have refused to remain silent. They have become some of the most effective and outspoken critics of executive abuses and government claims of secrecy to avoid accountability for abuses. The Connecticut librarians are so busy with speaking engagements around the country that they hardly have time to loan books and answer reference questions at their branch libraries. George Christian from Library Connection now drives a car with a vanity license plate that identifies him as "John Doe." Khaled El-Masri was finally allowed into the country and met with members of Congress and American citizens to tell his story and to fight for an end to illegal rendition. And Sibel Edmonds has formed a National Security Whistleblowers Coalition with over fifty members from multiple federal agencies, all committed to holding the government accountable for its national security abuses.

CHAPTER 12

Disorder in Military Courts

EUGENE R. FIDELL

T o most Americans, military justice conjures up grainy images from *The Caine Mutiny* or less grainy ones from *A Few Good Men.* But recent experience in Afghanistan and Iraq has taken the subject out of the movie theaters and video rentals and placed it on vivid display across the front pages of newspapers, on the morning and evening television news, and in the "blogo-sphere" with alarming frequency. People around the world have been scratching their heads about not only the seeming regularity of criminal conduct by American forces but also—and more disturbingly—by what certainly seem to be remarkably lenient outcomes in those cases that enter the military justice system, and perhaps even more so by the cases that never enter that system and are disposed of quietly by informal means.

Criminal conduct by deployed military personnel can have a severe adverse effect on any country's ability to conduct military operations effectively, since local support is critical to mission accomplishment. Moreover, what is sufficient to foster public confidence in the administration of justice in one era may not suffice in another. Wars often lead to changes in military justice. World War II led to the Uniform Code of Military Justice (UCMJ), which for the first time created a single criminal justice system for all U.S. armed forces, overseen, importantly, by a civilian court. The Vietnam War saw enactment of the Military Justice Act of 1968, which locked in place a uniformed military judiciary. Change will certainly emerge from the current conflict—whether it winds down, as hoped, or metastasizes, as feared. The questions are, what should that change be, and in what manner should change occur?

In addition to these questions, which have to do with the internal good order and discipline of our own uniformed personnel and are thus tremendously important in their own right, the nation's attention has been riveted at least as much if not more on another context in which criminal justice is dispensed by the armed forces: the military commissions with which the administration has sought to prosecute noncitizen "unlawful combatants" who were apprehended in Afghanistan and other places in the wake of 9/11. The original rules for the commissions were developed out of public view and had grave flaws. For example, they permitted the free use of hearsay, allowed evidence to be used that the accused never saw, imposed substantial constraints on defense counsel, and had no provision for appellate review by any court of law. Most of the Guantánamo detainees are not even slated for trial, and those who are face the prospect of continued detention even if they are acquitted.

The military commission rules—a far cry from the rigorous military justice system, which in important respects replicates trials of criminal cases in the federal district courts—were sufficiently flawed that some lawyers thought it better to boycott the process than to validate it by participating. The process was also disturbing to at least some of the foreign powers whose citizens had been brought to Guantánamo Bay not only for detention but for trial. Worse yet, the deficient military commissions were held up as a model by at least one foreign dictator as a basis for putting people on trial in a military forum. Few, if any, of our allies endorsed the commissions. Even some of those who are part of the coalition in Iraq have increasingly—and justifiably—held their noses on the subject. The cumulative effect of widespread discomfort with the military commissions, concern over apparent disregard for the Geneva Conventions, offense at the U.S. program of "extraordinary renditions" and secret detentions, and mounting anger at the Iraq War has been a serious erosion of our standing around the world. The United States has taken a few steps to mitigate this trend, such as returning detainees to those countries willing to take them, but those efforts have been limited, tardy, and grudging. Changes in the military commission rules and other measures affecting the detainees occurred only when some new adverse ruling from the courts seemed imminent.

Against this backdrop, it is hardly surprising that issues surrounding the military commissions consumed a great deal of energy in both the judicial and legislative branches. The Supreme Court held in 2004 in *Rasul v. Bush* that writs of habeas corpus could be issued to test the detention of alleged unlawful combatants held at Guantánamo Bay, Cuba, where the commissions have been located, and in 2006, *Hamdan v. Rumsfeld* invalidated the military commissions President Bush had authorized shortly after 9/11. Working at great—and entirely undue—haste,* Congress, after years of inactivity with respect to the military commissions as authorized by President Bush in 2001, belatedly got busy and

---

*There were hearings on the legislation during the summer of 2006, but in the end Congress succumbed to pressure from the White House. President Bush insisted that the legislation was needed and that, if it was not enacted before the fall election recess, he would have to suspend certain parts of the government's program for interrogating suspected terrorists.

passed the Military Commissions Act. This measure should go down in American legal history as a legislative low point.

A Bad Law

The Military Commissions Act was passed in direct response to the Supreme Court's *Hamdan* decision. Rarely has Congress acted so promptly and decisively to overturn a decision of the High Court. On issue after issue, the statute repudiates matters addressed by the justices, or at least attempts to do so. It seeks to close the doors of the federal district courts to habeas corpus petitions filed on behalf of Guantánamo detainees. It attempts to immunize government interrogators from prosecution for past conduct that may have violated the Geneva Conventions and therefore the War Crimes Act. It also substitutes for the early patchwork of isolated statutory provisions and executive branch regulations a detailed statutory code for military commissions, modeled on but in important respects different from the UCMJ, which applies to military personnel.

Almost immediately, the litigation process cranked up again, and it is inevitable that important aspects of the Military Commissions Act will percolate up to the Supreme Court. At the same time, the Defense Department has been at work on a *Manual for Military Commissions* comparable with the *Manual for Courts-Martial*,* has continued to move forward with preparations for as

---

*Indefensibly, the Defense Department did not plan to make the draft *Manual for Military Commissions* available for public comment, despite requests by the American Bar Association, the New York City Bar Association, and the National Institute of Military Justice. The stated reason for this was that the Military Commissions Act requires the implementing regulations to be submitted to

many as seventy-five to eighty military commission trials, and has plans for a multimillion-dollar, state-of-the-art courthouse complex at Guantánamo Bay.

Four developments render it nearly impossible to predict where the path leads for the military commissions. First, not long after the Military Commissions Act was signed, Secretary of Defense Donald Rumsfeld resigned and was replaced by Robert M. Gates. Dr. Gates, and whoever becomes his general counsel (assuming a change in that position), may have different views from Mr. Rumsfeld with respect to reliance on military commissions. Second, two new justices have joined the Supreme Court since the *Rasul* case was decided, and although Chief Justice John G. Roberts Jr. was unable to sit on the *Hamdan* case because he was on the U.S. court of appeals panel that had earlier heard the case, he will be able to sit on other military commission–related cases that reach the Supreme Court. Third, with the 2006 elections, control of both houses of Congress changed hands, and although the Democratic margin in the Senate is slender, this dramatic shift could see an effort to roll back some or all of the most controversial provisions of the Military Commissions Act. Finally, and perhaps least susceptible to analysis, is the fact that the longtime Cuban president, Fidel Castro, has suffered health problems of an unknown nature but of obvious gravity judging by his appearance in recent photographs and his failure to attend the public celebration of his own eightieth birthday in 2006. If, as seems fair to postulate,

---

Congress by January 16, 2007. Considering the extended time the entire process consumed since President Bush first authorized the military commissions, the time the department had the draft in the works, and the ease with which the department regularly obtains congressional acquiescence in missed statutory deadlines, this justification is utterly without merit.

the political scene in Cuba may well change in the near future, it seems equally fair to wonder whether Congress will wish to commit further resources to construction at an enclave in which we are not unlikely to renounce our rights-in-perpetuity before very long.

All of this suggests that the coming years will—and should—see continuing strong public and legislative interest in the administration of justice through military commissions. What, then, of the commissions' institutional cousin, courts-martial?

Nuts and Bolts

The present military justice system is a direct descendant of the system that existed under George III. The basic concept of the current system is that crimes by military personnel are punishable by the military itself (although in some circumstances they can also be tried in civilian courts).

The military justice system has both formal and informal parts. The formal parts are courts-martial. These are increasingly like federal courts. They have lawyer judges, jurors, prosecutors, and defense counsel. The strict rules of evidence apply, and the usual beyond-a-reasonable-doubt standard of proof governs. There are several tiers of appellate review. There is also a separate system of confinement facilities.

There are, however, numerous important differences between courts-martial and civilian criminal courts. Perhaps most fundamentally, courts-martial are not standing or permanent bodies. They are established from time to time by a commanding officer, known as the "convening authority," and hear only those cases that are referred to them. The convening authority decides who will be charged with what offenses, can enter into pretrial agreements, and must review the proceedings after trial. Unlike civilian courts, jurors are not selected at random; rather, they are, in theory, hand-picked by the convening authority, although their staff often heavily influences the actual selection. Military jurors, known as "members," decide not only guilt or innocence but also the sentence unless the accused opts for a bench trial. Military judges in some branches of the service have short (three-year) terms of office and in others have no fixed term, serving in effect at the pleasure of the judge advocate general of their branch.

Courts-martial can try any offense that is prescribed in the UCMJ. Some of the offenses mentioned there involve military discipline and obedience, but many are replicas of familiar civilian crimes, such as murder, assault, or rape. A court-martial can try a member of the service even for crimes that have no connection to the military aside from the fact that the accused is a member of the service. Some conduct that is punishable in the military would not be criminal in a civilian court. Examples include absence from work, dereliction of duty, disobedience, disrespect, and fraternization.

Successes and Failures

In the years since 9/11, the military justice system has gotten quite a workout. Although many have had misgivings as to the relatively mild sentences meted out in the Abu Ghraib abuse cases, the system as a whole has enjoyed a bump in public esteem as a result of the public stance of the judge advocates general in connection with the legislation that became the Military

Commissions Act. The "TJAGs," as the top uniformed lawyers are called, were to varying degrees publicly opposed to dilution of the prohibition on torture, drawing not only on settled international agreements on this subject but also on the practical consequences of any relaxation for military personnel who might in the future fall into the wrong hands.*

The armed services have shown, during the fighting in Vietnam, Afghanistan, and Iraq, that the UCMJ is versatile enough that justice can be dispensed even in wartime conditions. Hundreds of cases have been tried in Iraq, Kuwait, and Afghanistan, and still other cases involving offenses committed in those countries have been tried elsewhere. It does seem, based on the available data, that, whatever else is new in the current operational theaters, the UCMJ works. We will have a better sense of its function, however, as cases from that part of the globe begin to work their way through the military appellate process.

One interesting aspect of the last several years is that, for a time, there was a danger that military justice would be confused with the military commissions President Bush established in 2001 and to which Congress gave a statutory basis in the Military Commissions Act. As the news media grew more familiar with the entire legal landscape, the early confusion—fed in part by an unfortunate op-ed by Attorney General Alberto R. Gonzales—has abated, and the public now has no reason to conflate military justice of the court-martial variety with the military

---

*On the other hand, the TJAGs have not played a constructive role in facilitating media coverage of military justice trials. In a joint letter, they turned down a request to cooperate with the National Institute of Military Justice's National Court-Martial Docket Project. That project will provide one-stop, online shopping for information on what cases are being tried when and where.

commission variant. Indeed, Congress itself has been to a considerable extent at pains to keep the two separate.

For example, rather than adopting a sweeping provision that would simply apply court-martial procedures and rules to military commissions following the *Hamdan* case, Congress settled on a new, separate chapter of Title 10 of the U.S. Code to deal with the commissions. Moreover, it provided in that section of the Military Commissions Act that "[t]he findings, holdings, interpretations, and other precedents of military commissions . . . may not form the basis of any holding, decision, or other determination of a court-martial. . . ." "The findings, holdings, interpretations, and other precedents of military commissions . . . may not be introduced or considered in any hearing, trial, or other proceeding of a court-martial. . . ." Conversely, "[t]he judicial construction and application" of the UCMJ "are not binding on military commissions. . . ." In other words, the body of jurisprudence developed for courts-martial can be cited in military commission cases but is not dispositive. Nor is it a two-way street: military commission jurisprudence cannot even be used, much less form the basis of a decision, in a court-martial. We therefore face the odd prospect of two different bodies of military jurisprudence growing up more or less in isolation from one another, much like the separate species of finches Darwin found on islands in the Galápagos. The clear implication of the no-reference provision is that the quality of justice to be dispensed by the post-*Hamdan* military commissions will not equal that of our courts-martial.

The new arrangements for military commissions will of course be studied closely as the implementing rules are issued and actual trials move forward. Already, however, it is possible to note some ironic aspects of the legislation. In at least two respects it is an improvement over the UCMJ. Whereas some years ago Congress repealed a longstanding requirement that implementing rules for courts-martial be reported to the House and Senate Committees on Armed Services (as a paperwork reduction measure), it did include a reporting requirement for the implementing rules for military commissions. Although it is surely good that Congress has taken this small step to help it monitor the executive branch's use of its rule-making authority for the post-*Hamdan* military commissions, it remains to be seen how energetic Congress will be in its oversight role.

The other improvement concerns access to the Supreme Court. Considering the pains to which Congress went to preclude unlawful combatants from invoking the habeas corpus jurisdiction of the federal courts, it is certainly peculiar that decisions on appeal from military commission cases can be reviewed by the Supreme Court regardless of what the appellate court does. In contrast, comparable decisions of the U.S. Court of Appeals for the Armed Forces in courts-martial are reviewable by the Supreme Court only if the court of appeals has first granted review. If the court of appeals denies a petition for review, the only recourse is collateral review in the regular federal courts. Equally peculiar is the fact that Congress conferred appellate jurisdiction over military commissions on the U.S. Court of Appeals for the District of Columbia Circuit rather than the U.S. Court of Appeals for the Armed Forces, strange because the latter is the country's top specialized military court and would have appellate jurisdiction over trials by any *lawful* enemy combatants who fell into our hands and—as prisoners of war—were tried by court-martial for crimes they may have committed prior to capture.

The discrepancy in access to the Supreme Court is particularly ironic because one recurring theme that the administration and its partisans emphasized in the run-up to enactment of the Military Commissions Act was that unlawful combatants such as those to be tried by military commissions did not deserve the same treatment as honorable American military personnel. The fact that those unlawful combatants have a clearer track to the Supreme Court than do our own military personnel can only be described as bizarre.* The remedy is not to truncate review by the Supreme Court in military commission cases but to expand it for our own personnel—a point to which I will return.

The Numbers

For the period from 9/11 through August 26, 2006—nearly five years—the five most common offenses for army soldiers tried in Iraq, Kuwait, and Afghanistan involved (in descending order of frequency) alcohol offenses (108), false official statements (106), larceny of nonmilitary property (63), willful dereliction (53), and assault consummated by a battery (49).** These data involve only general and special courts-martial; many other minor (including some the public perceived as far more serious allegations of

---

*Another irony is that unlawful combatants tried by military commissions will have the benefit of appellate review by a court whose judges enjoy the "gold standard" protection of life tenure under Article III of the Constitution, whereas the judges of the Court of Appeals for the Armed Forces, who rule on cases of our own soldiers tried by court-martial, have the lesser protection of fifteen-year fixed terms.

**Data courtesy of the Office of the Clerk of Court, U.S. Army Judiciary, Arlington, Virginia.

prisoner abuse) offenses were handled through nonjudicial punishment or through administrative corrective measures. For comparison's sake, a study of the seventy-six cases that were decided
by the Court of Appeals for the Armed Forces by full opinion for
the term ending September 30, 2006, indicates that the seven
largest categories of cases that reached the highest court of the
military were (in descending order) sex offenses of every kind
imaginable, often involving children (29), drugs (again, everything imaginable, from marijuana to mushrooms) (20), false official statements or false swearing (9), nonsexual assaults (8), and
murder, larceny, and disobedience (a three-way tie at 7). Further
behind in the standings were child pornography (6) and unauthorized absence (6). Four cases involved obstruction of justice,
and three involved threats. The incidence of charges involving
drugs, pornography, and offenses against children are disquieting.
These are each hardy perennials in the garden of military justice.
At least with regard to the pornography cases, the free availability
of fast Internet connections on government computers has
proven a strong temptation for many soldiers and sailors.*

For comparison purposes, data available on prosecutions in
the British Army for the year ending January 2005 show that
the largest category by far is absence without leave (187), with
the next five largest categories being assault with intent to commit grievous bodily harm and obtaining property by deception
(both 87), battery (72), and indecent assault and theft (both

---

*Data in this paragraph are not scientific, since in military practice the same con-
duct may be charged in a variety of ways. For example, misuse of a computer for
the purpose of possessing, receiving, or distributing pornography may be charged
as conduct prejudicial to good order and discipline or service-discrediting, as conduct unbecoming an officer and a gentleman, as a non-capital federal crime, or as
a violation of the regulation on computer use.

55). There were eight prosecutions for racially aggravated words, assault, or harassment, four for ill treatment of soldiers, and one for disgraceful conduct of a cruel kind.

Which offenses should be prosecuted, and at what level of severity, is at the commander's discretion in American military justice as presently constituted. As a result, it is difficult to draw broad conclusions from the available data except to suggest that continued vigilance is needed in a few specific areas of indiscipline. Despite their infrequency, crimes of detention may have a devastating effect on the nation's interests overseas, as well as on domestic support for current military operations. The incidence of drug use is probably not something we should be surprised by, given patterns of drug use in the civilian community. Nonetheless, given the adverse effect of drug use on military readiness (and the danger posed to others in the already hazard-filled military environment) as well as the personal health needs of military personnel, it is not surprising that commanders take a very dim view of drug use.

Aside from reducing criminal conduct as much as possible, the military justice system does face important challenges. Primary among these is public confidence in the administration of justice. This is a function of both process and outcomes. On the process side, the more the public knows about the system, the more likely it will have confidence in the system and its results. One way to foster improved public confidence is to get the word out to the American people. To this extent, it was a very positive development that the public had an opportunity to see and hear from the TJAGs when they testified in connection with the Military Commissions Act. They were an excellent advertisement for the system. But more is required. The system itself must make greater efforts to engage the American people by becoming more transparent. The best way to do this is to take affirmative steps to facilitate intelligent coverage by the news media. The more journalists know about how the system actually works, and the more they are able to see the system in operation by covering hearings and trials in person, the better. To this end, the National Institute of Military Justice has begun a National Court-Martial Docket Project. When operational, it will provide Web access to data about what cases are being tried, when, and where. With this information, reporters and members of the public will be able to exercise their rights and actually observe proceedings and draw their own conclusions. It is possible that the armed services will decide that this is a function they ought to perform themselves, as some commands have already done. Regrettably, the National Institute of Military Justice has encountered initial resistance from the TJAGs. This resistance may require intervention by the new leadership of the Defense Department or by the congressional committees of the armed services.

Beyond the process, thoughtful observers have expressed concern about sentencing patterns that seem to be unduly lenient given the importance of demonstrating to others how serious we are about ensuring good order and discipline within the armed forces. Professor Gary D. Solis, a retired Marine Corps judge, has written compellingly on this subject, informed by his own earlier studies of the administration of justice in Vietnam-era war crimes cases. He writes: "Something odd is happening in courts-martial involving allegations of detainee abuse by American Soldiers and Marines. One takes no pleasure in noting that courts-martial in Iraq and Afghanistan seem to be acquitting individuals with unusual frequency. In courts that do convict, military juries frequently appear unwilling to impose sentences commensurate with the crimes of which Soldiers and Sailors have been convicted."

Because of concerns about unlawful command influence, there is little the government can do directly to overcome this problem other than to make certain that the necessary resources are available in these cases, including zealous attorneys on both sides who are willing to try cases rather than negotiate what may be improvident plea bargains. The latter may require a rethinking of the allocation of personnel, so that JAG Corps officers with an interest in military justice and a flair for the courtroom will not move out of that line of work as soon as they reach the grade of major or lieutenant commander.

Road to Reform

Both World War II and the Vietnam War led to substantial changes in American military justice. It is still uncertain whether the operations in Iraq and Afghanistan will do so as well. It would be wise, at least, to take a hard congressional look at the current system. After all, the UCMJ was enacted over fifty years ago, in 1950, and it is long overdue for an examination of how well it has served the nation and whether it would benefit from some changes. Sadly, Congress passed up the opportunity to use the fiftieth anniversary of the code for this purpose.

Congress should set aside time for sustained hearings on the administration of military justice. It should make a point of carefully studying the excellent report prepared by the Cox Commission on the occasion of the UCMJ's half-century. It should also hear from the TJAGs, commanders, present and former judges of the Court of Appeals for the Armed Forces, civilian practitioners, and scholars—including thoughtful observers from other countries. There would be no harm done from such an examination, and the system would likely benefit from it. We would not be alone in examining our system; Parliament in 2006 enacted a single military justice statute for the British Army, Royal Navy, and Royal Air Force, replacing the three separate "Service Discipline Acts" (the Army Act 1955, the Air Force Act 1955, and the Naval Discipline Act 1957).

Among the issues Congress should examine is whether the time has come to dispense with or modify the allocation of responsibility for deciding who gets prosecuted for what under the UCMJ. Is it time to jettison the role of the commander/convening authority? Should we have a single chief prosecutor for each branch of the service with the power to bring charges? Can we safely dispense with intermediate review by the service courts of criminal appeals and thereby save time in the appellate review phase? Should court-martial jurisdiction be rolled back to embrace only those cases that have a service-connection under the so-called "Relford factors,"* as a retired Navy JAG Corps officer proposed at a meeting of the Defense Department's Joint Service Committee on Military Justice in 2006?

Another significant issue concerns the lack of fixed terms of office for military trial and intermediate appellate judges. We would never tolerate at-will judges in civilian courts, yet we do

---

*The factors take their name from the decision in *Relford v. Commandant, U.S. Disciplinary Barracks,* 401 U.S. 355 (1971). Overruling *O'Callahan v. Parker,* 395 U.S. 258 (1969), the Supreme Court held in *Solorio v. United States,* 483 U.S. 435 (1987), that there is no need for an offense to be service-connected to exercise court-martial jurisdiction over a member of the armed forces.

so in the military. Is this defensible, whether or not it satisfies the due process clause (as the Supreme Court has held)? Alternatively, is it rational that judges in the army and coast guard have terms of office, albeit short ones and only as a result of voluntary service regulations, while those in the other services do not? Surely this kind of discrepancy, if not invalidated by the federal courts,* merits congressional attention.

Not everything that warrants consideration requires congressional action. For example, delay continues to be a serious issue in the administration of military justice. Cases in the navy and marine corps, in particular, have lingered years—literally—in the appellate process. Despite the best efforts of the Court of Appeals for the Armed Forces, this delay continues to be a problem. Fresh thinking on this and other issues is entirely possible at the Court of Appeals, given the addition of two new judges and the beginning of Judge Andrew S. Effron's term as chief judge in 2006. Perhaps the court will consider asking some of the many civilian lawyers who are admitted to its bar to accept pro bono assignments as appellate defense counsel to help the services catch up with their caseload once and for all. If the bar declines to serve pro bono voluntarily, and the court decides not to require such service as

---

*The inter-service disparity is the subject of a pending Fifth Amendment equal protection case in federal district court in Washington, *Oppermann v. United States,* Civil No. 06–1824 (D.D.C.) (pending). The argument has been repeatedly rejected by the at-will judges of the United States Navy–Marine Corps Court of Criminal Appeals but continues to be raised in navy and marine corps cases and is before the United States Air Force Court of Criminal Appeals. The United States Court of Appeals for the Armed Forces has, without explanation, declined to grant review of this issue. As a matter of full disclosure, the author is counsel for Lieutenant Commander Oppermann and a number of other navy and air force personnel who have asserted this equal protection argument.

a condition of bar membership, then it might indeed be necessary for Congress to create a system for compensating appointed civilian appellate defense counsel analogous to the Criminal Justice Act.

Finally, there are steps the executive branch can take unilaterally to improve military justice. Sentencing concerns could be addressed, at least to a degree, by a critical review of the maximum punishments for various kinds of offenses. The president has power to set punishment ceilings, but these are rarely altered. The administration should carefully review the existing maximums and make changes where appropriate. A good starting place would be the maximum punishment for dereliction of duty, which is only three months confinement for negligent dereliction. Considering the ability of members of the military to monitor and carefully supervise the performance of duty, and the dreadful effects that misconduct by unsupervised or inadequately supervised junior personnel can have on our ability to achieve our operational and political goals, three months seems entirely inadequate as an incentive to those higher up in the military chain of command to see to it that their subordinates behave properly.

The executive branch could also establish a better process for reviewing the *Manual for Courts-Martial* than the current insular committee. One alternative would be to create a broad-based committee that includes members of the civilian bar and law professors, along the lines of the committees on which the Judicial Conference of the United States relies. At present, the Joint Service Committee on Military Justice—like the statutory Code Committee on Military Justice—holds public hearings that are brief and perfunctory. The one conducted on September 18, 2006, lasted less than half an hour, having attracted only four spectators, only one of whom spoke.* Legislation would not be necessary to adopt this approach, but if the executive branch declines to act, Congress might have to step in.

The importance of military justice cannot be overstated. If it works well, our armed forces will be a model of good order and discipline. If it breaks down—or is perceived as having done so—it diminishes public esteem for the military and can erode public support for our men and women in uniform. We should have a first-rate system that meets contemporary standards, both our own and those of other advanced democracies. We have some work to do before we reach that goal, just as we have important work to do with respect to the military commissions. The good news is that there seems to be renewed congressional energy in these related areas. Whether that energy will be put to good use remains to be seen.

The opinions expressed in this chapter are those of the author alone and do not necessarily reflect the views of the National Institute of Military Justice. I would like to express my appreciation to my secretary, Allie Bernardo, for her assistance and to Colonel Dwight H. Sullivan, Professor Gary D. Solis, and my law partner, Matthew S. Freedus, for commenting on an earlier draft.

---

*I am indebted to Kathleen A. Duignan, Esq., Executive Director, National Institute of Military Justice, for this information.

Greg Anrig, Jr. is vice president of programs at The Century Foundation. He co-edited *The War on Our Freedoms: Civil Liberties in an Age of Terrorism*, *Social Security Reform: Beyond the Basics*, and *Immigration's New Frontiers: Experiences from the New Gateway States*. He is author of the forthcoming *The Conservatives Have No Clothes: Why Right-Wing Ideas Keep Failing*.

Ann Beeson is the associate legal director of the American Civil Liberties Union and director of its Programs on National Security and Human Rights. Ms. Beeson has argued twice before the United States Supreme Court, and has been named one of America's top fifty litigators by the *National Law Journal* and *American Lawyer*. She has successfully challenged warrantless wiretapping by the National Security Agency and the expanded surveillance provisions of the USA Patriot Act.

Alan Brinkley is Allan Nevins Professor of History and provost of Columbia University. His publications include *Voices of Protest: Huey Long, Father Coughlin, and the Great Depression*; *The End of Reform: New Deal Liberalism in Recession and War*; and *Liberalism and Its Discontents*.

David Cole is a law professor at Georgetown University and a contributor to the *New York Review of Books*, where this piece recently appeared. He is the author of *Enemy Aliens: Double Standards and Constitutional Freedoms in the War on Terrorism*, recently published in a revised paperback edition, and of *Less Safe, Less Free: Why We Are Losing the War on Terror*, to be published in 2007.

Eugene R. Fidell is head of the Military Practice Group at the Washington, D.C., firm of Feldesman Tucker Leifer Fidell LLP. Since 1991 he has also been president of the National Institute of Military Justice. He is a member of the ABA's Task Force on Treatment of Enemy Combatants and Standing Committee on Law and National Security and a director of the International Society for Military Law and the Law of War. Mr. Fidell served as a judge advocate in the Coast Guard from 1969 to 1972 and regularly represents members of the armed services. His current work in progress (with co-authors Elizabeth Lutes Hillman and Dwight H. Sullivan) is *Cases and Materials on Comparative Military Justice*.

Gary Hart, a former U.S. senator from Colorado, is the author of seventeen books, an international lawyer, a lecturer in national and international security affairs, and the former co-chair of the U.S. Commission on National Security for the 21st Century. He currently holds an endowed chair at the University of Colorado.

Aziz Huq directs the Liberty and National Security Project at the Brennan Center for Justice at NYU School of Law, where he conducts litigation and does policy work related to civil liberties in counterterrorism operations. Before joining the Brennan Center, he clerked for Justice Ruth Bader Ginsburg of the Supreme Court of the United States and for Judge Robert D. Sack of the Second Circuit Court of Appeals. His book *Unchecked and Unbalanced: Presidential Power in a Time of Terror* (co-authored with Fritz Schwarz) will be published in March 2007.

Patrick Radden Keefe is a fellow at The Century Foundation and author of *Chatter: Uncovering the Echelon Surveillance Network and the Secret World of Global Eavesdropping*. His articles on espionage, international security, and foreign affairs appear regularly in the *New Yorker*, the *New York Review of Books*, *Slate*, and other publications, and he is the recipient of a 2006 Guggenheim fellowship to research transnational criminal and terrorist networks and the globalization of crime.

Joseph Lelyveld was executive editor of the *New York Times* from 1994 to 2001. Previously, he served as the *Times* managing editor, foreign editor, and correspondent in London, New Delhi, Hong Kong, and South Africa. He is the author of the Pulitzer Prize–winning book *Move Your Shadow: South Africa, Black and White*.

Richard C. Leone, president of The Century Foundation, has held government, business, and academic posts, including stints as chairman of the Port Authority of New York and New Jersey, president of the New York Mercantile Exchange, and faculty member of Princeton University. His analytical and opinion pieces on public policy topics have appeared in the *New York Times*, the *Washington Post*, the *Los Angeles Times*, *Foreign Affairs*, and other publications. He was co-editor of *Social Security Reform: Beyond the Basics* and of *The War on Our Freedoms: Civil Liberties in an Age of Terrorism*.

Peter Osnos is the founder and editor-at-large of PublicAffairs books. He was publisher of Random House's Times Books Division from 1991 to 1996 and before that was a vice president and associate publisher of the Random House imprint. Authors he has worked with include former President Bill Clinton, former President Jimmy Carter, Rosalyn Carter, Nancy Reagan, former Speaker of the House Tip O'Neill, Boris Yeltsin, Paul Volcker, Kareem Abdul Jabbar, Donald Trump, Clark Clifford, Sam Donaldson, Morley Safer, Peggy Noonan, Molly Ivins, Stanley Karnow, Jim Lehrer, William Novak, Vassily Aksyonov, and journalists from the *New York Times*, the *Washington Post*, the *Los Angeles Times*, *Newsweek*, and *The Economist*. Before entering book publishing, Osnos spent nearly twenty years at the *Washington Post*, where he was variously Indochina bureau chief, Moscow correspondent, foreign editor, national editor, and London bureau chief.

John D. Podesta is currently a visiting professor of law at Georgetown University Law School and the president and chief executive officer of the Center for American Progress, a progressive think tank located in Washington, D.C. From October 1998 to January 2001, Podesta served as chief of staff to President William J. Clinton. He also served on the Commission on Protecting and Reducing Government Secrecy, chaired by Senator Daniel Patrick Moynihan, and previously held numerous positions on Capitol Hill, including chief minority counsel on several subcommittees for the Senate Judiciary Committee and counsel on the majority staff of the Senate Judiciary Committee, working closely with Senator Patrick Leahy to protect open government.

Stephen J. Schulhofer is the Robert B. McKay Professor of Law at New York University Law School. From 1986 until 2000, he was director of the Center for Studies in Criminal Justice at the University of Chicago, where he was the Julius

Kreeger Professor of Law. He served for many years as a consultant to the United States Sentencing Commission, and he has testified on terrorism issues before the 9/11 Commission and the U.S. Senate Judiciary Committee. He is the author of *Rethinking the Patriot Act*, *The Secrecy Problem in Terrorism Trials* (with S. Turner); and *The Enemy Within: Intelligence Gathering, Law Enforcement and Civil Liberties in the Wake of September 11*, together with many articles on the nexus between liberty and national security. He also writes extensively on other aspects of police practices, criminal law, and criminal procedure.

Stacy Sullivan is a senior editor at the Institute for War and Peace Reporting, a media development organization that trains journalists in two dozen countries. She covered the Balkans for *Newsweek* magazine in the 1990s and is the author of *Be Not Afraid, for You Have Sons in America*, which tells the story of a Brooklyn roofer who emigrated to the United States from Kosovo, then spearheaded a major fundraising effort to launch the Kosovo Liberation Army. Her articles on various human rights issues have appeared in the *New York Times Magazine*, *New Republic*, *New York Magazine*, *Men's Journal*, and the op-ed pages of the *New York Times*, the *Washington Post*, the *Boston Globe*, and other major newspapers.